BARRIE COOK

Twin Spheres 2003, Acrylic on canvas, 40x22 inches

0 October -
0 November 2003

emon Street Gallery
3 Lemon Street
uro, Cornwall TR1 2LS
+44 (0) 1872 275757
info@lemonstreetgallery.co.uk
lemonstreetgallery.co.uk

atalogue available on request.

IAN HUMPHREYS

ART IRELAND
RDS, Dublin
21-23 November 2003
Stand E2

Cladach
Oil on canvas
157 x 132 cm
2003

Cunnamore Galleries
Cunnamore, Skibbereen
Co. Cork, Ireland
Tel +353 28 38483

CUNNAMORE
G A L L E R I E S

www.cunnamore.com

Bonhams
¹⁷⁹³

NEW BOND STREET

20th Century
British Art

Tuesday 2 December 2003
New Bond Street, London

Patrick Heron (1920-1999)
Lamp and lemon
oil on panel
Estimate: £10,000 - 15,000

We are currently accepting entries for this sale.
For further information about selling or buying at
auction, or to order a catalogue, please contact:

Matthew Bradbury on 020 7468 8295
Magnus Renfrew on 020 7468 8263
Siobhan O'Connor on 020 7447 7400
britart@bonhams.com

The deadline for consignments is 17 October 2003

Bonhams, 101 New Bond Street, London W1S 1SR
www.bonhams.com

MODERN PAINTERS

AUTUMN 2003

BRIEFING

COVER
Susan Rothenberg, *Crying*, 2003, oil on canvas.
Courtesy Sperone Westwater, New York

MODERN PAINTERS

Founded and edited by Peter Fuller, 1987–1990

3RD FLOOR, 52 BERMONDSEY STREET ■ LONDON SE1 3UD ■ TELEPHONE 020 7407 9247 ■ FAX 020 7407 9242 ■ INFO@MODERNPAINTERS.CO.UK ■ WWW.MODERNPAINTERS.CO.UK

Editor
KAREN WRIGHT

Deputy Editor
REBECCA WILSON

Creative Director
VINCENT WINTER

Editorial Board
BILL BERKSON
DAVID BOWIE
WILLIAM BOYD
LANCE ESPLUND
MARTIN GAYFORD
MARTIN GOLDING
HOWARD JACOBSON
PHILIP JODIDIO
NORBERT LYNTON
RICHARD MISRACH
JED PERL
CHARLES SAUMAREZ SMITH
DAPHNE WARBURG ASTOR
RICHARD WOLLHEIM

EDITORIAL / DESIGN

Contributing Editors
SIMON GRANT
CHARLOTTE MULLINS

Art Director
LUCY WARD

Assistant Editor
CRAIG BURNETT (020 7407 9246)

Personal Assistant to Editor
SERENA AHANGAMA (020 7407 9247)

Special Projects
SHANE WALTENER (020 7407 9244)

Intern
ANGELA ROBERTS

PUBLISHING / MARKETING

Production Manager
TARA HALE (020 7407 9245)

Advertising Manager
HOLLY STEVENS (020 7407 9249)
holly@modernpainters.co.uk

US Advertising Representative
LOUISA KEARNEY (516 883 2828)
ldkpub@aol.com

Reprographics
PRECISE@ICON REPRODUCTION
Crowne House, London

Printing
SOUTHERNPRINT LTD.
Poole, Dorset

Accounts
JO HALL

SUBSCRIPTIONS

UK/Europe
£20.00/€37.00 for one year
£36.00/€71.00 for two years

US/Canada
US$41.00/Can$54.00+tax for one year
US$82.00/Can$108.00+tax for two years

World
£30.00/US$50.00 for one year
£56.00/US$93.00 for two years
All prices include postage

**UK/Europe/World
(excluding US/Canada)**
Please make £/€/US$ cheques payable
to 'MODERN PAINTERS'. Send to:
Modern Painters Subscriptions, Cary Court,
Bancombe Trading Estate, Somerton,
Somerset TA11 6TB.

Freephone: 0800 085 2757
Local: +44 (0) 1458 271231
Fax: +44 (0) 1458 271146

Freepost
MODERN PAINTERS, Freepost LON15765,
Somerton, TA11 6ZA
(only in the UK)

US/Canada
Please make checks payable to 'EXPRESS MAG'. In
US send to MODERN PAINTERS, c/o Express Mag,
PO Box 2769, Plattsburgh, NY 12901 – 0239. In
Canada send to MODERN PAINTERS, c/o Express
Mag, 8155 Larrey Street, Anjou, Quebec, H1J 2L5

Toll free: 1 877 363 1310
Fax: (514) 355 3332
email: expsmag@expressmag.com

MODERN PAINTERS, ISSN number
0953-6698, is published quarterly
(4 times per year: December, March, June,
September,) by Fine Art Journals Ltd. at 1320
Route 9, Champlain, NY 12919 for US$41.00
per year. Periodicals postage
paid at Champlain, NY
POSTMASTER: Send address changes to
MODERN PAINTERS, c/o Express Mag, PO Box
2769, Plattsburgh, NY 12901-1329

CIRCULATION

MODERN PAINTERS can be ordered across
the counter from any UK/Eire newsagent

UK Newsagents and global distribution
Comag Specialist
Tavistock Road
West Drayton
Middlesex UB7 7QX, UK
Tel: 01895 444 055

Galleries and bookshops
Central Books
99 Wallis Road
London E9 5LN, UK
Tel: 020 8986 4854

USA and Canada
IPD Source Interlink Companies,
10 East 40th Street, Suite 3110,
New York, NY 10016, USA
Tel: 212 683 0376 109

New Zealand
Propaganda, CPO Box 582
Auckland 1001, New Zealand

Publishing
Fine Art Journals Ltd, England
ISSN 0953-6698

MODERN PAINTERS does
not assume responsibility
for unsolicited manuscripts,
photographs or illustrations.

Copyright worldwide of all
editorial content is held by
the publishers, Fine Art
Journals Limited.

Reproduction in whole or
part is forbidden save with
the express permission in
writing of the publishers.

**MODERN PAINTERS
is published quarterly:**
December, March, June
and September.

21,022
Average net circulation
(July – December 2002)

CONTRIBUTORS

JULIAN BARNES

KATE BUSH

ALAN CUMMING

EMMA DEXTER

ANOUCHKA ROGGEMAN

JOHN ASHBERY's most recent book of poems, *Chinese Whispers,* was published in 2002 (Farrar, Straus & Giroux).

KENNETH BAKER is the art critic for the *San Francisco Chronicle*. He has recently completed a book on Walter De Maria's 'Lightning Field.'

JULIAN BARNES is the author of nine novels. His collection of stories, *The Lemon Table,* will be published in March 2004.

KATE BUSH is Senior Programmer at The Photographers' Gallery, London. In 2002 she curated 'Reality Check', which featured 16 young British-based photographers and video artists.

DAVID CARBONE's work recently appeared in 'Drawing Conclusions' at the New York Arts Gallery.

MATTHEW COLLINGS' television series about the Old Masters will be shown on Channel Four this autumn. The accompanying book will be published by Weidenfeld and Nicolson.

ALAN CUMMING has appeared in numerous films and plays. His first novel, *Tommy's Tale,* was published in 2003 (Penguin).

PETER DAVIES is an artist based in London.

EMMA DEXTER, a Senior Curator at Tate Modern, was the co-curator of 'Cruel and Tender, Twentieth-Century Photography and the Real'.

ROBERT ENRIGHT is writing a book about the making of Guy Maddin's film *The Saddest Music in the World*. He is Editor-at-Large for *Border Crossings* magazine.

LANCE ESPLUND is a regular contributor to *Art in America* and *The Yale Review*. He teaches at the Parsons School of Design in New York.

MORGAN FALCONER is a journalist and critic who writes regularly for the *Times Literary Supplement* and the *New Statesman.*

MARTIN GAYFORD is art critic of the *Sunday Telegraph* and is writing a book about Van Gogh.

RUTH GUILDING curated the exhibition 'Marble Mania' at Sir John Soane's Museum in London in 2001 and is currently writing a book on this subject.

VICTORIA HARDIE is a play-wright. She has written the libretto for Michael Nyman's opera *Facing Goya* which opens in London in 2004.

MICHAEL HASTINGS has written 17 plays, including *Tom and Viv*. His new play *Calico* opens in London in January 2004.

DARIAN LEADER is a psychoanalyst. His most recent book is *Stealing the Mona Lisa: what art stops us from seeing* (Faber).

JAMIE MCKENDRICK's most recent book of poems, *Ink Stone,* was published in 2003 (Faber).

MARK RAPPOLT is the editor of *AA Files,* the current issue of which focuses on post-colonial London.

PAULA REGO lives and works in London.

ANOUCHKA ROGGEMAN is a freelance journalist based in Paris. She writes about contemporary art for *Connaissance des Arts* and *l'Art Aujourd'hui.*

PHILIP ROTH is the author of many best-selling novels. In 2001 he received the highest award of the American Academy of Arts and Letters, the Gold Medal in fiction.

SUKHDEV SANDHU is chief film critic for the *Daily Telegraph* and the author of *London Calling: How Black and Asian Writers Imagined a City* (HarperCollins, 2003).

SHANE WALTENER is an artist based in London where he has recently created site-specific installations for 'Moral Combat' at St Leonard's Church and 'Bootleg' at Spitalfields Market in Shoreditch.

Ochre Bathers, Oil on canvas 152.5 x 152.5 cms

LISA WRIGHT
POOL PAINTINGS

2ND OCTOBER - 31ST OCTOBER 2003
illustrated catalogue available

www.beardsmoregallery.com
email: info@beardsmoregallery.com

22-24 PRINCE OF WALES ROAD, LONDON NW5 3LG. TEL: 020 7485 0923 FAX: 020 7485 0975

Tourist (recto), 1940, ink on paper, 22 x 15 cm / 8 ½ x 5 ¾ inches

Lucian Freud:
Drawings 1940
10 September–10 October
Timothy Taylor Gallery

24 Dering Street London W1S 1TT   Telephone 020 7409 3344   Facsimile 020 7409 1316

KEN CURRIE
20 SEPTEMBER – 19 OCTOBER 2003

RECENT WORK

Flowers East
32 Kingsland Road
London E2 8DP
Telephone 020 7920 7777
Facsimile 020 7920 7770
gallery@flowerseast.com
www.flowerseast.com
Tuesday – Saturday 10 – 6pm
Sunday 11 – 5pm

Flowers

Homage to Naum Gabo 1948   oil on canvas   16 x 20 ins/40.5 x 51 cm

JOHN WELLS
1907 – 2000

Retrospective
Oct 15 – Nov 7

Colour catalogue £15

Jonathan Clark & Co Fine Art

18 Park Walk London SW10 0AQ

t: +44 (0) 20 7351 3555
f: +44 (0) 20 7823 3187
w: www.jc-art.com

Marlborough
Paula Rego

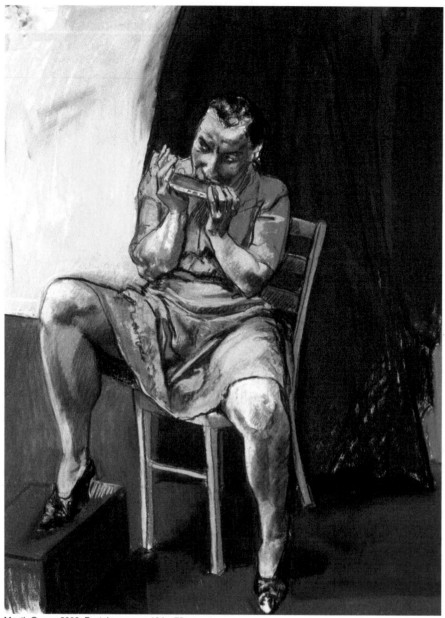

Mouth Organ, 2003, Pastel on paper, 104 x 79cm

Jane Eyre and Related Stories
pastels and lithographs

15 October – 22 November 2003

Fully illustrated catalogue available

This exhibition coincides with the publication of a fully illustrated catalogue raisonné
of Paula Rego's graphic work by T.G. Rosenthal, published by Thames & Hudson

Marlborough Fine Art (London) Ltd.
6 Albemarle Street, London W1S 4BY
Tel: 020 7629 5161   Fax: 020 7629 6338
mfa@marlboroughfineart.com
www.marlboroughfineart.com

Untitled 25 x 27" oil on canvas, 1957

HACKETT
MODERN
FREEDMAN

250 SUTTER STREET

SAN FRANCISCO

CALIFORNIA 94108

415.362.7152

FAX 415.362.7182

David Park

A Singular Humanity

September 4 – November 1, 2003

EXHIBITION PREVIEW: www.hackettfreedmangallery.com
56-PAGE COLOR CATALOGUE, $30.00 PPD.

mhackett@hackettfreedmangallery.com

KAREN WRIGHT

Experiencing Art

*The sweltering heat of the summer raises questions
about what we are influenced by when we look at art.*

THE MEDIA COVERAGE OF THIS YEAR'S VENICE BIENNALE was dominated by one thing – the heat. The heat during the opening in June was brutal, filling your mind with its miasma. It blinded the critics to what in fact was a Biennale packed, as always, with both good and bad pavilions, as well attendant exhibitions. When I returned to Venice in August, the atmosphere had transformed. It was still over 100 degrees but the Giardini was now tranquil, the only visitors 'art tourists' who were engaging with the work in a way that the critical art world during the opening press week weren't. Chris Ofili's erotic paintings celebrating his recent wedding glistened, albeit in the harsh Adjaye light, and convinced in a way they had not done previously. Olafur Eliasson in the Danish Pavilion was a favourite among visitors, and the rapture generated by his work bodes well for his forthcoming installation in the Turbine Hall at Tate Modern. Francesco Bonami's painting show at the Museo Correr, reviewed in this issue by the painter Peter Davies, was well worth a second visit, confirming his view '*not* that painting is back but that it never went away'. Veteran Alex Katz looked fresh and Dumas mysterious in their respective solo shows. I was glad I made it to the Absolut extravaganza if only to get the free Richard Wentworth postcard and the now obsolete Damien Hirst poster announcing solemnly: 'never trust an artist who doesn't drink' – that from a newly converted teetotal Christian.

The overwhelming heat followed me to Gallasteo near Santa Fe, New Mexico, where I went to interview Susan Rothenberg for this issue – her painting *Crying* adorns our cover. It was 97 degrees when I landed in Albuquerque at 9pm and well over 100 degrees the next day when I arrived at the 600-acre ranch Rothenberg shares with her husband Bruce Nauman. Together they have created an oasis in the desert with their long low-slung ranch house painted a cool green, surrounded by a lush garden. The first night Nauman, Rothenberg and I relaxed on a rooftop overlooking the ridge-back, drinking iced neat vodka laced with kumquats. The quiet of the evening was punctuated by swooping swallows and hummingbirds lining up in an orderly fashion to sip

water from a nearby feeder. All of a sudden Nauman's twenty-five horses appeared, passing in front of us in a single line as if connected by an invisible rope. Nauman slowly intoned the breeds of the horses: 'strawberry roan, pinto, palamino, buckskin'. Last to appear was a mule, which Nauman had given Rothenberg for her to learn to ride on.

It is impossible for artists to remain detached from their surroundings, and the landscape of Gallasteo, as well as her marriage to Nauman, has had a profound impact on Rothenberg's work. Every day, in the cool of the morning, she walks through the desert accompanied by her three dogs, Gertrude Stein, Mink and Boots, all rescued from the local pet sanctuary. 'The shifting perspective caused by seeing things from different heights is something that feeds directly into my work,' she explained. In the distance mountain ranges give off a blue shimmer and the desert floor is an unmistakeable shade of red, a colour which repeatedly finds its way into Rothenberg's paintings. She takes these morning walks in order to see things happen, incidents which subsequently appear in her work: she once came across Nauman tending a horse's foot and in her next painting his disembodied arm mysteriously emerged.

In her recent work – very different from the iconic paintings of horses from the 70s which propelled her onto the world's art map – she has, despite her dislike of the word 'narrative', allowed the personal to 'intrude' into the canvas. Nauman's profile appears as if by magic in the foreground of a recent landscape. But, as Rothenberg explains, it's not specifically Nauman's, just a general human profile which, if you look carefully, is not really a profile at all. Rothenberg is still wrestling with the tensions between abstract and figurative painting. One of the great strengths of her new work is that it both illuminates and describes emotions – arguably one of the special qualities of great art.

This relationship between biography and art – between experience and the work subsequently produced – is the dominant theme in Julian Barnes' exploration of Vuillard, who is the subject of a major touring retrospective over the next year.

> **The desert floor is an unmistake-able shade of red, a colour which repeatedly finds its way into Rothenberg's paintings.**

Nauman's profile appears as if by magic in the foreground of a recent landscape.

Susan Rothenberg, *Headscape,* 2003, oil on canvas, 77.5 x 91.5in. Courtesy Sperone Westwater, New York

It surfaces again in this issue when Bill Viola talks about the importance of water in his work. When he was six years old he almost drowned when he jumped off a raft and sank to the bottom of a lake. 'I'll never forget what I saw under there,' he says. Not surprisingly this experience influenced his video piece *Five Angels for the Millennium*, which he describes as 'literally a drowning'.

Returning from New Mexico to a sweltering London I went to see Paula Rego in her exotica-stuffed studio to ask her to create the artist's installation for this issue. Rego collects dolls, objects and costumes, and her son-in-law, the artist Ron Mueck, has made strange furry beasties for her which sit incongruously next to mannequins dressed in bizarre costumes. We settled on *Little Red Riding Hood* as the subject for the installation, a tale which in Rego's mind is filled with rape and incest. She has produced specially for MODERN PAINTERS a version of the story like no other, using her regular cast of sitters, transformed by her fertile imagination.

As well as artists being influenced by their surroundings, viewers of art too are swayed by mood and the weather – as was certainly the case at the Venice Biennale. In this issue Alan Cumming is mesmerised by Douglas Gordon's installation 'Play Dead; Real Time', in which two screens show a revolving tracking shot of an elephant. His fascination is, surprisingly, shared by his dog who, though usually more interested in gallery floors, is also transfixed by this powerful image. Could it be possible that it's really who you are with that can make or break the experience of looking at art? **MP**

Anxiety

A critic frets that his multi-layered Coleridgean musings will be misrepresented by the editorial introduction under the main heading.

Colour good

This coming November I was supposed to be having a show in Melbourne of abstract paintings done in collaboration with my wife, Emma Biggs. But now we've put it off till next year because the paintings are so hard to do. The content is pure pleasure but the process is torture. There are a lot of differences, really a great many of them, which all have to work harmoniously. The more it works the less you can tell any torture went on. The beginning point is a format that E. Biggs has already laboured over, and then the next stage is that I make that idea into a painting. Just the making of it mucks it up so the idea has to keep being stirred around, and done and done and re-done, until there's an arrival back to something like the original rightness. I have the role of the painter and EB is the mind: she comes in the studio and says to change things and I say no, you must be mad! But then I have to, because that's the rule. On the whole I don't have any certainty when I'm working, only ability. And in this context because EB is a mosaicist and not a painter she doesn't have any ability. But she does have certainty even though it's usually only certainty that something's wrong.

Waldy confusing

Another factor that made it hard to finish all the paintings on time was that this summer I've been working on the book that goes with my TV series on Old Master painting. Last week the commissioning editor at Weidenfeld & Nicolson phoned to tell me he was surprised to see Waldemar Januszczak adopting my TV persona in his programmes about Gauguin. I agreed it was alarming because when my programmes come out in November the reviews will say I've adopted *his* persona.

Black bad

Since that call I've been having a further anxiety, which is that the colour proofs of the pictures for the book are dark. It isn't an anxiety dream – 'Help! My illustrations are going black! Phew! It's only a dream!' – but an anxiety reality: these pictures really are very dark. I immediately fired off a lot of emails and phone calls to the Weidenfeld people. But whereas they'd been contacting me like crazy to get me to look at the proofs in the first place so everything could be happily passed, now that there's a problem they're all suddenly unavailable.

The word 'black' seldom appears in the text of the book. Once I talk about the cat in *Olympia* being a touch of black Manet thought the picture needed, and somewhere else I compare the uniform solid blacks in Caravaggio with the different kind of darkness you get in Rubens' crucifixions of the 1610s, a few years after Caravaggio's death – within the dark areas of these paintings there are always sheens of colour, so the darkness appears to be warm and vibrating. But in the reproductions there isn't a cat at all in the Manet because that whole area of the painting, where there should be a black cat against a green curtain, appears entirely black; and the paintings by Rubens are so utterly tonal – kind of black, white and greenish – that they might as well be by Caravaggio.

The reason blackness doesn't feature

Emma Biggs and Matthew Collings, *I Boss You Around*, 2003

much in the story is because the point of the book is to sing the praises of painters who on the whole are great colourists. Even Hogarth, who has a whole chapter, is an underrated rococo-ist, forever balancing subtle muted complimentaries against thoughtfully orchestrated blasts of brightness. So all these figures are in the business of putting patches of colour next to each other and making them vibrate so something visually surprising and delightful happens. But according to these colour proofs the artists don't do that. Instead they do a kind of painted version of sculpture, hacking greenish-white form out of blackness.

Is art for masses or only a few?

I felt happier today because some creative and intelligent solutions to the blackness problem have come up. That Weidenfeld team is hot stuff! Another thing I've been working on is a one-off TV programme about the history of the Turner Prize. In my mind the Turner Prize is a bit of harmless mass-media flim-flam: it doesn't have anything important about it except for the four exhibitions, which are now each so large you can almost take them seriously. And I have to admit they could be a good stepping-off point if someone wanted to find out about contemporary art from a position of knowing nothing at all about it. Or at least knowing only what they see on TV. But that's already a problem, because one of the things they see on TV is the annual live broadcast from Tate Britain on the night of the Turner Prize award, which in my view is not really what art is about.

For me art is about a few colours placed nicely together. It's a lifetime's work to get that kind of thing to be successful and as a viewer of it I believe you've really got to have your head in order. You've got to know something about what it is you're looking at. But the Turner Prize is defined by its willingness to suck up to whatever arbitrary stuff is already in people's heads anyway from watching TV all the time and reading the culture sections of the Sunday papers and *Time Out*. That is, it's defined by populist giddiness: the whole point of it is that anyone

should be able to join in. And every year more and more people do in fact engage with it, or become fascinated by it, or enjoy it in some way.

I suppose they enjoy the party, the celebs, the sense of a race, the anticipation of something shocking or disgusting coming up, the feeling that some corruption might be going on, and the interchangeably slightly incoherent, strained, awkward interviews with the artists, which are that way because the artists are confused about what the gig is when they're

being interviewed: should they be pretending to be intellectuals or should they just be themselves? Should they say whatever occurs to them or should they use a range of terms that they don't understand themselves and which they wouldn't normally dream of using unless they were in a group crit. in one of the art schools they occasionally teach at, situations where it's normal for no one ever to utter a sentence that can be understood by anyone else?

I don't think art can be explained anyway: it's not really about explanations. And, actually, being incoherent isn't even all that bad in this context. The point is you can't just tap into the context artificially and expect the whole thing to be revealed and make sense in the same way it would if you'd had an organic relationship with it for years. And

everything I say on those Turner Prize programmes, from 'Good evening, welcome to...' to '... See you next year!' is designed to get that point over: I'm a campaigner for that position. I campaign for seriousness in painting, as well.

Of course there can't be a campaign if no one realises it's going on. But I think if you've got something to say you've got to be aware of what you're up against and work out your moves based on that. So in art's popularisation over the last fifteen years or so two main campaigning modes can be identified: gung-ho missionary and moronic hip. I think sounding a bit standoffish from either should have a good effect and get your campaign noticed. I know it would if I was the audience. I'd think, 'Hmm, I haven't heard that tone so much – maybe there's something there?'

Usual phoneys

You'd think others would have caught on too but in fact I'm always amazed at how curators I find myself milling amongst on art junkets abroad are always zombie-ing me with their boggle-eyed bullshit about how serious and worthwhile they find Tate Modern – where they work – to be. Or conversely how the little sillies on the constipated

(Above)
Chris Ofili, installation shot of British Pavilion, 2003. Courtesy British Council

(Left)
Fred Wilson, *Speak of me as I am,* 2003, 50th Venice Biennale. Courtesy MIT List Visual Arts Center. Photo: R.Ransick/A. Cocchi

The more the paintings work the less you can tell any torture went on.

art monthlies continue to name-drop daft new artists, art movements and galleries loudly in my earshot, in the mistaken belief that it will sound as if they're in touch with something important. And they all behave towards me as if I want something from them!

Wolfgang Tillmans, *If one thing matters, everything matters,* 2003, Tate Britain. Photo: Joanna Fernandes

I thought it was good that the music was challenging, but bad that the art was completely vacuous.

Back to masses

In any case, with this Turner Prize special I've been finding it rewarding to be forced to analyse the Turner Prize phenomenon from a personal point of view: my ideas on art and the mass audience, etc. The director says, 'Well if you don't think art can be explained why do you do those programmes?' And I reply, 'Well, I'm one of life's natural explainers!' This goes back and forth, we write it down, change it a bit, a script gradually appears, and then we film it. My only fear is that the programme is scheduled to come out a week before the Old Masters series and I might unwittingly undermine the campaigning effort I put into those programmes by appearing to be shallow in this one, when what I thought I was doing was coming up with illuminating paradoxes.

Feeble conformist almost good

One of the places I had all that inappropriate blasting of peoples' deluded self-images at me, which I was mentioning earlier, was the Venice Biennale press view in June. I don't remember much else

about the event. The overall tone of the art was feeble, conformist, unthinking political correctness, and some artists did it OK. The Fred Wilson display at the US pavilion was good outside, where he had some leather shoulder bags laid out with a black guy selling them, but bad inside, where he had some photos of Venetian paintings in which a black face or two appears, and he'd somehow highlighted the face. You thought: 'Yes, I'd noticed there were some black guys in Tiepolo, too: so what?' As political consciousness-raising it seemed like it hadn't yet got off the ground. It needed a bit more effort put in. The selling-bags scenario outside was good because of opposite reasons: the transition between a daily life experience and an absurdly grandiose gallery experience was so smoothly effortless that the anarchy of the context-switching really hit home strongly.

Zzz

There were times during the three-day Biennale opening when I thought 'This is so absurd it's impossible.' One of these was a public lecture held in the Arsenale, which was part of the Biennale's official explanation of this year's aims. The seats were all on a transparent floor. Through it you could see opened-out books and intellectual pamphlets and art catalogues. On a stage in front of the audience four people explained their ideas to each other in ridiculous self-preening fake intellectual language. They spoke into microphones and a screen showed a film of them talking as it was actually happening. There were two more people in the audience than there were on stage, and half of these were asleep.

Bongo wrong

Another impossibility was a thing called 'Utopia Station' where a lot of people were playing bongos and some others were sitting in trees. And another was an exhibition of international painting from the last few decades, which was put on in the Museo Correr off St Mark's Square, which, besides being visually incoherent and arbitrary, had explanatory wall-labels that plumbed new

depths of pretentiousness and literal simple-mindedness: like the one for Francis Bacon where it stated flatly, as if it was telling you what type of white spirit he used, that Bacon paints his own anxiety. In another museum nearby there was a carefully presented, intelligent exhibition of paintings by Alex Katz since the 1950s. Katz puts the concerns of the Abstract Expressionists into a context of portraits of his friends and family, bland people who you wouldn't ever want to meet, at least from this impression of them – in fact I've met them and they're pretty nice. But in any case, somehow recontextualising gives the concerns a sting and freshens them up. You don't see the neckties and sundecks and hair bands and white teeth; you see colour and handling. Back in the main part of the Biennale, the Chris Ofili pavilion had good paintings in an over-designed situation. Or it was a well-designed situation but there wasn't enough work, so the situation appeared over-designed.

Disturbing diversion

Another thing I remember was the music at the MODERN PAINTERS party on the Giudecca, which drove the guests away and made them ill. Plus there was some art at the party with buckets of water. I thought it was good that the music was challenging, but bad that the art was completely vacuous. But this party left a weird impression of modernity, as if MODERN PAINTERS really is gearing up to grooviness. People not in the know went away saying 'Ooh that was groovy!' (Or a new phrase that has the same meaning.) And I noticed even some people in the know said it too. I wasn't sure how this development would affect my various campaigns, but in any case when I got back to London I emailed the MODERN PAINTERS office to get my name taken off the editorial board.

Fake artist go away

Yesterday I went round the Wolfgang Tillmans and Bridget Riley exhibitions at Tate Britain. I love Tate Britain but my role in life is to be critical. I didn't like the WT show because in a way it was *only* love – it was WT's natural untransformed relationship to his subject matter. I think with art you have to do a bit of transforming of the subject to make the art worth having. But all you're seeing with WT is what you get in fashion magazines. You feel something is being sold to you in a superficial way. With a fashion mag that's fine because that's what they're for. But with art you definitely don't want that. Unless you're confused, which is what the bosses of the Tate are.

I reject the shaven-headed ninnies WT hangs out with, and his titles that say things like 'I went to an anti-Nazi demo.' But it's not the subjects that are the real problem but his treatment of them, the pretentious relationship to 'lifestyle' that he's selling. And it would be just as objectionable if the pitch were right wing instead of left wing. What's wrong is the pampered oblivion, the inner blindness, the inability to tell the difference between anything and anything (which all usually amounts to being a bit right wing anyway). The message of this show is that WT admires society like a fluffy donkey and society gives him its saccharine worthless admiration back again.

Great artist not quite right

The Riley show brings up a whole different lot of issues because she's a serious figure instead of an ephemeral pet, and you feel she'll always be good on some level. Even so this show left me wishing it had been different. With the early work you see her achieving something like the magic, all-over ripple of the painterly Old Masters, from Titian to Goya – and the flat-colour version of that in Delacroix, the Impressionists and Post-Impressionists, Mondrian, Paul Klee and Jackson Pollock – by using a modern graphic language of blips, stripes and dots. And this stuff is genuinely powerful. Then as the individual units start to spread and the touch becomes more uniform and industrialised and less wobbly and tentative, and the small units become actual colour-areas, things start to fall apart slightly.

Generally, although BR has grande-dame status so she gets a lot of big shows,

attention and respect now, the audience doesn't respond to these new paintings. Normally I don't care what the audience thinks but in this case maybe they're right. They probably don't know it's the colour that's awkward, just as they don't know why they responded well earlier: they assumed they were responding to fashion. But it was an original, advanced expressive quality they were responding to. Until the late 1970s there'd either be only black or white in the paintings or if there were colours it would be a small amount, not a large area, and with the colour separated from other colours by black or white (which is the formula for Damien Hirst's successful dot paintings, incidentally). But when she starts putting a real blast of colour next to another blast it's quite chancy if the pairing is going to work: one might be OK, another not. She seems not to see what the colour's doing and how texture is affecting colour.

There's definitely something to these 1990s paintings, a dynamic movement across the surface, which connects them to her work of the past. And that feeling of consistency is good. But you've got to be in control of all the effects, not just a few. And these colour juxtapositions are simply weird. Some are neutral, some are nice and some are positively repulsive. None is helped by the uniform, chalky, matt surface.

If you say anything about colour to anyone they fall asleep immediately. It just doesn't have any currency as a modern theme. BR often writes about it in a lucid and convincing way. Her official apologists are always going on about it too. In fact, only this week some dinner party gasser was going on about it in the *TLS*. But for these guys gassing is all it is. For BR it's obviously more fraught: it's right in her head but wrong on the canvas – because these 1990s paintings are neither lucid nor convincing, even if they're sometimes a bit oddly compelling just because of the verve of that wavy rhythm she does.

Presumably the problem is personal

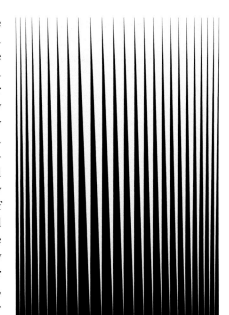

as well as cultural. She has her own ideas: she knows perfectly well that when she was applauded in the past it was probably for non-profound reasons. She feels she should plough her own furrow and think for her self. This individualism is part of what makes her good, but now it's turned slightly bad and someone whose judgement she trusts ought to challenge her.   ▥

Matt's Old Masters, written and presented by Matthew Collings, starts on Channel Four on Sunday 9 November. Matthew Collings' book of the series, with full-colour illustrations, is published by Weidenfeld & Nicolson on 6 November, £20.
Twenty Years of the Turner Prize is on Channel 4 on 31 October.
'**I Boss You Around: Paintings by Emma Biggs and Matthew Collings'** is at PavModern, Melbourne, Australia, next year.

(Left)
Bridget Riley,
Breathe, 1966,
Emulsion on canvas,
29.7 x 20.8 cm.
Courtesy Museum
Boijmans Van
Beuningen,
Rotterdam. © 2003
Bridget Riley

(Above)
Bridget Riley,
Harmony in Rose I,
1997, oil on linen,
164.5 x 227.7 cm.
Private collection,
Switzerland

The Ultimate Invisible World

Bill Viola *talks about how video has given visual artists a unique access to the mysterious dimension of time.*

MG A couple of years ago I went to Carmignano in the hills above Florence to see Pontormo's *The Visitation*. And there on show next to the church was your piece *The Greeting*, which takes as its starting point Pontormo's picture. It was extraordinary to see them side by side, but what led you to base a contemporary work in a high-tech medium on a picture from the 1520s?

BV I first came across the Pontormo in books and was completely taken by this image. But I wasn't interested in re-staging it, only in using it as a guide to make something new. My cameraman Harry Dawson and I analysed it a lot and discovered that it was impossible to recreate Pontormo's scene with a single lens. For the top half of the picture you would need to use a telephoto lens that flattens the figures so they stack up against each other, and for the bottom half, from the women's waists down, you would need a wide-angle lens so that the space bows out and away from you. We realised that the picture has multiple geometries – which gives it that strange, subjective quality.

MG Do you know David Hockney's thesis that some painters were employing lenses centuries before the discovery of photography?

BV I love the fact that Hockney, as a

(Above left)
Jacopo Pontormo,
The Visitation,
1528-9, oil on wood,
202 x 156 cm.San
Michele, Carmignano
(Florence)

(Above right)
Bill Viola,
The Greeting, 1995,
video/sound installa-
tion; three channel
colour video triptych.
Production still ©
Bill Viola. Photo:
Kira Petrov

living practitioner of art, is shaking up the art historians. One thing that fascinates me about the so-called Old Masters is that they were not old masters – they were young radicals. Most of the Renaissance artists we know were doing wild, incredible stuff when they were in their twenties, applying and sometimes inventing radically new visual techniques in the process. They were innovating right at the edge of what was possible.

Perspective in the early fifteenth century

was like 3-D computer graphics was 20 years ago – the cool new thing. It was an amazingly fertile time – science, art and technology were all coming together, just like they are now.

MG Is that one reason why you are drawn to take Renaissance paintings as a point of departure for film and video pieces? *The Greeting* was one of the first, but at the National Gallery this autumn you are also showing a series of pieces, 'The Passions', derived from works by Bosch, Dürer and Masolino.

BV There are several reasons. First, as I've said, I am fascinated with that historical period of intensive innovation, a complete shift in the basis of image making. Imagine if you were living in Florence in 1427 when Masaccio, at the age of twenty-six, unveiled one of the first perspective pictures at the prestigious venue of the church of Santa Maria Novella. At the time, most artists were still using a different system to make images, with roots in the Middle Ages. Single-point perspective was mostly unknown outside of a few university research institutes. It would be as if, for us, as recently as the 1990s realistic images had been based on a fundamentally different assumption of what constituted 'real'. The advent of moving pictures at the turn of the last century was in some ways a similar ground shift.

Second is the socio-political side of it. The Old Masters were disturbed by things that were going on in the world around them, just as I am by events like the Iraq war. Take a look Signorelli's 1504 fresco cycle in Orvieto cathedral, in particular the panel of 'The Rule of the Anti-Christ,' with the false Christ preaching to the people as the devil whispers in his ear.

Third is the importance of content. These artists were not only making formal innovations and strong social statements, they were applying these new concepts to the stale religious tradition of their time, re-visualising and reinterpreting some of the world's great spiritual texts and stories for contemporary viewers. A new humanism was being born that revolved around the deepest human issues: birth, death, compassion,

cruelty, suffering – in short, life itself.
MG In *Dolorosa*, one of 'The Passions' series, you show a man and a woman weeping in slow motion. Obviously, it evokes the diptychs of the fifteenth century in which the Virgin mourns over Christ. And even before *The Greeting* you had used the three-part format of the Renaissance altarpiece for one of your most celebrated pieces, *Nantes Triptych* from 1992, showing birth, life and death on three screens.

BV In coming to terms with Western art of the past, the last stage that fell into place for me was to make peace with the overtly Christian iconography and to understand those works in another, deeper way. In my case, this was very personal because I met birth and death head on in the 1990s – my children were being born at that time and my parents were dying. I finally understood what is going on in those pictures through this raw emotional and intensely personal contact with them.
MG Had the art of earlier centuries always meant so much to you?
BV No, at least not in terms of European art. In art school, I sat in art history class mostly bored and disinterested. It was just not relevant. I grew up with movies and television. I was among the first generation of TV kids who took it for granted that there was this image machine in the living room. At the time I enrolled in art school in 1969 nearly every rock concert you went to included a light show projected behind the band. Multi-media environments were just appearing, special large-scale events with music, film projections and architectural elements.

(Above from left)
Bill Viola.
Photo: Kira Perov

Bill Viola, *Dolorosa*, 2000, colour video diptych on two free-standing hinged LCD flat panels, 40.6 x 62.2 x 14.6 cm. Production still © Bill Viola. Photo: Kira Petrov

Bill Viola, *The Arc of Ascent*, 1992. © Bill Viola. Courtesy Haunch of Venison, London.

The so-called Old Masters... were not old masters – they were young radicals.

At the time, I was playing drums in a rock band and was creating my own media environments, so conventional painting and sculpture seemed too confining. Video was the new thing. A few seminal books on it had just been published and video art was only a few years old. We were all reading McLuhan, Youngblood and Norbert Weiner. A media revolution was in the air, and that was what I wanted to do.

As a graduation present my mother gave me the Time-Life series on art. It was the typical 'dumb mom' gift, this set of popular books on the Old Masters. I said thank you and never opened them. Then, in the early 80s, I learned that one of my favourite artists, the experimental filmmaker Michael Snow, was talking about Vermeer, so I pulled that volume off the shelf and started reading it. I couldn't stop and soon began to plough through the whole set.

These were books for the general reader so they were not involved with formal analysis or current critical theory.

Instead they focused on biographical details and the social and political milieu of the artist's life. I learnt all these interesting personal and cultural facts about the Old Masters – it really brought each person to life. Finally, here was something from the point of view of the living artist. Around that time I had the opportunity to go to Spain and I went to the Prado with this new awareness to see some of the works first hand. It changed my life.

MG But your own medium is not derived from paint and canvas, but from lenses and electronics.

BV If I were to trace my technological genealogy back, I would go to the development of the microscope in the early seventeenth century. The idea of extending the senses through artificial means, particularly vision, is really my branch of the family tree. The microscope is an instrument that not only extends the senses, but extends knowledge. So is the telescope. People like Hooke and Galileo were seeing things no one had seen before, but most importantly, things that exist.

When I first came across video, I wanted to use it like that – to see the unseen. I came of age in the late 60s and my generation was quite conscious of the fact that we were pushing the boundaries of what was apparent – trying to go beneath the surface, or surfaces. I realised then that new media tools like video have an extraordinary ability to do this. They are to time what the microscope is to vision. The full potential of the moving image is only coming to fruition today, after a century of evolution, but its full flowering is being severely hampered by the current corporate hegemony of our visual landscape.

In our world, the personal computer is the icon of individual media empowerment, at least for the time being, and it maintains this power from the fact that it is fundamentally not a visual instrument. It is an instrument of code. So we are, I believe, leaving the world of optics and visually derived images and arriving at the threshold of a new world that is based on codes and hidden informational substructures. Here the image

Bill Viola,
Observance, 2002, colour high-definition video on plasma display mounted on wall, 120.7 x 72.4 cm. Bill Viola studio, Long Beach, CA © Bill Viola Photo: Kira Perov

When I first came across video, I wanted to use it to see the unseen.

is literally the tip of an iceberg, a temporary surface manifestation of an underlying reality of invisible strata and branching root systems, webs of relationships and histories that we, as social beings, are immersed in but have never been able to represent or model before.

This is fundamentally a Platonic space of ideal forms and multiple, shifting points of view, where philosophy is reality and the real world is inherently symbolic and imaginary. It's incredibly exciting and it connects art back to its roots in earlier ages. We are inexorably moving into this non-visual world, one determined by invisible forces.

MG A good deal of your work has to do with stretching time - for example, *The Greeting*, in which the women approach each other in extreme slow motion.

BV Time is the ultimate invisible world. It's all around us. It literally is our life. We live in it like fish in water, yet we can't taste it, see it, touch it, smell it. It is a fundamental mystery, defining who we are as human beings in the most profound ways. The video medium has given visual artists access to the dimension of time.

But, like all media, video has specific technical limits as to how it can capture

and represent that time. When working on a new piece for Documenta in 1992, *The Arc of Ascent*, I had an idea to shoot an image of a man falling from a 10-metre high diving platform, but the problem was that with video I didn't have enough frames – individual increments of time – in the one second of his fall to make the sequence work. So I was forced to use film, a sacrilege for a video artist, and shoot the action at 300 frames per second, ten times the frame rate of video. That allowed me to extend time and smooth out the slow motion in ways not possible before. It was also the first time I worked with a full crew and collaborated with Harry Dawson. It opened up a whole new way of working for me. Most of 'The Passions' was shot on film for these same reasons.

MG It's that transformation of time that gives your work a similar strange, subjective quality to the one that you described in the Pontormo. But obviously one of the fundamental differences between a painting and a film or video is that a painting does not move.

BV True, but even so I think those artists were very aware of time. The tension in Pontormo's *The Visitation* as Mary and Elizabeth are about to embrace is a perfect example. And certainly, in the nineteenth century, the transitional group of the Impressionists and Post-Impressionists – who, not coincidentally, were working during the advent of photography – felt that time was one of the most essential things they were dealing with in painting. Cézanne said, 'Right now there is a moment of time passing by. We must become that moment.'

Notice that he didn't say we must represent that moment or paint that moment. He said, 'we must become that moment.' He's out there in the landscape with his brush, the light is fading, and he's trying to touch it – to BE it. This is not about a camera or vision – it's about Being. That's a very Zen-like statement, to be so conscious of the fleeting nature of reality like that.

MG Many painters have talked about their medium as a way of pinning down a moment in time as it slips past.

BV Yes, but with video you don't catch the moment – the image rides along with it. The fundamental nature of my medium is the living, transforming image. Video – as opposed to film – has as its origin and nature the live camera. That's the quintessence of time continuously slipping away.

If your interest is to hold onto time, then you will regard it as something slipping away, that's being lost. But if your interest is transformation, growth and change – wanting to ride the wave as it's cresting – then there is no problem. You are immersed within the flow of time, and you are dripping wet!

MG You were talking a moment ago about *The Arc of Ascent*. In fact, water and immersion in water are as much a leitmotif in your work as the slowing of time. Is that connected to the drama that you've described in your childhood?

BV I almost drowned when I was six years old. We were on holiday on a lake in upstate New York and I jumped off a raft and didn't hang on to my little inner tube, so I sank to the bottom. My uncle rescued me. I'll never forget what I saw under there.

Water for me is the ultimate medium for the image – it has a vivid, captivating surface, and it has a dark, uncertain depth. In prehistoric times, when human beings knelt to drink before a little pool or stream and the water was still, they saw their own face in reflection. Just imagine that moment – the first self image. It's no coincidence that the myth of Narcissus has been so powerful for millennia. This phenomenon, and its complement, the shadow, maintain a very deep connection within us.

However, water by nature is seldom still and so the images you see in it are distortions. The Buddhists call this 'the World of Appearances'. Like the images on the walls of Plato's cave, we only see the reflection, not the actual thing itself. Many analogies have been made between video and water, especially in the early days of analog signal processing – the kinds of visual disturbances that occur within the magnetic field on a television monitor. Nam June Paik, video art's original master, perfected these techniques of image distortion and spontaneous signal processing in the tradition of John Cage.

Because the magnetic field and electronic circuits that were doing the distorting are made up of electrical waves, they can create visual patterns that closely resemble rippling water. In art school I quickly realised that I needed to study wave theory as one of the fundamentals of my craft – in this regard we were way ahead of our professors, making up the curriculum as we went along.

At that time I also did a lot of work with live cameras, creating architectural spatial setups that worked with the multiple, simultaneous viewpoints of self and space made possible by this technology. Coexisting with images of myself from various positions fascinated me, philosophically as well as aesthetically. Water and mirrors are the only two other ways to do that. I just kept going deeper and deeper into this medium and at every turn it seemed I found something that reminded me of water.

(Above)
Bill Viola,
Emergence, 2002, colour high-definition video rear projection on screen mounted on wall in dark room, 200 x 200 cm. Commissioned by the J. Paul Getty Museum and the Getty Research Institute, Los Angeles © Bill Viola. Photo: Kira Perov

(Below)
Bill Viola,
Six Heads, 2000, colour video on plasma display mounted on wall, 102.1 x 61 x 8.9 cm. Bill Viola Studio, Long Beach, CA © Bill Viola. James Cohan Gallery, New York. Photo: Fred Scruton

MG You could make a huge exhibition about reflections in water – including Vermeer, Monet and Mondrian. It's been a fundamental subject in art.

BV I'd love to see that. A piece I made recently, *Five Angels for the Millennium* – which is currently at Tate Modern – originated in a series of images that I shot in water in 1999. The five 'angels' are various views of a man plunging into a darkened swimming pool, seen from under and over the water surface. It is one of several pieces that I drew from this material. If you look at what is going on in the piece, beyond the very simple image manipulations, you'll see that it's an image of a body falling into the water and sinking to the bottom. Literally, it's a drowning. He never comes up for air.

I edited the images very intuitively. I would spontaneously do things like turn the image upside down so that he was rising upwards instead of sinking down. Other times I would run time backwards so that he was being drawn up and out of the water like a bird in flight. At every turn an image of death was unconsciously being transformed into an image of birth. I guess that's what art is – turn something upside down and the world changes, and you along with it. ◼

'Bill Viola: The Passions', 22 October – 4 January 2004, National Gallery, London.

The Message is the Medium

Frank Gehry's *revolutionary architecture merges building and content into one vast spectacle.*

THE STORY OF THE ROCK BAND Mötley Crüe begins in a house in LA. 'It was 1981, and we were broke, with one thousand seven-inch singles that our manager had pressed for us and a few decimated possessions to our name. In the front room sat one leather couch and a stereo that Tommy's parents had given him for Christmas. The ceiling was covered with small round dents because every time the neighbours complained about the noise, we'd retaliate by pounding the ceiling with broom handles and guitar necks. The carpet was filthy with alcohol, blood, and cigarette burns, and the walls were scorched black. The place was crawling with vermin.' The band put much of the scorching down to using an excessive amount of lighter fuel while rehearsing the climax of their performance – setting fire to their bass player Nikki Sixx – and spend the first two chapters of their official history, *The Dirt*, gleefully elaborating on the acts of destruction that made their house so special.

As their account progresses, the carpet seems to play a particularly important role. It becomes a canvas on which they can present a permanent physical testimony to the impermanent combination of 'booze, drugs, chicks, squalor and court orders' that defined rock and roll as they saw it. And they invited everyone to admire the months of living recklessly conserved on a few square metres of festering fabric. It sounds like a work of art,

(Above)
Frank Gehry.
Courtesy Gehry
Partners, LLP

(Above right)
Experience Music
Project, Seattle

but it was better than a work of art because it was real, because it showed how genuinely rock and roll they were. It was the unofficial version of the Official Notice of Violation, issued to them by the LA Health Service Department on account of a massive pile of garbage in their back garden. That notice was the first public recognition of the band's nonconformity. It was a treasured proof of the house's

existence, one that they rather improbably kept as an illustration for the book they would write twenty years later, when they were famous.

Perhaps their foresight in preserving this important document only tells us that the band always knew that it was their house, rather than anything contained on their seven-inch singles, that provided them with their true rock-and-roll credentials. And if it tells us that, then it also tells us that Mötley Crüe are a lot smarter than most people think.

In 2001, when the band published their autobiography, there was evidence to suggest that for the first time for many years they might really be onto something. Their musical career had hit the skids a decade earlier, but in 2001 architecture was looking like the new rock and roll. Perhaps not the kind of rock and roll that their carpet was describing, but rock and roll in the sense that critics of culture tend to mean it: something that is popular and accessible. If you wandered around New York's cultural centres in

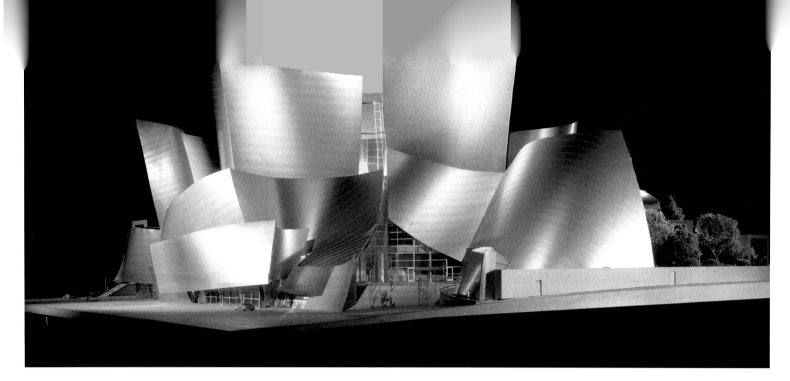

the late summer of that year, you could not help noticing that architects had replaced artists in the big galleries. An endless trail of models, drawings and collages by Mies van der Rohe littered both MoMA and the Whitney Museum, while the Guggenheim presented 'Frank Gehry, Architect'. The title alone had a mixture of grandeur and simplicity that Mötley Crüe might have appreciated.

And perhaps Gehry reached some bizarre pinnacle of triumph when, in January 2002, *World Architecture* magazine celebrated the opening of the Rem Koolhaas-designed Guggenheim Museum in Las Vegas by using a cover photograph that showed only the glittering prow of the Gehry-designed installation that it housed. The headline was 'Va-va voom: Koolhaas' Vegas Museum' – the inaugural exhibition was Gehry's 'Art of the Motorcycle' – and its unconscious suggestion was that while Europe's greatest architect had designed the museum, it was America's greatest architect who brought the va-va voom. If no one could remember what they had seen inside Gehry's Guggenheim Bilbao, they would *only* remember what they had seen inside Koolhaas' Guggenheim Las Vegas.

After the completion of the Guggenheim Bilbao (upon which every accolade up to and including 'building of the millennium' has been heaped) Frank Gehry was definitely the most rocking architect of them all. In 2000, he had even completed Seattle's Experience

Music Project, named after *The Jimi Hendrix Experience*, to prove it. And when it came to spinning his own rock-and-roll credentials off this project, it wasn't just that Gehry talked about the obvious qualities of the building – the form as a whole suggested a shattered guitar and one section was 'shiny with a purple haze, which is like Jimi Hendrix' (actually it looks more shiny like Liberace). Somehow he managed to come up with a tale that suggested he was no longer simply rocking in the sense that critics mean it; he was rocking for real.

The story of the EMP, as recorded in the rather pompously titled *Gehry Speaks*, begins with the architect's confession that, being a classical music lover, he didn't know much about rock when he received the commission. But he knew that a couple of people in his office played guitar and so, with their help, he set about 'educating' himself. 'They brought it all to me, all the books and the records, and I listened,' he recalls in an almost biblical manner.

Having ensured that he had seen enough guitars to be suitably inspired, Gehry presented his client with a model that depicted a fragmented accumulation of colourful buildings. And, of course, the client loved it. In fact he loved it so much that he approved it on the spot, despite Gehry's protestations that 'it looked like broken crockery' and that he would really like to work at it some more.

In the end, Gehry did continue to

evolve the design, but when the client saw the more integrated version that was the result his response was one of shock: it was too messy. At this moment Gehry proudly recalls the punchline that was his reply: 'Well, rock and roll is messy.' On the one hand he seemed to be demonstrating that he was really 'out there', that he rocked more than rock itself. On the other hand he showed that he, like Mötley Crüe, had understood the dirt – that rock and roll wasn't really about playing a guitar, it was about how well you could smash one.

Of course, Gehry had demonstrated that understanding much earlier in his career. Three years before Mötley Crüe set about modifying their house Gehry had performed a similar operation on his own. And despite the fact that when the remodelling was completed (in 1978) he

(Above)
Final design model of Walt Disney Concert Hall. Courtesy Gehry Partners, LLP

(Left)
Model of Walt Disney Concert Hall foyer. Courtesy Los Angeles Philharmonic

Walt Disney Concert Hall from the southeast. Courtesy Los Angeles Philharmonic

had already been in practice for 16 years, Gehry's official history as a great architect always begins here, with the house that spawned his act.

It was, in Gehry's words, 'a dumb little house' (he has fully mastered rock star speak) in an anonymous part of Santa Monica. And in Gehry's hands the house, constructed in the Dutch colonial style, was stripped back to expose its structure and then encrusted with an apparently bizarre accumulation of tumbling boxes made out of exposed everyday materials such as chainlink fencing and plywood, all contained by a corrugated sheet-metal fence. Now his little house was both dumb and intelligent (whether or not it was articulate depended on your point of view). Its materials made it an essay in LA vernacular architecture, while its structure was a tribute to the city's disorganised urban growth. The old asphalt drive had now become the floor of the dining room, and the house as a whole a gesture of defiant non-conformity.

Gehry described living in the house as like living in a painting, but even though he was openly inspired by art (and the list of inspirational artists – from Cézanne to Carl Andre – is, as the critic Beatriz Colomina has pointed out, enormous), his house remained better than art because it was real. Because he lived there and he ate his breakfast on the remains of an asphalt driveway.

Exploring a rock and roll of square and cuboid forms, the exterior surface (and the kitchen's asphalt) had become Gehry's equivalent of Mötley Crüe's carpet. It showed that he could take simple, square things and make them outrageous (later he would make them curvy too). It showed that he could turn grit into glamour, an accumulation of worthless architectural crap into priceless architectural gold. And where Mötley Crüe had a notice from the LA Health Service Department, Gehry had the story of a neighbour who tried to sue him for ruining the area, for leaving what some considered a mountain of architectural garbage in his back yard. He also had the architectural tourists who came to see his masterpiece, drawn by magazine articles expressing either revulsion or

A neighbour tried to sue him for ruining the area, for leaving what some considered a mountain of architectural garbage in his back yard.

admiration, all the while informing their readers that the house would tell them everything they needed to know.

By the time of his 2001 retrospective, everything you needed to know about Gehry was a collection of chainlink, cardboard furniture, pinwheel plans, curves and swoops, exploded architectural forms and shiny, shiny metal that spiralled up the ramp of Frank Lloyd Wright's iconic Guggenheim Museum interior as it traced Gehry's revolutionary progress from Santa Monica to Bilbao. And amid it all there were still traces of the dirt: a few of Gehry's messy, scribbled drawings, one of which was executed on the back of a napkin, and his battered process models, featuring crumpled bits of paper and fabric that might not have looked out of place on Mötley Crüe's floor.

Of course in physical terms the dirt was very hard to find on the shiny surfaces of Gehry's more recent work. He really seemed to have become like some glittering rock star, dropping a spangly sequin of metallic architecture at various gigs around the world. Even when Gehry became the subject of an architectural 'controversy' earlier this year it was as a result not of any of his warped metal buildings, but of his alleged association with the rock band U2. In an affair that seemed to highlight an utterly bizarre reversal of roles, whether or not Bono and the Edge had hung out with Gehry at his LA studio became the subject of an investigation by Dublin authorities, following a complaint by an anonymous architect, who, like Gehry, planned to enter a competition for a landmark tower

in the city. And, as if to ram home the truth that rock stars think like architects and architects think like rock stars, one of the judges of the competition was to be U2's Adam Clayton.

Gehry even has groupies who, in a singular display of devotion, promised to reconstitute a world map in terms of his architectural deposits on their website. (The projected completion date for this construction was May 2002 but, in a demonstration that Gehry's number one fans truly understand the architectural process, the 'Frank Gehry World Map' has yet to appear.) Many critics, on the other hand, worry that, high on CATIA (the computer program that has, over the last decade, enabled Gehry's scribbly drawings and messy models to become buildings that stand up) and commercial success, Gehry, like every ageing rock star, may simply have sold out. To them he seems to be operating as little more than a carnivalesque hall of mirrors, producing an architecture that is merely the wonderfully bent and fabulously distorted reflection of his wealthy clients' corporate dreams.

That one of the primary sponsors of Gehry's Guggenheim retrospective was Enron, who proudly stated in the catalogue that they 'share Mr Gehry's ongoing search for the moment of truth', is merely grist to the mill. And it doesn't help him that Paul Allen, the client for the EMP building, wasn't really a rocker at all, but a billionaire businessman who had made his fortune at Microsoft. It doesn't help him that he works for Disney. Because these days we all know that big business is bad.

To the critic Hal Foster, Townsend Martin Professor of Art & Archaeology at Princeton University, the issue at stake in Gehry's work is rocks (ones that are worth money), not rock. At his best, Foster concedes, Gehry produces architecture that brings 'elite design to the common culture' (which seems a pretty damning indictment of both design and popular culture); at his worst Gehry exploits this ability to produce architecture that is little more than an ingratiating 3-D billboard. Obvious examples are works like the Aerospace Hall at the California Science Centre (1982–4), which has a fighter jet clamped to its side in order to exhibit what it is exhibiting. You might also consider the Chiat Day Building (1985–91), designed (with Claes Oldenburg) for an advertising company with a monumental pair of binoculars as its entrance. For Foster (and others), buildings like this, in which the message is offered as a stylised ready-

Much has changed since the exhibition of Gehry's work at the Guggenheim. Big business has felt the pinch. The Guggenheim Las Vegas has closed and Gehry's proposed Guggenheim for New York appears to have been indefinitely postponed. But now that the epic saga that has been the realisation of LA's Walt Disney Concert Hall (begun in 1987) has concluded, the world will get a chance to debate his architecture again.

'An investment in the heart of Los Angeles' are the words that introduce the Concert Hall's website. The building was founded on a $50 million gift from Walt Disney's widow, Lillian, and has an ultimate project cost of $274 million. It occupies a full city block in LA's Bunker Hill area. Like many of Gehry's buildings, it uses this space to make a flamboyant statement of swoops, waves and curves. It aims at being the Guggenheim of concert halls, not simply because Gehry designed it, but

He seemed to have become like some glittering rock star, dropping a spangly sequin of metallic architecture at various gigs around the world.

of the Angels, which opened for business last year, is part of an attempt to reshape the image of downtown LA via landmark buildings. Both cathedral and concert hall provide unconventional packaging for traditional offerings. The cathedral is situated next to a freeway, and at night its illuminated crucifix acts like a giant billboard addressing the traffic. It's a Christian beacon of light updated for our times. But next to the what-the-fuck-is-that appeal of the Concert Hall, Moneo's building appears incredibly old-fashioned. And the fact is that a building constructed in honour of the man who gave us Mickey Mouse will probably outshine a building that honours the deity who gave us Jesus.

But do we really need to worry about it? Or hasn't Gehry always shown that architecture is merely something on which to stick dirty proofs of human existence? Sometimes we sweep it away (Gehry has continued to remodel

made, an integral architectural component, brazenly reflect the sinister way in which design is used to fuse aesthetic pleasure with commercial (in every sense) consumption. It reaches its most sinister level at Bilbao, where there are no ready-made pieces of pop iconography to signal this presence. Gehry doesn't even tell you he's doing it. Instead, building and content merge seamlessly into one vast spectacle. The medium is the message: the building is the museum's logo and a symbol that eclipses the entire town (because no one can think of any other reason for going there).

also in terms of creating an identity for the area and for the LA Philharmonic who will work inside it. And naturally this new identity will be exploited to sell the LA Philharmonic's product to new audiences. It's about classical music ('clad in wood, the 2,300-seat auditorium recalls the warm surfaces of a violin' according to one description) with a rock and roll finish. And Gehry's an architectural Jesus turning cultural water into 100 per cent proof cultural wine.

The original Jesus has a new home in LA too. Along with the Concert Hall, Rafael Moneo's Cathedral of Our Lady

Walt Disney Concert Hall. Courtesy Los Angeles Philharmonic

his house, notionally to suit his changing lifestyle) and sometimes we leave it on display. But one way or another it's always there, whether it's a festering carpet, a driveway-cum-dining room, a pair of ridiculous binoculars, a critic's diatribe, or a curvy, shiny, reflective love note to a big corporation. Even Mötley Crüe were smart enough to realise that. And they and Gehry just play with two different kinds of heavy metal. **MP**

The Walt Disney Concert Hall opens 23 October.
'Frank O Gehry: Work in Progress',
7 September 2003 – 1 January 2004,
Museum of Contemporary Art, Los Angeles.

Art in Motion

Merce Cunningham, Catherine Yass, Radiohead *and* **Sigur Ros** *confound the orthodoxies of collaboration by not working together – until the opening night.*

Catherine Yass, *Descent: 1/4s, 23°. 0mm, 15mph,* 2003, translucent inkjet on opera plastic, 30 x 60ft. Courtesy Goldenshot Ltd. Merce Cunningham 2003. Photo © Mark Seliger. Courtesy Brooklyn Academy of Music, Brooklyn

Merce Cunningham Dance Company performing *Fluid Canvas,* 2003, music by Radiohead and Sigur Ros. Photo © Tony Dougherty. Courtesy Brooklyn Academy of Music, Brooklyn

ROCK MUSICIANS have always been rather sniffy towards contemporary dance. They see it as alien, pretentious, perfumed. Rock likes to think of its own kineticism as spontaneous and untutored. It's an escape from choreography, from design. Punk ideology insisted that all non-DIY creative expression was hopelessly middle class and stank of prog-rock pomposity. Far better to shake, rattle and roll, to jump up and down like you just don't care.

Nearly thirty years have passed since Pan's People and Legs and Co, nice girls seemingly fresh out of the Lucie Clayton College, appeared weekly on 'Top of the Pops' with their freeform interpretations of Top 40 blockbusters. The explosion of rave culture at the end of the 1980s pretty much put an end to the idea that dance music should be accompanied by anything so formal as dance steps.

Yet renegades have existed. David Bowie, who trained under Lindsay Kemp and was in a dance troupe called Heathers at the end of the 1960s, performed in the 1980s with La La La Human Steps. Kate Bush, though she rarely stages live shows, has in her videos eschewed the post-R&B footwork of most pop stars and instead drawn on Theophile Gautier, Martha Graham, even Powell and Pressburger's *The Red Shoes* (1948). The Fall, Mark E Smith's band of avant-lumpen refuseniks from Prestwich, had a largely successful collaboration with Michael Clark called *I Am Curious, Orange* based on the Glorious Revolution of 1688.

October sees an addition to this slim tradition with the staging of *Split Sides* at the Brooklyn Academy of Music in New York. It's a four-way collaboration between choreographer Merce Cunningham, Turner Prize-nominated artist Catherine Yass and the rock bands Radiohead and Sigur Ros. Collaboration, however, is a slightly misleading word. The participants have never all been in a room together and will meet for the first time only on the opening night. As to guidelines: they haven't been given any.

They will be producing art in the dark.

Such are the joys of working for Merce Cunningham. Probably the most celebrated choreographer alive today – his 75th birthday in 1994 was designated Merce Cunningham Day by the then Mayor of New York, Rudolph Giuliani; more recently he has been honoured as a 'Living Legend' by the US Library of Congress – 2003 marks the fiftieth anniversary of the self-titled dance company he founded at Black Mountain College in North Carolina.

His genius, as contentious now as it was back in the 1950s and 60s, is for confounding the orthodoxies of ballet. He insists that his works have absolutely nothing to do with thinking or with images or ideas. They tell no stories. They express no political ideals. They do not even try to embody emotional or psychological states of mind. Rather their meaning lies purely in the motion and form of the human body. His oeuvre is, as writer James Davidson has argued, 'one of the most almighty and sustained acts of abstraction performed in this age of abstraction'.

Visual artists, Robert Rauschenberg, Jasper Johns and Andy Warhol being among the most distinguished of them, have always played an important role in the staging of Cunningham's works. Musicians too – John Cage, David Tudor, Alvin Lucier, Charlemagne Palestine, all avant-garde composers widely admired by the more questing, sonically adventurous members of the rockist fraternity for their efforts to forge sonic palettes more experimental than those found in the metronomic, rhythmically anorexic confines of the pop charts.

Small wonder then that Radiohead are involved in the project. Some of their fans may bemoan the fact that they are still shying away from the straight-ahead guitar-rock of The Bends and exploring the oblique, left-field strategies found on divisive LPs such as *Kid A* and *Amnesiac*. Others will find it admirable that a band so critically and commercially popular is willing to throw itself into new ventures, to cede centre stage, and agree to play what is an important but still only contributory part in a collective project.

Radiohead, 2003. Photo: Jason Evans. Courtesy Parlophone Records.

In some ways the trajectory Radiohead have taken in recent years makes them perfect for a venture of this kind. They've been willing to switch off the default settings for The Song – hooks, choruses, anthemic chords – and to shift from rock modalities to new textures, influenced by the abstract logorhythms of electronica acts such as Autechre, but also by click-and-cut glitch, modern composition and free jazz. Thom York's vocals, rather than anchoring individual songs, are now used as just another instrument in the mix. It's less the lyrics that convey meaning, and more the grain of his treated and reconfigured voice.

The effect, some disgruntled fans claim, is wilfully opaque and inhuman; exactly the same has been said of Cunningham's work, not least since he began experimenting with a software program called LifeForms in order to try out virtual dance figures. But the loss in traditional sonorities and comforts is more than made up for in the new forms that begin to brew up. What starts off as discomfiting or alienating soon creates its own kind of rapture.

That's what Catherine Yass is hoping anyway. Yass is responsible for the

Baseless buildings range across the purple and black backdrop, conveying a sense of swoony beauty and off-kilter dread.

photographic backdrops for *Split Sides*, alongside eighteen-year-old camera obscura experimenter Robert Heishman. When I went to meet her at her studio off Columbia Road in London's Hackney she still seemed rather taken aback by the speed at which the whole project had been conducted: 'Someone from the Museum of Modern Art suggested me only six months ago. I was totally shocked, hot-footed it over to New York and had an intensive week of talking to Merce's people and watching the dancers rehearse. It's quite bizarre really. I do my thing, and the set design and the music people do their thing, and somehow it all comes together on the night. When you watch it it looks completely synchronous. It's all to do with a chance meeting.'

If the commission came as a surprise, the artistic process itself is also far less coherent and structured than anything to which Yass is accustomed. The uncertainty this creates seems to worry and excite her in equal measure: 'When I went over there I wasn't even expecting to make a new image, but I thought I may as well try and take some photos while I'm in New York. It seemed to me that there

Sigur Ros, 2003.
Photo: Alex Torrens.

Not that Sigur Ros were too familiar with Cunningham's work initially. Bassist Georg Holm admits: 'I wasn't a big fan of modern dance and didn't know much about it. It didn't surround me or my friends at all. But after we were asked to contribute we went to see a show in Reykjavik, *Rainforest*, the one with Warhol's silver balloons. We were very impressed and got more and more interested. It was definitely a mind-opener.'

I put it to Holm that his band shares with Cunningham a zen for non-referentiality. Their last album was entitled ( ), eschewed song titles, employed a made-up language called Hopelandic, and at one point features 36 seconds of silence that baffled some listeners but also echoed the famous *4'33"* by Cunningham's partner John Cage: 'I can relate to that. We definitely have something in common there. We're not going to tell anybody what to think with our music. It's more important that people make up their own mind, so that people become part of the music. We provide the basic tones and people then come to fill up the space.'

Sigur Ros are fond of playing unorthodox venues such as galleries and churches. But *Split Sides* is a bolder project still. How good it is to see a band break out of the album-tour, album-tour routine. How good that, just at the point in their careers when many established groups tend to become set in their ossified ways and are closed off to new ideas and influences, they – like all the artists in this collaboration – are happy to embrace risk. They are allowing themselves, and what they perceive they stand for, to be remixed and disfigured.

Holm says: 'It just sounds like a genuine and original idea. We work a lot on instinct. When we heard about this it sounded different. This is great. This is something. We haven't produced anything so far. We won't until the last minute. That's the way we work best. All I can say is that we're really looking forward to actually performing it – it's really different and exciting.' MP

'Split Sides', 16 - 18 October, Brooklyn Academy of Music, Brooklyn.

I understood something about Merce's sensibility and the way he uses structure. I'm so unmusical, and I'm probably misunderstanding everything, but I got a sense that there was some kind of structure going on that I was hearing in the music and in the dance. But how do you translate that sense of rhythm in a photograph if you don't know what the dance is going to be?'

The designs Yass shows me are woozy and evocative. Baseless buildings range across the purple and black backdrop, conveying a sense of both interiority and exteriority, swoony beauty and off-kilter dread. 'It's got the rhythms of the building going across, and you can imagine them being a musical score. I always thought that Abstract Expressionism makes this rhythm across the surface of the canvas but it also has a kind of depth. Here the fifteen dancers are going to be dancing under the space where the buildings should be, as if it was a weight on them.'

It's clear that the end results will be a revelation to the artists as well as to the audience. Yass points to an image on her computer screen: 'What will happen to the pixellation and grain when it's blown up? It's got to be back-lit and I've never worked on this particular material. I've no idea how it's going to translate: this image has already been transferred from photographic colours into printing colours, so already it's very different. I think I'm just going to have to accept that it changes from how I originally envisaged it. It's really strange working remotely. I sent them the images and they've assembled them in parts. You need trust and faith. Your own meticulousness only counts for so much when it's being assembled thousands of miles away and when its full scope only becomes clear when other parts – music and dance and light – are also applied. Your identity becomes subsumed; you're a sort of team player.'

That ethos isn't entirely alien to Sigur Ros. The Icelandic band emerged from the *Smekkeysa* (Bad Taste) collective in Rekyjavik that also gave birth to the Bjork-fronted band The Sugarcubes. Bad Taste produce poetry, art, music – whatever grabs their fancy. At a recent show at East London's Spitz venue, one of the collective's bands played a song whose tune was known to only two of its members (one a pre-pubescent toy-trumpeter). Such an embrace of the aleatory and random recalls the way Cunningham uses I Ching, computers and the toss of a coin to determine the structure and order of his pieces, but it also contributes to the 'enlargement of possibilities' that the choreographer sees as a fundamental part of his work.

Cunningham uses I Ching, computers and the toss of a coin to determine the structure and order of his pieces.

masterpiece so that it lasted a whole day. Not really a crowd pleaser, I thought, when a friend suggested we catch it (or a bit of it – I think watching it in its entirety was only for the really fervent), but I went along and it was, well, mesmerising and hypnotic and disturbing. Art is about making us feel things, I think, and if this is all that any artist can hope their work to achieve then Douglas Gordon is a great artist. He's also one of the bright young things of the video art world whose work sells for a fortune and who party like it's 1999 – it's not only the socio-logical and cultural aspects of video art that emulate rock and roll. My research for this piece uncovered a plethora of hard-drinking, drugging and shagging stories that make the televisions-thrown-into-the-pool antics of their musical cousins seem schoolboyish and mimsy by comparison.

Last year Doug Aitken, who started his career making pop videos, showed a piece called *New Skin* at the 303 Gallery in New York. It was about a woman who was obsessed with images, and rightly so as it turns out she was going blind. The video was even projected onto a moving elliptical screen representing the eye. This combining of several different disciplines – video, performance and sculpture or architecture (or however you care to think of Aitken's moving screen) – is where I think video art becomes really interesting, as it is no longer bound by the confines of a mere canvas or screen.

This idea of bringing together video, performance and sculpture is not new, however. Tony Oursler has been doing it for years. His show at Metro Pictures this summer consisted of a collection of weird-shaped objects with weird-shaped faces projected onto them. Their voices were imploring, cooing, and inviting us to come closer as if we were babies, but the faces, made up of two eyes and a mouth that seemed to move independently of each other, weren't inviting at all. The effect was both funny and disturbing. I loved it.

If we're talking rock and roll we need look no further than Matthew Barney. Barney is über-big. In fact Barney is the Elvis of video art. This year's Guggenheim

exhibition presented his sculptures, photographs and video installations, as well as screening his Wagnerian *Cremaster* film cycle. It is pretty rare for the Guggenheim to devote its entire space to a young artist, but such is the power of Matthew Barney. Like a true rock star, he has managed to forge a multi-layered identity that is a feast of mythology, sexuality and gender, semiotics and personal Matthew Barney stuff. He also has the rock chic trait of getting other amazing artists to join him in his films, like Richard Serra, thereby both collaborating and confirming his deity at the same time. As if this wasn't enough, he is really sexy and is always taking his clothes off and climbing things, and he goes out with Björk to boot. He couldn't get any more rock and roll.

Other artists who would feature in my video art top 10 include Candice Breitz, Pierre Huyghe, Shirin Neshat, Paul Pfeiffer, Pipilotti Rist, Eija-Liisa Ahtila and Janet Cardiff. She had a show at PS1 last year that blew my mind. Not only had she created ingenious video installations where you walked behind a curtain and entered a room in which a tiny projection of a woman on stage made you feel like you were in the gods of some huge old theatre, but she also talked to you through a headset as you wandered round the museum, guiding you down dark corridors and through ominous doors. It was really spooky and a daring act of trust between the artist and her audience. Never have I felt so penetrated by an artist's will – she was literally inside my head telling me what to do. In fact, I suppose Cardiff isn't strictly speaking just a video artist. She is a sort of aural suggestive artist too, if such a thing exists. She is a crossover artist in the video world. Think Faith Hill or Dolly Parton. Actually don't, but you get the idea, I hope.

I would also have to include from the old guard Bill Viola, one of the legends who have influenced young artists and still stun, but are now more mellow and reflective. Bill Viola is the James Taylor of the video world – a ground breaker, always inspiring and always cool. My favourite Bill Viola experience was

Doug Aitken,
New Skin, 2003,
4-channel,
4-projection video on
elliptical x-screens
with sound, 12 min.
Courtesy 303
Gallery, New York

when I walked into a darkened room and suddenly a whole wall in front of me crashed into life and I saw a man drop into a tank of water in slow, slow motion. Every little air bubble and wave became apparent and, even though the man can only have been there for the length of one breath, it felt like he was there forever and was surely going to burst. Like Douglas Gordon's *24-Hour Psycho*, Bill Viola was using the technology of video to make us re-examine what we thought we already knew.

Viola's recurring themes of water and playing with time were particularly apparent in PS1's exhibition of early video work belonging to Pamela and Richard Kramlich, who have been avidly collecting video art since 1967. Luckily for us, their collection contains key pieces of a whole new art movement in its early stages. (God knows where they keep them all. I hope they have a big house. And a lot of televisions.) Here were video art pieces that were made even before video came into being. Some of them had originally been shot on film, and the sound of the film looping was carefully added to the exhibits to recreate the experience of seeing them for the first time in their original state.

The most outstanding works for me involved the performance artist Marina Abramovic, whose piece, *Art Must Be Beautiful, Artist Must be Beautiful*, consisted of her brushing her hair so hard you felt it was all going to fall out, and you really wanted her to stop. She used to do really wild and often violent and naked pieces with the artist Ulay in which the two of them would run into each other or slap each other again and again and again. Recently she starved herself for twelve days in a gallery in New York. The public could go in and observe her and wish, no doubt, that she would stop. I'm glad I didn't see it as, much as I appreciate what she's trying to do, I think my Scottish upbringing would have forced me to throw her a doggy bag or bring her some soup in a flask.

They even have video art in my local bar! I originally thought that there was something wrong with their satellite system, but no. I soon realised that the

(Right)
Douglas Gordon, *Play Dead; Real Time*, 2003, DVD on monitor, dimensions variable. Courtesy Gagosian Gallery, New York (Chelsea)

(Below)
Janet Cardiff and George Bures Miller, *Berlin Files*, 2003, film and sound installation, dimensions variable. Courtesy the artists and Luhring Augustine, New York

Matthew Barney is the Elvis of video art.

screens showing two men standing the Royalton Hotel in New York, constantly shaking hands for twenty minutes at a time, were actually video art installations. It was mesmerising. Yes, that word again. My fellow drinkers and I became obsessed with it. Eventually I had to look away as it made me feel a bit weird in my tummy. Who would have thought art in a bar would do that?

But that, I think, is the amazing thing about video art. It can surprise and provoke us because we aren't quite sure what makes something a piece of video art as opposed to a film. We're all so familiar with some of its elements and the ways in which it is presented that artists are able to manipulate us and lure

us further down new roads than we might otherwise have allowed. Because I mean, what actually is it? Is the *Cremaster* cycle video art or a film? Would Sam Taylor-Wood's film of Robert Downey Jnr wandering around an empty house be considered video art if he wasn't lip-synching to Elton John's *I Want Love*?

Isn't it great that this young breed of artists have taken the newest and most all-conquering art form in our history and used it to inspire, challenge and explore? Despite the links I've tried to make with their musical cousins, they do not merely seek to entertain or pander to the lowest common denominator in order to sell their product. The similarities are only in style, not content. Vivat, vivat, video art! MP

'Janet Cardiff and George Bures Miller', 12 April - 7 September, Tate Liverpool, Liverpool.
'Janet Cardiff and George Bures Miller', 7 June - 24 August, Whitechapel, London.
'Janet Cardiff and George Bures Miller: The Paradise Institute', 5 June - 21 September, Baltic, Gateshead.
'Douglas Gordon: Letters, Telephone Calls, Postcards, Miscellaneous, 1991 - 2003', 13 September - 31 December, Vanabbe Museum, Netherlands.
'Tony Oursler', 3 May - 21 June, Metro Pictures, New York.
'Bill Viola: The Passions', 22 October - 4 January 2004, National Gallery, London.

RICHARD HARRISON

10 SEPTEMBER – 4 OCTOBER

ALBEMARLE GALLERY

49 ALBEMARLE STREET LONDON W1S 4JR Tel: 020 7499 1616 Fax: 020 7499 1717
www.albemarlegallery.com Email: info@albemarlegallery.com Monday – Friday 10 – 6 Saturday 10 – 4

Seeing in the Dark

Richard *and* **Pamela Kramlich** *have amassed the most extensive collection of video art in the world.*

Pamela and Richard Kramlich. Courtesy ICA, London

PAMELA KRAMLICH HIT AN ICON on a bedside touch screen and a soft churning of motors lowered shades smoothly and simultaneously over the three master bedroom windows.

A second touch brought down a wide projection screen opposite a nearby sofa. Then, opposite the big screen, a video projector dropped from a nearly invisible ceiling panel. 'It's Stan Douglas's *Television Spots,*' said Richard Kramlich, when a moving image appeared from the late-80s compilation of mini-dramas that Douglas made for insertion among Canadian TV commercials, to the bafflement of viewers.

In the past 16 years the Kramlichs have made an international reputation as collectors of video art and projected image installations. Their Tudor-style house in San Francisco's posh Presidio Heights neighbourhood has been wired from top to bottom. Flat-screen monitors and carefully closeted electronics keep a rich menu of video works on DVD available for viewing in almost any room at almost any time.

Two institutional exhibitions have celebrated the Kramlich Collection, one of the most extensive private holdings of its kind anywhere: in 1999 'Seeing Time' filled a floor of the San Francisco Museum of Modern Art with installation pieces from the collection, and in 2002, PS1, a venerable New York alternative space now affiliated with the Museum of Modern Art, presented 'Video Acts:

Single Channel Works from the Collections of Pamela and Richard Kramlich and the New Art Trust'. A trimmed-down version of 'Video Acts' has been showing at the ICA in London since

July. It includes things often cited in the critical literature but seldom shown, including early works by Peter Campus, Vito Acconci, Bruce Nauman, Joan Jonas, Richard Serra, John Baldessari, Nam June Paik, Gary Hill and others now recognised as pioneers of video.

'We were very surprised that PS1 wanted to do the show,' Richard Kramlich told me. 'We thought it would bore people beyond belief. We thought it was great reference material of historical importance, but it was really Glenn Lowry' – director of MoMA – 'who convinced us to do it. He said, "I know my constituents and they want to go back to the roots and understand who these artists were." And it's been wonderful to see how important the show was to art students.' Public response to the PS1 show exceeded even Lowry's expectations. The institution's vast square footage permitted curator Klaus Biesenbach to devote an individual monitor or projection space to nearly every work, so visitors could wander among them at whim, seldom having to wait to see a piece playing. The ICA has arranged a similar presentation, which minimises visitor impatience, a cause of the general public distaste for video art.

'Video Acts' draws upon both the Kramlichs' personal holdings and those of the New Art Trust, a non-profit archive they have founded that shares its resources with three museums, SFMoMA, MoMA New York and Tate Modern. Pamela Kramlich developed the idea with Thea Westreich, the New York art consultant who until recently advised the Kramlichs on acquisitions. 'We realised that when an institution collects [video], it's going to be the last thing the budget goes to and the first thing from which it goes away. The Walker Art Center let their video curator go and SFMoMA has put Benjamin Weil' – its curator of new media – 'on part time. It's a very vulnerable kind of work in terms of support. And if we gave it away to any institution in the quantity we have now, it would be very costly to maintain. So unless Dick and I could completely endow the collection, we wouldn't be able to give it away. We were already thinking in terms of three institutions, but we didn't want to split the collection up, so we came up with idea of their sharing an archive.'

'The idea is to donate the whole collection to the trust over time,' Richard Kramlich added. 'That way we can make it available to these museums and it'll get a lot more exercise. And if we can get the Napa house built in, say, two more years, and donate it to the trust, then it can become a study centre, we can have an artist-in-residence programme, the whole shot.'

The Kramlichs have commissioned Herzog + de Meuron, the architects who made a derelict London power station into Tate Modern, to design a new residential showcase for their collection in Napa County, an hour north of San Francisco. After five years, the house is still a construction site. The project reached what the Kramlichs describe as a 'cross point' at which they decided to scale back their original plans for it. Now that the 21,000 square foot bottom

floor, partially underground, has been completed, they are redesigning the upper floor. Controls and settings for displaying video work will be integrated into the new house from the ground up. But the collection has not really dictated the house's design. 'We had to build a special space for a James Coleman piece because it has a specified distance between projector and screen,' Pamela Kramlich said, 'but otherwise we've conceived it like a Kunsthalle, where we could install whatever we want to show.'

Her husband's venture capital business rode high during the boom years of Silicon Valley. But the sharp downturn in the California economy has touched even top financiers, though the Kramlichs did recently buy a New York apartment and have been busy deciding what art works belong there.

The Kramlichs began collecting video work in the late 80s. They credit John Caldwell, then chief curator of SFMoMA, and Antonio Homem of New York's Sonnabend Gallery, with setting the course their collection has taken. 'We started with drawings, which kind of led us into conceptual things,' Pamela Kramlich said. Works on paper by Bruce Nauman, Jenny Holzer and Joseph Beuys punctuate the main floor of their home. A double self-portrait and a *Shadows* painting by Andy Warhol face each other across the living room, flanked by vitrines full of paraphernalia from Matthew Barney's *Cremaster* cycle, which they keep loaded on a concealed disc player. 'Once I started to look at video art', she went on, 'I realised that it wouldn't have been accepted without the way being prepared by conceptual art. Conceptual art was something I had to go through before I could get into video. I always thought Beuys was right in there because I think this collection comes out of Fluxus. Nam June Paik too and of course Warhol, because he started with the movie camera. Later on, when Dick felt comfortable spending the kind of money it takes, we got an Yves Klein because it involved a performance element. And we started with Matthew Barney really early on because of the museum's [SFMoMA's] interest in him.'

A performance-made canvas in

(From top)
Vito Acconci,
Walk Over, 1973.
Courtesy Electronic Arts Intermix (EAI), New York

Richard Serra,
Prisoners' Dilemma, 1974. Courtesy Richard Serra.

Bruce Nauman,
Art Make-Up, 1967-8.
Courtesy Electronic Arts Intermix (EAI), New York

International Klein Blue greets visitors who ascend the staircase between the house's two main floors. Long poles dropping from the ceiling into the stairwell support the several monitors and speakers of Dara Birnbaum's multi-channel *Tiananmen Square: Break-In Transmission.*

The Kramlichs' first new media acquisition was a video transcription of Peter Fischli and David Weiss' film *The Way Things Go,* which they saw at

Mike Kelley and Paul McCarthy, *Heidi,* 1992. Courtesy Electronic Arts Intermix (EAI), New York

Documenta in 1987. Pamela Kramlich ordered it over the phone from Sonnabend in New York. It cost US$350. 'We were in a fortunate position because nobody then was trying to put a collection like this together,' she said. 'The museums weren't yet buying it in any serious way and there was almost 30 years of material to review. So then we went on, trying to convince Dick that we could spend more than $10,000 because it seemed like we had a very limited budget early on.'

In 1990 they bought Bruce Nauman's *Raw Material – OK, OK, OK* because, according to Pamela Kramlich, 'I thought we needed a benchmark for the collection in terms of quality standard.' A gruelling performance in which the artist, seen in tight close-up, apparently stands on a spinning turntable shouting 'OK, OK, OK, OK...', it plays, when activated, on two stacked monitors and a projection screen in a large ground-floor space where the Kramlichs frequently entertain. The same room holds Jeff Wall's photo *The Argument,* a version of Nam June Paik's *TV Buddha,* Bill Viola's super slow-motion homage to Pontormo, *The*

The artist, seen in tight close-up, apparently stands on a spinning turntable shouting 'OK, OK, OK, OK...'

Greeting, and a slide projector word piece by Robert Barry.

But the Kramlichs acknowledge that they seldom sit down alone at home and watch an artist's video work. 'It's much more socially interactive than painting, for example,' Pamela Kramlich said. 'When you walk into a room, you don't automatically talk about the Warhol or whatever. But when you walk in to look at video art, you're already talking about it and somebody wants to see something. It becomes a choice that you make with other people to turn it on. Unless I'm going to look at it for some research reason or because I've forgotten some detail and want to look for it, I don't turn things on. We have a lot of people who come through who are curious about how we work with this material, and that's when we'll turn something on. Otherwise we pretty much live with dark screens.'

Collecting work in new media, the Kramlichs have encountered issues of conservation and authenticity that no one had ever anticipated. Part of the New Art Trust's brief is to develop standard practices for the preservation and

conservation of artworks in video and digital media. The trust has already sponsored two international symposia on presentation and conservation topics, involving artists, curators and conservators.

'We've realised through mistakes we've made that we need a whole checklist of questions every time we buy an artwork, so we know exactly what we're getting,' Pamela Kramlich said. She recalled one example: buying on the secondary market a highly regarded video work by Canadian artist Rodney Graham. 'We paid US$110,000 and all we got was a DVD – no equipment – and it didn't work,' she said. They got no satisfaction from the seller, a reputable London dealer, and so had to rely upon an American dealer they know to appeal to the artist to restore the defective disc.

'Not even institutions have been through the kinds of experiences we have,' she said, 'because they don't own the same quantity of material. So we're trying to set up guidelines to apply to everything we buy. We've slowed down in purchasing now because we've got so much going on, what with the show and construction. It's cost us a lot of money.'

The obsolescence of display technology may be one worry they can put behind them for a while. 'With the current digital formats, it's pretty stable,' Richard Kramlich said. 'The tape is what puts us in a bind right now,' Pamela added, thinking of the originals in 'Video Acts'. 'How much do you go back and preserve?' The work in 'Video Acts' was completely re-mastered digitally, presenting viewers as well as curators and the artists themselves with the question: how much, if anything, is lost when a work made on tape migr-ates to digital format? **MP**

'**Video Acts: Single Channel Works from the Collections of Pamela and Richard Kramlich and New Art Trust',** 30 July - 19 October, ICA, London.

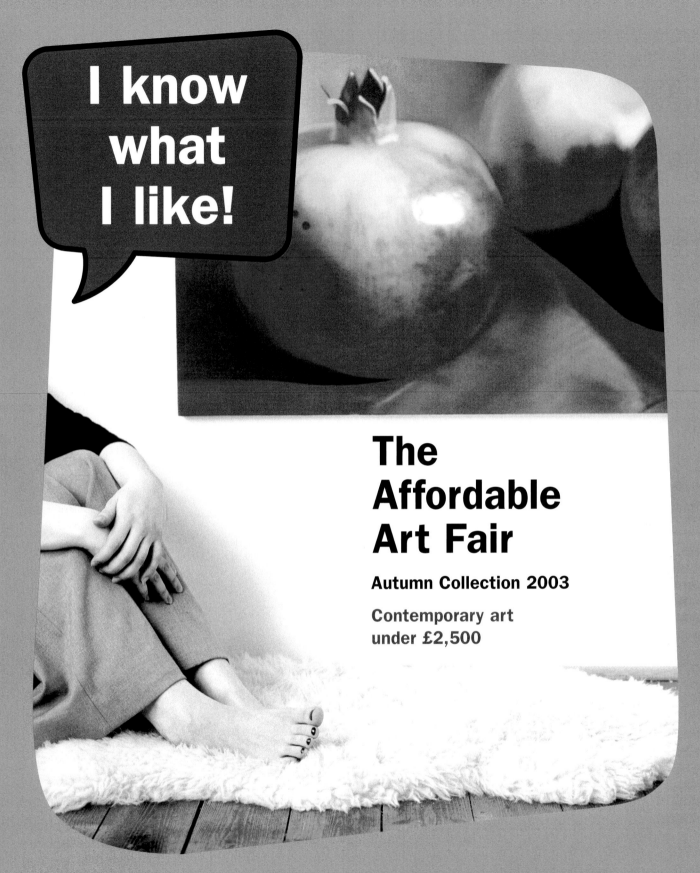

A Cultural Laboratory

The Palais de Tokyo opened 18 months ago but it still has a long way to go to convince the public and the art world.

FOR MANY YEARS, PARIS HAS lacked a space dedicated to contemporary creation, which would reflect new trends in art. That is until last year when on 21 June the Palais de Tokyo, the much awaited 'laboratory of emerging cultures', opened its doors. Within a week of its highly publicised opening, 50,000 visitors ventured through the immense leaden door of the building, first erected in 1937 for the International Exhibition of Arts and Techniques of Modern Life. Immediately the whisperings of awe spread throughout Paris and scores of articles expressing a range of opinions appeared in newspapers and magazines all over the world. Some compared it to New York's PS1; others described it as a fake artists' squat, or mocked this strange French creation which, although it tried to distinguish itself from existing institutions, ended up resembling them. A year and a half after its opening, and about thirty exhibitions later, opinions about the Palais de Tokyo are divided. Some denounce it and even boycott it. Others shower it with praise and declare it a place where one can feel at home. Opinions aside, the fact remains that the site has so far attracted 350,000 visitors, many of them young people and children who, thanks to programmes designed specially for them, go there to try to understand contemporary art.

For the majority of Parisians, who think of the site as a museum, comparing

Palais de Tokyo. Photo: © Stephane Lemouton.

it to the Musée d'Orsay or even the Museum of Modern Art which is located in the other wing of the building, the Palais de Tokyo is full of surprises. There is nothing solemn about it, no feeling of silence, nothing is fixed, everything moves, makes a noise. Video, television and electronic music are among the many media exhibited. The latest trends and those who typify them are celebrated, like the Berlin-based artist Daniel Pflumm, whose videos incorporate advertising's techniques of persuasion. There is also a taste for chaotic artworks: the exhibition 'Hardcore', accompanied by the noise of military combat, featured torn posters, a burnt-out car, and a model of an aeroplane transformed into a bomb.

There is no permanent collection, only temporary exhibitions, some displaying a single installation. Visitors can talk as much as they want. They can smoke in the building (excluding the exhibition halls), have a drink, browse in the bookshop and discover the latest trendy objects from Japan in the Black Block boutique. They can wander through the vast exhibition space of almost 40,000 square feet: there are no walls to stop them and no security guards. Here, guards are replaced by 'mediators', young art students who are there to provide explanations of the exhibitions. Above all, visitors can take advantage of the atypical opening hours: noon till midnight.

The Palais de Tokyo is, without doubt,

a unique project. For a start, it was created on the initiative of the Ministry of Culture and is run by two directors who are fully responsible for the exhibitions and the management of the site. While the Ministry provides 45 per cent of the entire budget (3.9 million Euros), patrons and sponsors, following the American model, finance its projects. 'The government doesn't interfere with our choices. That would be frowned upon,' explain the directors, Nicolas Bourriaud and Jérôme Sans.

Appointed for three years, the directors set the pace and tone of this 'personalised institution'. But sometimes the programming seems so personal that it fails to deal with central issues of art today. In response to the 'GNS: Global Navigation System' exhibition, which presented the hypothesis that topography is a major issue in current artistic creation, a journalist asked Bourriaud if topography was a particular passion of his. 'Without obsession or personal architecture', he responded, 'it is impossible to discover that of others.' Provided the correct balance is found, of course.

Inspired by the Moroccan square, Djema-el-Fnaa, the architects, Anne Lacaton and Jean Philippe Vassal, transformed almost 90,000 square feet (including exhibition and commercial areas) into a space which, to many, looks like a construction site: wire fence walls and a camping trailer masquerade as ticket windows at the entrance, and the exhibitions' titles are chalked up on a blackboard. Wandering through the enormous exhibition space with its crude, unplastered walls, it is easy to see why some visitors feel uncomfortable. 'You always feel like you've arrived at the wrong time. There is still scaffolding up,' explained a student from Lyon. But this is how the Palais de Tokyo was conceived: the installations are constantly being put up and dismantled even while you are there. Occupying the majority of the space, the café-bar, the restaurant, the boutique and the bookshop are for many visitors the most welcoming spots. They unite trendiness with conviviality especially in the bar, where large cushions

are strewn over the floor created by Michael Linn.

The programming at the Palais de Tokyo, as well as the works exhibited, has not been unanimously well received. So far thirty exhibitions have been presented with more than 200 artists participating, including Dominique Gonzalez-Foerster, Jota Castro, Tobias Rehberger, Thomas Hirschhorn, Rebecca Horn and Louise Bourgeois (whose very sparse exhibition caused a scandal). People have complained that some of the work is too obscure. 'If this is the art of today, I don't understand anything,' remarked a young woman standing in front of a Lars Nilsson. Some art professionals have criticised the lack of consistency between the exhibitions and the absence of any real investigation of ideas. Where's the defiance? Where's the novelty? People were already asking these questions at the opening exhibition, notably when faced with Wang Du's giant garbage can filled with papers and televisions. For the art critic Françoise Monnin these issues are still unresolved: 'They promise innovative artists, but the choices made are politically correct and follow current international trends. The way in which the Palais de Tokyo tries to show that it is on the fringe is extremely caricatured. Thus, among the artists chosen are the essential ethnic minorities threatened by political conflicts. If you are sixteen or ninety-six-years-old, black, Jewish, homosexual and Afghani, then you have the ideal profile for exhibiting your work there!' Others have found the exhibitions stimulating. 'While museums are trying to identify with art centres by showing "trendy" work and art centres are becoming stuffy and museum-like, the Palais de Tokyo is one of the only places that has succeeded in creating its own, special dynamic,' explained Franck Scurti, a French artist who has exhibited at the centre.

Undeniably, there is a feeling of freedom that the public is enjoying. During the demonstrations which paralysed Paris in May, angry teachers flocked there to protest. 'We welcomed them, we let them come in and express themselves. For them the site represents

Installation view of 'GNS: Global Navigation System', Palais de Tokyo. Photo: © Marc Domage

'People feel so comfortable that we have repeatedly had to ask them not to write on the walls.'

a symbol of the freedom of expression,' the centre's press officer told me. Lost in this sense of freedom, visitors, wandering somewhat aimlessly, at times forget certain basic rules of civility: 'They feel so comfortable that we have repeatedly had to ask people not to write on the walls,' says Bourriaud.

All criticism aside, the centre has succeeded in its role as a catalyst, bringing together people of all ages and all types at all hours. With more than 3,500 mentions in the press in one year, the Palais de Tokyo can boast of having piqued the curiosity of both the French and international communities. 'It is a place that is in the spotlight. I have never had so many articles written on my work as when I exhibited at the Palais de Tokyo. It didn't stop,' said Scurti.

In addition to exhibitions, the Palais organises events, concerts and shows, and offers access to a virtual Tokyo TV station. 'The moment for evaluation has certainly not arrived. Give us until 2005,' concludes Bourriaud. 'The Palais de Tokyo has not yet fulfilled its potential. The ship has just left the harbour.' Some nasty rumours say that there is little chance the government will renew its support of the Palais de Tokyo and that its survival depends on its ability to attract private investment. It may be necessary for it to learn to steer its own course – and without a captain since the honorary president of the centre, the highly regarded art critic Pierre Restany, died in May.

'Chen Zen: Silence Sonore', 1 October – 18 January 2004, Palais de Tokyo, Paris.

Peter Davies VENICE

The Pleasure of Paint

*A painter gives his perspective on a celebration of
the last forty years of painting at the Museo Correr.*

Takashi Murakami, *Superflat Jellyfish Eyes 1 & 2*, 2003, wood, silk, acidic dyes, foil, metal, platinum, paper, 200 x 397 cm. © 2003 Takashi Murakami/ Kaikai Kiki. Courtesy Galerie Emmanuel Perrotin, Paris. Photo credit: Lucia Veronesi

THE PAINTING EXHIBITION AT the Museo Correr was for me the highlight of this year's Biennale. It takes as its starting point Robert Rauschenberg's historic win of the prize for painting in 1964 when the Europeans to their horror saw the powerbase in the contemporary art world shift to America, and ends in 2003 with Takashi Murakami. Housed in the elegant rooms of the museum above Piazza San Marco, the concise and well-chosen show provides a refreshing antidote to the otherwise sprawling nature of the Biennale.

Curated by Francesco Bonami, the overall director of the Biennale, his natural affinity for painting is immediately apparent. In 1999 he curated, with Judith Nesbitt, 'Examining Pictures' at the Whitechapel Art Gallery in London. This show started a wave of exhibitions devoted to painting: 'Cher Peintre' at the Pompidou in Paris, 'Painting at the Edge of the World' at the Walker Art Center in Minneapolis, and 'Painting On The Move' at the Kunsthalle in Basel. Although multi-disciplinary and not purely a painting show, Dave Hickey's 'Beau Monde' at Site Santa Fe shared with the Museo Correr show the premise that it is okay to like something because of the way it looks and celebrated visual pleasure for its own sake. As Bridget Riley, who contributed to the show, put it, this

was a show for people for whom, 'looking is a pleasure, a continual pleasure'.

This cluster of recent shows has been particularly encouraging for me as a painter. Together they have given people a broader sense of the huge range of different kinds of painting that are currently being done. No single show

could ever achieve this. It is only through more large group shows curated by differently minded people that we will get a clear sense of what painting is about.

The exhibition at the Museo Correr follows Bonami's previously successful format adopted for 'Examining Pictures': one painting by each artist is on show.

Not each piece would necessarily have been on my personal wish-list. Perhaps different works might have been chosen; some artists might have been omitted; others might have been added. But encouraging people to respond in this way is a good thing; it gets you involved and it's also fun to think about which paintings you might have selected from the last forty years if the choice had been yours. But of course, this was a very personal selection – that of the curator's

of works. In the first room Rauschenberg, Ryman, Fontana, Twombly, Warhol, Buren and Riley set the tone of the show. In another Schnabel, Clemente, Kiefer, Kippenberger and Basquiat hang side by side. This show includes more grand figures and fewer emerging artists than Bonami's earlier show, which gives it a greater sense of authority and weight. But there are a few rooms devoted to the works of younger artists such as John Currin, Peter Doig, Jenny Saville,

(Above left)
Franz Gertsch,
Patti Smith IV, 1979, acrylic on cotton, 285 x 420 cm. Courtesy Galerie Haas & Fuchs, Berlin

(Above right)
Beatriz Milhazes,
Elefante Azul, 2002, acrylic on canvas, 189 x 299 cm. Courtesy Galerie Max Hetzler, Berlin

the lesser-known Enrico Castellani.

The exhibition, on until November, is a broad survey with its own idiosyncrasies and won't satisfy everyone. But it gives a powerful sense of what has been happening in painting over the last forty years as well as offering the chance to understand the traditions out of which many artists working today have emerged. As a viewer the personal nature of the selection by a highly regarded curator draws you into the exhibition and you can almost feel the presence of a knowledgeable, welcoming guide. As a painter it's the sort of show you'd aspire to be in. Unlike many contemporary exhibitions, all the work is self-explanatory; as Kippenberger said, 'everything we can see and understand is already on the canvas.'

There are a number of exciting painters in other parts of the Biennale: in the Giardini, Beatriz Milhazes, Dubossarsky and Vinogradov, Mamma Andersson, Chris Ofili and Ellen Gallagher, and in the Arsenale, Magnus Von Plessen, Dana Schutz and Hakan Gursoytrak. But most exciting of all was seeing a big painting show within the context of a large international exhibition dominated, as you would expect, by video installations. It was an enjoyable, even life-affirming, show which emphasised the fact not that painting is back but that it never went away. **MP**

– and it is precisely this that made it so interesting. Given the difficulties with works not always being available or there being restrictions about works travelling, it was a sign of the curator's considerable reputation that so much is in the exhibition. Bonami's choice shows a sensitivity and enthusiasm for the works, and the pleasure and excitement which these paintings have evidently generated in him is wonderfully infectious. This was one of the major achievements of the exhibition.

Another is the idiosyncratic groupings

Margherita Manzelli and Takashi Murakami whose enormous *Superflat Jellyfish Eyes 1 & 2* is spectacular. Other highlights include Richard Hamilton's *Fashion Plate,* a Franz Gertsch picture of Patti Smith, Gerhard Richter's painting of Gilbert and George, and an eerie Kai Althoff. It was great to see Jorg Immendorf included, an apparently out-of-fashion artist whose work nevertheless seemed to resonate with many of the art world's current concerns and trends. Another surprise was the space-age Fontana-like abstract by

(Above)
Mamma Andersson,
Minnesluckoma öppnas alltid från söder / The blank memories always open from south, 2002, oil on canvas, 80 x 280 cm. Collection Vicky Hughes and John Smith, London. Courtesy Galerie Magnus Karlsson, Stockholm. Photo credit: Per Erik Adamsson

Pittura / Painting: From Rauschenberg to Murakami, 1964 - 2003', 15 June - 2 November, Museo Correr, Venice.

Great Danes

Paintings from Denmark's Golden Age raise issues about the relationship between national identity and art.

TO APPRECIATE A NATION'S ART and artists, it helps to visit the place – walk the streets, eat the bread, drink the wine. On my first rainy-grey day by the Seine, as I fell in love with Parisian light, I fell more deeply in love with Corot. Corot's greys, I realised, are Parisian greys. Corot's light is Parisian light. The more intimate I became with Paris, the closer I felt to French painting. It was then also that I got closer to Braque. I understood Braque's love of greys – Braque's connection to Corot.

It can be dangerously reductive, I suppose, to equate people's cadences of speech or movements on the street with rhythms on the canvas; the temperament of a people with that of its art; the colour of a place with the palette of a painter; and yet, comparisons are inescapable. Renoir, after his Italian journey, remarked: 'The Italians don't deserve any credit for great painting. They just have to look around them. Italian streets are crowded with pagan gods and biblical characters. Every woman nursing a child is a Raphael Madonna.'

Having returned recently from a trip to Denmark, I have been thinking a lot about national identity as it relates to art and artists. In Denmark, I was immersed in nineteenth-century Danish art from Denmark's Golden Age, specifically the paintings of Christoffer Wilhelm Eckersberg (1783–1853), whose retrospective will open at the National Gallery of Art in Washington, DC, this November. Denmark is a beautiful country and Eckersberg is an accomplished painter; but I wonder how his work,

(Above)
Christoffer Wilhelm Eckersberg, *Langebro Bridge in Copenhagen with Running Figures,* 1836, oil on canvas, 45.5 x 33.5 cm. Statens Museum for Kunst, Copenhagen

(Right)
Amalienborg Palace, Copenhagen. Photo: Ireneusz Cyranek

seen outside his homeland, will be received.

Danish art has rarely been exhibited outside the country. The Eckersberg retrospective in Washington will be the first in twenty years devoted solely to the artist, and the first ever to be held outside Denmark. Eckersberg, who painted mostly landscapes, seascapes and portraits, is not Denmark's greatest painter, and he is little-known outside his country. (Christen Købke, Eckersberg's student, is a better painter than

Eckersberg, and is certainly better known.) Yet, Eckersberg deserves attention. He was Denmark's most influential teacher, introducing plein-air painting into the country and into the curriculum of the Royal Danish Academy, and he founded a school of painting that fostered a national sense of identity and regionalism, as it spawned the 'golden age' of Danish painting.

Eckersberg's canvases have an impeccable sense of compression. His landscapes are idyllic and precise, and his portraits are frank and generous in spirit. I was most taken, though, by his nudes. One in particular, of a seated woman putting on her slippers, feels psychologically complex. The woman is huge in the room, yet she also feels dropped down into the floor, as the space of the interior closes in on her. Some of the spatial complexity could be merely problematical. It is difficult to say, but it is here that it seems Eckersberg is closest to the neo-classicism of David and Ingres.

Like many Danish artists during the nineteenth century, Eckersberg went to Paris and Rome to absorb neo-classicism. In Paris, he studied with David, and in Rome he probably crossed paths

with Ingres. But I do not believe that Eckersberg, ultimately, ever wanted to compete with, let alone, be, Ingres. Ingres' temperament is not Eckersberg's. Ingres is Raphael reborn in France. Eckersberg is Danish, through and through.

Before visiting Denmark, I paid little attention to Danish painting and sculpture, but while there I found much to love in Danish art. Yet, I suspect that if I had initially seen Eckersberg outside Denmark, and I had compared him to Ingres and David, I would have thought of Eckersberg as a kind of neo-classical country-bumpkin, as a less talented version of his contemporary French masters. And this assessment, ultimately, would be a misconception, I believe, of what actually drove Eckersberg and his fellow Danes as artists.

Part of Eckersberg's charm, and the charm of most Danish art from its Golden Age (1816–48), is part of the charm of Denmark itself, which lies in Denmark's provincial sense of national autonomy and purpose. American folk art, which, unlike Danish painting and sculpture, is born almost entirely of the provinces and is often self-taught, appeals to that same sense of level-headed, utilitarian simplicity. Both Danish and folk art speak, seemingly, first and foremost for the people. The memory of the French and the ancient Greeks, though discernible in Danish art, is suffused – cleansed by Danish austerity.

Eckersberg obviously knew that the French and Italians did what they did very well, but French painting would never take hold in Danish soil, Eckersberg understood, unless it was reclaimed and made uniquely Denmark's own. Eckersberg could not compete with his European forefathers, and he probably realised that long before he returned, in 1816, to Copenhagen from Paris and Rome. Eckersberg, it seems, had another agenda.

In Rome, Eckersberg, through the plein-air process of painting Roman ruins, had for himself discovered and reclaimed antiquity. Going out into the Danish landscape to paint, he could discover and reclaim Denmark, not only for himself but for the Danish

people. American artists, also Puritan in origin, have consistently rejected European culture for similar reasons, preferring not only a more plain-spoken voice that is theirs alone, but one that, though it may be informed by Europe's weightier, more culturally sophisticated past, is fresher and pioneering in spirit – American, above all else. Pollock is a case in point; and once you have been to New York and also driven across the country, Pollock's choices, what he embraced and rejected, begin to make more sense. Eckersberg, seen in the greater context of Denmark – among its beautiful architecture and design, its landscape and art, among the Danes themselves – proves to be inventive, original and strange, as his paintings convey the essential qualities and temperament of the Danish people.

To understand Danish art, which is humble and unpretentious yet self-assured, it helps to know something about the Danes themselves. Across the proscenium of Denmark's Royal Theatre in Copenhagen is the Danish phrase, 'Ei Blot Til Lyst' (Not Merely for Amusement). There is something very northern, or at least Protestant, about being reminded, just before the curtain goes up, to keep the 'amusement' in check. There is a sense in Danish art that too much feeling may lead to disorder; that individual expression could undermine the common good. When Chardin is claiming to paint with his 'heart', and Renoir with his 'penis', the Danes feel as if they are painting with their heads.

This kind of utilitarian response in Danish art is most evident and successful in their architecture and design. Danish buildings, furniture, glassware

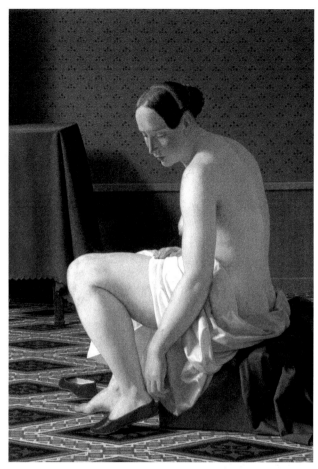

(Above)
Christoffer Wilhelm Eckersberg, *Woman Putting on Her Slippers*, 1843, oil on canvas, 65.5 x 46 cm. Ny Carlsberg Glyptotek, Copenhagen

(Below)
Interior of Ny Carlsberg Glyptotek, Copenhagen

Eckersberg's paintings convey the essential qualities and temperament of the Danish people.

and fixtures are among the most beautifully designed and useful objects created; but this approach is less successfully applied to Danish painting and sculpture, which at times can feel so modest and quiet that it can seem aloof, almost mute. Sometimes, it can feel in Danish art, as it can sometimes in American art, that too much of the important lineage to Europe has been severed.

Købke, who is certainly not without powers when it comes to composing with light, and who is often compared to his contemporary, Corot, can feel as if he is holding his emotions in check, in favour of expressing something more sensible and unromantic. Købke paints light rather than illumination. Light in Købke is rarely enigmatic or alive with possibility, and it never reaches that sublime resonance felt in Corot, whose light, as it naturally passes through the landscape, suggests that somewhere an annunciation might be brewing. Certainly, not everyone is Corot. The Hudson River School painters went so far in the direction of melodrama that every sunset can feel as if it's the Second Coming – but they

gave themselves over to their subjects. Købke's light can feel as if it is expressed first and foremost as a practical necessity. Light rarely feels fully embraced, which is the first step towards transformation.

This stoicism is also a Danish strength. During Denmark's Golden Age, Copenhagen was, and still is, one of those rare port cities: essentially European yet detached, highly cultured yet provincial, undeniably modern yet old-world. Copenhagen's insular stability comes out of a culturally clear sense of self. Danes and Danish art are quiet, but it is an inner calm, both self-reflective and self-assured. In the eighteenth century, Copenhagen's busy harbours were receiving a plethora of exotic, other-worldly objects from as far away as India, Africa and the West Indies. And yet, unlike New York and London during the Victorian era, Copenhagen seems to have looked beyond its borders with a subdued enthusiasm. The Danes may have taken in the world but they were not taken in by it.

Copenhagen, even before neo-classicism took hold, was neo-classical in temperament, but its neo-classicism arose out of two equally important impulses – one Lutheran, one Greco-Roman. Copenhagen's sense of order, though often symmetrical and Doric, was born as much out of a revival of antiquity as it was out of Protestant moderation and functional restraint. When, in 1794 and 1795, respectively, two devastating fires wiped out most of Copenhagen, the capital was rebuilt intentionally to emulate neo-classicism, to the

(Above left)
Christoffer Wilhelm Eckersberg, *View through Three of the Northwestern Arches in the Third Storey of the Colosseum in Rome,* 1815–1816. oil on canvas, 32 x 49.5 cm. Statens Museum for Kunst, Copenhagen

(Above right)
Christen Schiellerup Købke, *The North Gate of the Citadel,* 1834, oil on canvas, 79 x 93 cm. Ny Carlsberg Glyptotek, Copenhagen

(Above)
Søren Kierkegaard Square and 'The Black Diamond', the latest addition to the Royal Library. Photo: Cees van Roeden

point that the buildings were often painted an unassuming white or in Pompeiian hues of yellow, orange, red or green; and yet, so as not to overpower the church towers, the buildings were not allowed to exceed five storeys. And for pure practicality, the buildings also were bevelled at their corners so that fire engines could more easily pass through the streets. The repetition of those unassuming, obtuse corners gives the buildings a polite recession, as if the city were constantly bowing away from you, giving you the right of way. The effect gives Copenhagen the quality of being the most civil city I know of. Add to this that Copenhagen's traffic is made up mostly of bicycles.

I do not mean to imply that Denmark is culturally lacking or unsophisticated. Denmark has a world-class ballet company, great architecture and design, and spectacular collections of Danish and world art – all housed in monumental museums. These include the Ordrupgaard and Hirschsprung Collections and the Lousiana Museum of Modern Art, which is set on a beautiful site by the sea and has one of the most startling Giacometti installations I have encountered. There is also the Bertel Thorvaldsen Museum (part-Pompeiian villa and part-Sir John Soane's Museum in London), which houses the sculptor's work and his collection of antiquities, the Ny Carlsberg Glyptotek, and the Danish National Gallery. And there is the Tivoli Gardens,

a magical, through-the-looking-glass world – as much art installation as theatre – that is best seen at night.

I mean only to imply that Denmark is 'other'. It makes perfect sense to me that existentialism was born there, within a culture that, though insular, honours equally both its sense of independence and its sense of personal accountability. When I visited the collection of Kierkegaard's artefacts in the Museum of the City of Copenhagen, I was encouraged to go ahead and actually touch Kierkegaard's desk. Touching it, for the Danes, became purely a practical matter: if I had come all this way to see it why not take the next logical step? I can see why Kierkegaard was very at home in Copenhagen. Living there, in that unique climate, as opposed to, Paris, for example, allowed Kierkegaard to take that next, essential step inward. In *Stages on Life's Way*, he wrote:

Copenhagen... refreshed as it is by the sea... is as favourable a place as I could desire to dwell in. Big enough to be a great city, small enough to have no market price set upon men, where the tabulated comfort one has in Paris that there are so and so many suicides, where the tabulated joy one has in Paris that there are so and so many persons of distinction, cannot penetrate disturbingly and whirl the individual away like foam, so that life acquires no significance... MP

'Christoffer Wilhelm Eckersberg',
23 November 2003 - 29 February 2004,
National Gallery of Art, Washington, DC.

Not Just Another Place in the Sun

Valencia's Biennale offers the chance not only to survey the visual arts but also to explore the city's exciting urban developments.

V ALENCIA OUGHT NO LONGER TO BE Spain's unsung hero. Three hours from Madrid, Barcelona and the Balearic Islands, Valencia's location is one if its great assets. The city has the fastest developing economy in Spain, reflected in the major architectural projects the city has undertaken in the last decade. It is a compact city, with a population of barely one million, which means you can walk from one side of the centre to the other, grab a tapa, and still be on time for your appointment. Appropriate then to have 'The Ideal City' as the theme for Valencia's second Biennale. Its aims this year were to 'investigate communicative creation' between a wide range of creative areas. Five major exhibitions were programmed, in addition to a social project and various events and performances.

'A&M: department of proper behaviour', a show featuring the work of Will Alsop and Bruce McLean, occupies the Convento del Carmen. The large installation in the old Carmelite convent presents itself as a shop of experiences. Visitors are invited to sit, chat, sip a cocktail, get a haircut and even purchase the exhibits.

Mike Figgis, part-time Valencian resident for the summer, is responsible for 'The Museum of Imperfect Past', an exhibition at Los Palacios, a derelict 16-room mansion in the city centre. The film director-turned-multi-media artist has created specific narratives in each of the rooms, exploring the concept of dreaming by deconstructing the medium of film and cinema through the

> Visitors are invited to sit, chat, sip a cocktail, get a haircut and even purchase the exhibits.

Bertrand Lavier, *Relief-Peinture n. 14,* 2003. From 'Solares'

use of projections, photographs, sound and found objects. The installations include numerous showroom dummies, surprisingly low-tech exhibits for a Hollywood man.

Sebastiao Salgado presents 100 portraits of Valencians at the Museu de la Illustració i la Modernitat (MUVIM), ranging from fishermen, members of the

aristocracy and recent immigrants to the city. These images resulted from a democratic selection process in which the artist set up photographic studios throughout the city, inviting residents to have their photograph taken. The musical accompaniment and lack of labelling brought a necessary element of fiction to an otherwise arbitrary photographic

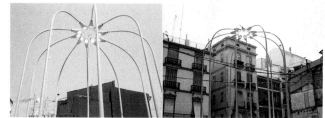

sociological survey.

At the newly refurbished Reales Atarazanas 'micro-UTOPIAS', curated by Francisco Jarauta and Jean-Louis Maubant, remains true to the Biennale's intention of focusing on communication across the creative fields. The show features work by artists and architects exploring contemporary architecture and notions of utopia. Contributions by ASYMPTOTE, Nigel Coates, Frank Gehry, Vito Acconci, Joop Van Lieshout, Tobias Rehberger, Jason Rhoades, François Roche successfully encourage viewers to analyse the exhibits and measure these utopic creations against our understanding of public environments and social change.

Visitors to Valencia soon become aware of numerous empty spaces in the city, which noticeably break up the continuity of its urban planning. Most of these are the result of buildings having been destroyed by floods prior to the Turia river being redirected away from the city in the late 50s. Art historian and philosopher Lorand Hegyi, recently appointed curator at the Palazzo Roccella in Naples, commissioned a large number of artists to create outdoor works to interact with these abandoned urban spaces. The resulting show, 'Solares (or on optimism)', includes amongst others Marina Abramovic, Gilbert & George, Ilya & Emilia Kabakov, Dennis Oppenheim, Orlan, Kim Sooja, Michelangelo Pistoletto, and Wim & Donata Wenders. Part of the success of this exhibition, probably one of the most visible at the Biennale, derives from

the way it interacts directly with the fabric of the city and questions the value of spontaneous processes of urban transformation as opposed to considered city planning. The question as to whether these empty plots are simply an omission to the urban regeneration masterplan is particularly pertinent in a city that has seen many recent changes, not least 'the City of Arts and Sciences', a challenging architectural project by local architect Santiago Calatrava designed to revitalise the former river bed south of the city.

In addition to these five major exhibitions, 'Sociopolis' offers visitors a chance to view a multi-media display of plans for a 50,000 square-meter 'social campus' in Valencia. Responding to the immediate needs of the city and its inhabitants, leading international architects have devised plans for housing, work places, and other urban services. Construction on this project is due to start, providing the city approves the plans, within the next two years.

During the Biennale, a number of performances have been organised in and around the city, directed by illustrious names in film and theatre such as Bigas Luna and Peter Brook. *Odyssey 2003*, a Mediterranean art ship, also sailed from the port of Valencia to other destinations around the Mediterranean, reinforcing links between the city and elsewhere.

The exhibition 'Ephemeral Architectures' has similar intentions. A number of structures containing magazines and brochures featuring articles on the city and the Biennale have been installed in the local airport and in a number of bus and train stations, with the idea being that travellers will take them to their onward destinations.

The Valencian government has invested considerably in the modernisation of the city in the last decade: historic buildings have been restored, projects

have been started and new exhibition areas opened. The Biennale has prompted further developments in the city including five monumental exhibition sites – Convento del Carmen, El Almudin, La Gallera, San Miguel de los Reyes, Reales Atarazanas. IVAM (Valencian Institute of Modern Art), formerly under the direction of Vincente Todoli, plans to complete its major extension project by 2006 which is set to rival Bilbao's Guggenheim. The Biennale offers people the chance not only to survey current artistic practice but also to explore the city's recent building projects and the role that cultural events can play in shaping the process of urban development.

Despite these exciting changes, the Biennale has been under attack from its local community and has polarised the city. It has been attacked by the press and numerous posters were pasted throughout the city, denouncing the elitist nature of the Biennale, which is ironic since a good number of the exhibitions are being held in non-art venues. Some, such as 'Solares', are on permanent public view and others, such as 'Can the children save us?', are the result of a direct collaboration with the local community. Valencia is, however, a bastion of conservatism in Spain. Let's not forget that the other main cultural event in the city is Fallas, a strictly Catholic festival celebrated every March. Maybe this goes some way to explain the local resistance to the innovation and spirit of change endorsed by the Biennale.

Valencia doesn't have the hip glamour of Barcelona, nor the capital status of Madrid. However, the Biennale has played a huge part in helping to redefine the city's identity. Valencia might not be an ideal city, but it is far from just another place in the sun. **MP**

'Valencia Biennial. Communication Between the Arts: The Ideal City', 8 June - 30 September 2003, Valencia.

MODERN PAINTERS

Julian Barnes on VUILLARD, Philip Roth on GUSTON,
Susan Rothenberg interview, Marlene Dumas, Guy Maddin, Bill Viola
PLUS John Ashbery on cult films & Alan Cumming on video art

Take out a 2-year subscription and receive 4 back issues absolutely free. Please print media code NY023 on your order slip. The offer extends to the end of November 2003, subject to availability.

SUBSCRIBE NOW

UNITED KINGDOM AUTO3UK

TWO YEAR SUBSCRIPTION (8 issues) ☐
SAVING 25% OFF COVER PRICE

UK	£36.00

ONE YEAR SUBSCRIPTION (4 issues) ☐
SAVING 17% OFF COVER PRICE

UK	£20.00

ALL RATES INCLUDE POSTAGE
INSTITUTIONAL AGENTS WILL RECEIVE A 10% DISCOUNT

To subscribe:
- Email **modernpainters@cisubs.co.uk**
- Telephone freephone **0800 0852757**
- Fax **01458 271146**

Please quote media code **AUTO3UK** or post this completed form.

Personal Subscription
Name
Street/no.
City
Postal code   Country
Telephone   Email

Gift Subscription
Name
Street/no.
City
Postal code   Country
Telephone   Email

Method of Payment
Visa ☐ Mastercard ☐ Amex ☐ Eurocard ☐ Switch ☐ Cheque† ☐
Card no.
Issue no.   Expiry date   Total cost
Signature   Date

(†Make cheques payable to **MODERN PAINTERS**)
Please tick if you prefer not to receive occasional mailings from selected companies ☐

US & CANADA MOD33

TWO YEAR SUBSCRIPTION (8 issues) ☐

US	US $82.00
Canada	Can $108.00*

*Price inclusive of taxes:
Quebec and Maritime Provinces Can $124.22
Ontario and Western Provinces Can $115.56

ONE YEAR SUBSCRIPTION (4 issues) ☐

US	US $41.00
Canada	Can $54.00*

*Price inclusive of taxes:
Quebec and Maritime Provinces Can $62.11
Ontario and Western Provinces Can $57.78

ALL RATES INCLUDE POSTAGE

To subscribe:
- Email **expsmag@expressmag.com**
- Telephone toll free **1 877 363 1310**
- Fax **514 355 3332**

Please quote media code **MOD33**, or post this completed form.

Personal Subscription
Name
Street/Apt.#
City
Zip code   Country
Telephone   Email

Gift Subscription
Name
Street/Apt.#
City
Zip code   Country
Telephone   Email

Method of Payment
Visa ☐ Mastercard ☐ Amex ☐ Check† ☐
Card no.
Total cost   Expiry date
Signature   Date

(†Make checks payable to **EXPRESS MAG**)
Please tick if you prefer not to receive occasional mailings from selected companies ☐

EUROPE & WORLD AUTO3

TWO YEAR SUBSCRIPTION (8 issues) ☐

Europe	£46.00	€71.00
Rest of World	£56.00	US $93.00

ONE YEAR SUBSCRIPTION (4 issues) ☐

Europe	£24.00	€37.00
Rest of World	£30.00	US $50.00

ALL RATES INCLUDE POSTAGE
ALL PAYMENTS ARE BANKED IN STERLING AND ARE
SUBJECT TO FLUCTUATION OF CURRENCY

To subscribe:
- Email **modernpainters@cisubs.co.uk**
- Telephone **+44 (0) 1458 271231**
- Fax **+44 (0) 1458 271146**

Please quote media code **AUTO3**, or post this completed form.

Personal Subscription
Name
Street/no.
City
Postal code   Country
Telephone   Email

Gift Subscription
Name
Street/no.
City
Postal code   Country
Telephone   Email

Method of Payment
Visa ☐ Mastercard ☐ Amex ☐ Cheque† ☐
Card no.
Issue no.   Expiry date   Total cost
Signature   Date

(†Make cheques payable to **MODERN PAINTERS**)
Please tick if you prefer not to receive occasional mailings from selected companies ☐

MODERN PAINTERS

MODERN PAINTERS
FREEPOST LON15765
Somerton
TA11 6ZA

'No other magazine has played such an influential role and none since the War has stimulated such debate' –NICHOLAS SEROTA, Director Tate Modern

MODERN PAINTERS

MODERN PAINTERS
c/o Express Mag
PO Box 2769
Plattsburgh
NY 12901 - 0239
USA

'MODERN PAINTERS gives me a warm feeling in an unlikely place' – STEVE MARTIN

MODERN PAINTERS

MODERN PAINTERS
Cary Court
Bancombe Trading Estate
Somerton
Somerset
TA11 6TB

'Possibly the most infuriating art publication to come out of Britain. It's a pleasure to write for it, whatever the hell it is' – DAVID BOWIE

Reserve your copy today!

If you would prefer not to subscribe but want to be sure of future copies of **MODERN PAINTERS** magazine, you can just fill in your details below and hand this slip into your local newsagent.*

☐ Please reserve/deliver** a copy of **MODERN PAINTERS** on a regular basis commencing with the Winter issue.

The Winter issue will be on sale from **December 8th**.

If you have any difficulty placing your order through your local newsagent, just call this hotline number **01895 433 800**.

* service only available to readers based in the UK
**delete as appropriate

Mr/Mrs/Ms
....

First name
....

Surname
....

Address
....
....
....

City
....

Postal code
....

Daytime telephone
....

Fax
....

The Standard

Hotels

"An excellent place to do **business**... just as good a place to **unwind**" -Business Traveller

"Tongue in **Chic**" -LA Times

"The *in* spot as much for it's playful irony as for it's **location**" -Elle

"Setting the standard" -W

"Trendsetting yet budget conscious- fun and functional"

-Condé Nast Traveller

"Wacky and self assured" -Playboy

"Riffs on mid-century **corporate America's love affair with modernist design**" -Vanity Fair

The Standard Hollywood 8300 Sunset Boulevard Hollywood Ca 323 650 9090   The Standard Downtown LA 550 South Flower Street Los Angeles Ca 213 892 8080

www.standardhotel.com

Back issues of MODERN PAINTERS are highly collectable and a valuable research resource

Back issues

MODERN PAINTERS

JOHN CHAMBERLAIN

EARLY WORKS

OCTOBER 28 – DECEMBER 20, 2003

CATALOGUE AVAILABLE

AllanStone Gallery

113 East 90th Street, New York, NY 10128   T. 212.987.4997   F. 212.987.1655   www.allanstonegallery.com

Hatband, 1960, painted metal, 58 1/2 x 53 x 38 inches

Ben Butler
September 6–October 5

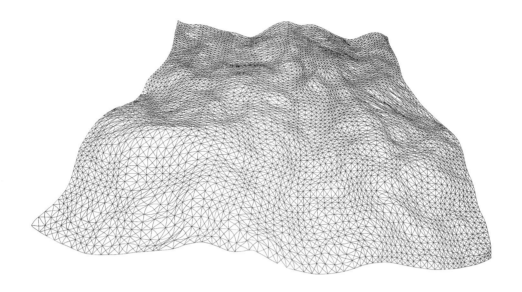

Kristine Marx
October–November

P L A N E   S P A C E

102 Charles Street New York, New York 10014 917.606.1268 F:917.606.1265 www.plane-space.com

Four
PORTRAITS OF THE ARTIST

from nyrb NEW YORK REVIEW CLASSICS

BLACK SUN · Geoffrey Wolff

Harry Crosby was at the center of the wild life of the lost generation until, in 1929, he shot his girlfriend—the recent bride of another man—and then himself. A masterful picture of a brilliant man **who sought to make his life into a work of art.**

Paperback · ISBN: 1-59017-066-0 · **$16.95**

RENOIR, MY FATHER · Jean Renoir, introduction by Robert L. Herbert

A delightful memoir of the Impressionist painter Auguste Renoir by his son Jean Renoir, director of such cinematic masterpieces as Grand Illusion. "One of the most **engaging** biographies ever written about an artist." —*Art in America*

Paperback *includes 12 pages of color plates & 18 pages of black and white images* · ISBN: 0-940322-77-3 · **$16.95**

MISERABLE MIRACLE · Henri Michaux, introduction by Octavio Paz

"This book is an exploration. By means of words, signs, drawings. Mescaline, the subject explored." Here French graphic artist Henri Michaux has created **a breathtaking vision of interior space** wrested from the grip of the unspeakable.

Paperback *includes 40 pages of black and white drawings* · ISBN: 1-59017-001-6 · **$13.95**

THE UNKNOWN MASTERPIECE · Honoré de Balzac, introduction by Arthur C. Danto

The story of a painter who, depending on one's perspective, is either an abject failure or a transcendental genius. The story, which has served as an inspiration to artists as various as Cézanne, Henry James, and Picasso, is, in critic Dore Ashton's words, **"a fable of modern art."**

Paperback · ISBN: 0-940322-74-9 · **$12.95**

Order these and other titles online at **www.nyrb.com**
or call 1-601-354-5306

ALIGHIERO E BOETTI
GREG COLSON
HANNE DARBOVEN
NICOLA DE MARIA
WIM DELVOYE
KIM DINGLE
LUCIO FONTANA
GUILLERMO KUITCA
WOLFGANG LAIB
JONATHAN LASKER
CHARLES LEDRAY
RICHARD LONG
PIERO MANZONI
MARIO MERZ
THE ESTATE OF FRANK MOORE
MALCOLM MORLEY
NABIL NAHAS
BRUCE NAUMAN
MIMMO PALADINO
SUSAN ROTHENBERG
TOM SACHS
RICHARD TUTTLE
NOT VITAL

SPERONE WESTWATER

415 West 13 Street New York 10014
212/999-7337 (fax) 999-7338
www.speronewestwater.com

50 Shades of red

Susan Rothenberg talks about the liberating force of the light and colours of New Mexico, where she now lives with her husband Bruce Nauman.

KAREN WRIGHT

KW How did your paintings of horses from the 70s come about?

SR I had been experimenting with 'wholes and parts' and was doing things like tearing pieces of paper out of a whole sheet of paper and putting them next to each other. Then I started putting unstretched canvas on the wall, just nailed up there. Then I started ripping the canvases. I was new to New York and picking up everything I was seeing and trying it on. Instead of ripping I decided to draw the outer edge of what a rip would look like with a pencil line. That was that, no more tearing. The first horse was on an unstretched piece of canvas. It had a pencil line down the middle and the image of a horse wasn't symmetrical. Whilst riding home from the beach one day I'd been thinking, what if everything was the same colour? What if the trees were the same colour as the sky, the sky the same colour as the bush? And that's where that fleshy burnt sienna and white colour came in, making the image and the ground the same colour.

When did you start working with stretched canvases?

The first horse I did was about 7 feet by 5 feet unstretched, so basically it looked like a rag on the wall and then I thought, 'Oh gee – I'm gonna have to get a stretcher' to see how it looked when placed in the context of how other paintings look. It was too much like a tapestry but not built with the care of a tapestry. It just looked like a piece of pinkish cloth with the image of a horse on it. So the stretchers came, the ideas came on the back of an envelope, different positions, shadows, double images, and then black and white. This went on from about 1973 to 1980 and then it was over and I didn't have another idea that wouldn't have been repetitive. So I did some other kinds of paintings. I did a chair with a pair of red slippers next to it. I did my daughter's teddy bear with a huge black line around it. I decided to experiment with circles that were almost like bands, instead of lines, for my separations. I always think a painting should have three elements: the figure, the ground and the third thing.

Susan Rothenberg,
Red Studio, 2002-03,
oil on canvas, 160 x
147.3 cm. Courtesy
Sperone Westwater,
New York

What's the third thing?

It can be a shadow, it can be the double image, it can be the band around the bear that separates the image or holds it in the space.

But your images aren't representational?

I never drew from a horse. I have said this before – it is probably comparable to a series of gestures or numbers. But I needed this figurative image. Of course the human figure used to revolt me in those days. A nude?!!

Why was that?

Figurative painting wasn't exactly happening at all anyway then and I wouldn't have known how to do what I did from a purely figurative perspective. Maybe some day the great American nude will finally pop out of me.

In the 80s there was a period when you were painting Mondrian. What was it about him that led you to this?

I did a non-specific large black and red drawing on the wall of a male figure naked to the waist in black trousers and in the light of the window. I wasn't thinking anything, but I stood back from it and I said, 'God, that looks like photos I've seen of Mondrian.' It was an accident. So I decided, he's a guy that likes essences, I like essences, and I wondered if I could have a little dialogue with him. I knew he loved to dance so I painted him dancing. I have the greatest admiration for the last three paintings of his life. If there was a painting I could own in this world it would be the last boogie-woogie. So it was a side step and didn't mean much of anything. I got fascinated with light and light on a figure, and it was the first time I was trying to be contextual, putting furniture in, putting a floor in, painting an interior. Before, my backgrounds were always non-specific.

Which other artists have influenced you as a painter?

Early on it was Jasper Jones for sure. Guston has also been very important to me. I have a little thing going again with Matisse, which I think I have to get over. I'm trying to clear my brain of all the names of people I have looked at over the years. Van Gogh has been very influential. I like Auerbach, I like the early Bay Area painters like David Clarke, I like Soutine very much.

Do you make sketches before you actually start painting?

Sometimes but I usually use a dirty brush. I have an idea and I use one of my brownish, greyish dirty brushes to start laying things out in a drawing-like way. You know, the dog is here, the leg is here, the couch is there. And then I start applying the paint. I try to leave the canvas with some of that dirty drawing showing through.

Why do you use dirty brushes?

I'm lazy. I tend to keep the red brushes in the red dirty can and I tend to keep black and white a little bit separate so that I can get a clean white. I have lots of clean dog food cans so if I want to get a clean colour I start a new can.

In your more recent work the dogs seem to be making an appearance.

That's because I'm here painting in the studio and they're here with me. It's this thing of thinking what have I got to paint? I don't have anything. I'm not going to paint the bowl of fruit, what have I got? I've got my head and my hands to work with, so I used them as images for the large head and hand paintings I did after the horses. The dogs are the same – but this won't go on too long with the dogs. I haven't really got an attitude to this landscape or any other landscape.

Do you feel you've just had enough looking at it?

I don't know. I had an idea to mix up lots of things from the landscape – the railings, horses' legs, dogs' legs, human arms pointing, rabbits running. It's in the back of my mind that I should find a way to integrate elements of the outside and animals. I thought my painting *The Chase* was a brand new beginning and that I was going to do 100 paintings that had that circular, empty sort of space and I never got anywhere with that idea because I couldn't visualise how to do it and I didn't want to re-do that painting.

That seems to be a common theme of the work – you do a certain thing, you exhaust it, you stop and then you come back to it – like the horse with the severed arm in this new show, which is reminiscent of both the horse paintings but also the severed arm paintings.

Don't say severed!

How would you describe it?

Dislocated. There is nothing violent about them.

In fact they are actually very sensual images. And they have a figurative element to them too. But you don't feel you are a figurative painter, do you?

No. I want everything to be looser in space. I want there to be enough for you to get what I'm talking about but I don't think I have to spell everything out. It's a matter of editing. In the

(Above)
Fifty shades of red on Rothenberg's studio wall

(Right)
Susan Rothenberg.
Photo: Juergen Teller
Courtesy Juergen
Teller Ltd

Susan Rothenberg,
Smoke Rings, 2003,
oil on canvas, 88.9 x
254 cm. Courtesy
Sperone Westwater,
New York

Domino paintings I didn't need the shape of the skull, only the eyes, the nose, the lips, the hands. Why would I need head or hair or clothes? That was a very happy period for me, for about a year or two, because I knew what I was doing, I knew how to expand it from painting to painting. I was learning something new about green which I'd never worked with before. It creates a particular mood. Bruce and I would quietly play dominos. The saturation of the green was the perfect environment to play in.

You seem to adopt a similar principle in the Studio paintings – you're in the paintings to a degree but only suggestively.

Yes, in *The Red Studio* it's as close as I get to putting myself in a painting. I wanted to say, 'Here I am in my studio, this is me.' But just my clothes, not my arms. I have shoes, but I didn't need my face or anything approaching that.

Is this a problem for non-figurative painters in that you are trying to capture something without capturing it? What is the process of transformation?

I like melodrama in my world and I can't sit around waiting for someone to get hurt out there or to have an event to paint.

New Mexico. You're high, low, up, down, looking around a bend, you can see things happening down below. It's not flat New York or flat Long Island. The change in actual levels of land in my walking has caused this change in perspective.

Has the light affected your work too?

I hated the light here at first. That's why I don't have very many windows. I also wanted lots of walls, but when we built the fireplace in the living room, I said to Bruce I want to live in there. I want a space that's dark. When we first lived in Pacos it was a much more forested area and before we moved here it didn't occur to me what I was getting into. After I spent weeks and weeks staying here the red and the white and yellow really started to come into the work. I started to try to be a colourist, although secretly thinking of myself as somewhat of a black and whiteist. In the black landscape painting I put in a lot of earth tones – raw umber and a lot of greys – so it became a tonal painting rather than a black painting.

There's a wonderful story from when your daughter was young about using a certain kind of red so that you could get

ACRYLIC IS THE TEXTURE OF YOGHURT, OIL IS THE TEXTURE OF TOOTHPASTE.

I have to create my own event. These just happen to be in the studio and then I transfer them into the living room – look at the couch, it's like, TV, dinner, dogs all over, books, papers, glasses.

A domestic scene.

Yes but weird, from an aerial point of view – that has been a big issue for me lately. It comes from living and walking in

it off her hands easily.

I was trying to work with oil and I was getting pigment, mostly burnt sienna and white, and grinding it with oil to make my own paint. It felt earthier to use the real stuff, not the mixed-up kind. I stopped that when my baby was born because I had to pick her up to nurse her. So to avoid all the sticky mess and turpentine I switched to acrylic.

Susan Rothenberg,
Butterfly, 1976,
acrylic and matte
medium on canvas,
173.75 x 207.5 cm.
Collection Maggie
Trakas

Why did you change back to oil?
In 1982 Elisabeth Murray, one of my contemporaries in New York, told me to. She said you can get so much more texture in oil. Acrylic is the texture of yoghurt, oil is the texture of toothpaste. She thought that the oil paint would hold my texture better.

Was that the case?
I started painting like an Impressionist at first. I was so shocked that every stroke counted. That stayed with me for a long time, that realisation, and I made every stroke count. Now I don't like that. I want bigger brushes and swathes of paint. I found a whole new way to paint with the Domino paintings. I use bigger brushes and also have an additive which thins the paint. I make a pool of paint on a table-top, then I make sure there are lots of other colours around the pool so that I can bring them in when I want to.

I love the story of how you used to paint on the floor but now you don't because you say you got too much paint on your feet.
Some of my paintings were very, very big and when you got to the bottom of the canvas, instead of reaching up to your paint table, it was easier to just throw some paint on the floor and paint from the floor.

The act of painting is very physical, isn't it?
Yes but most of my painting is done sitting in a chair with a book. I'd say it's 80 per cent sitting and reading, 10 per cent eating and 10 per cent painting. You can't spend the whole day painting and painting and painting. You have to sit back, look at what you've done, be puzzled by what you've done, ask what it needs next. Sometimes you look at the painting and you're not hearing it so you have to go back to your book and try again.

So when you moved here from New York, what were the other big changes apart from the light and the landscape?
The animals. We had one dog in New York and at one point we had 7 dogs here. What else changed? I never needed to look good, here, I was madly in love so everything was supported and nurtured by the feelings that I had done something brave and amazing and had a partner to do it with. While we were building the house I was painting almost exclusively with palette knives, as I watched the builders put adobe onto the house with the big adobe plastering knives. The palette knife is less important to me now but still if I want a really quiet area in a painting I brush the paint on and then I knife it so it doesn't speak of the strokes.

There's a story about Bruce buying you fifty different shades of red.
It was my Christmas present. I tried them out on the Christmas wrapping paper and there it is on the wall.

You say that you lead quite a separate artistic life from Bruce, that you don't actually talk about what happens in your individual studio spaces.

(Left)
Susan Rothenberg,
Green Studio,
2002-03, oil on canvas, 188 x 292.1 cm.
Courtesy Sperone
Westwater, New York

(Above)
Three stages of
progress on
Rothenberg's
Green Studio

I ask, 'Did you do anything today?' He says, 'I'm thinking about it but no,' and I say, 'Oh, around 3pm I got going and worked till 5.30.' And that's it. I'm not very good in the mornings. I usually don't paint until about noon. I am looking, thinking and thinking beyond what I am doing right now to what I'm going to do next.

In your most recent paintings I notice that you've allowed his image in.

His profile is not unlike my father's and I think that's become what a profile is to me with that emphasis on the nose. It's not Bruce so much but it is in my head and the figure is ambiguous in terms of gender but it has to have a nose. I am strongly attracted to noses. Man is nose and may be even woman.

didn't have any women in it at all.

That made me really mad and then I made a statement that I have never been called upon to act on – that I would never be the only woman in any group art exhibition again.

Why do you think that so few women make it as artists?

It's a very strange thing to me because there are so many women dealers, there are a fair amount of women curators, there are a few women directors in America and I don't know how many in Europe. Since that club has now been penetrated, why isn't there the support for women artists? It should be coming from all these women who hold power. There should be a greater sense of making an extra effort to look at women artists and give them space in exhibitions. It's still

MOST OF MY PAINTING IS DONE SITTING IN A CHAIR WITH A BOOK.

Jean-Christophe Ammann, referring to your work, once said that 'painting is stronger than its subject matter and that painting is its subject matter. Painting is an immense feeling which is why painting is scarce, because the immense feeling cannot be redeemed if people are no longer willing to risk despairing over the immense feeling. Painting is the most difficult thing to do.' Do you agree with this?

Yes, it's great.

How do you feel about working in such a male-dominated world? For example, you were the only woman in the 'Zeitgeist' show in Berlin and in the 'New Spirit of Painting' show

way too much of a boys' club.

What do you feel is special about the way an artist sees things and the way someone else sees things?

I think there has to be an interesting transformative process between your perception of reality and making the paintings. If you are just trying to render what you see you are not entering into a transformative process. And that's what makes a good painting: the process of transforming and the willingness to leave reality behind. **MP**

'Susan Rothenberg', 29 October – 22 November, Waddington Galleries, London.

Once considered mere illustration, photography in the 'documentary style' can articulate the world in as complex a way as any art.

Maximum Clarity

THE FLURRY OF PHOTOGRAPHY EXHIBITIONS IN LONDON'S major institutions this summer – 'Cruel and Tender' at Tate Modern, Philip-Lorca diCorcia at the Whitechapel, Wolfgang Tillmans at Tate Britain, Walker Evans at The Photographers' Gallery and Cindy Sherman at the Serpentine (as well as important shows in the spring such as William Eggleston at the Hayward and David Goldblatt at Modern Art Oxford) – would seem to confirm what has been, over the last decade in the United Kingdom, a slow but accelerating process: the institutional and market acceptance of photography as a fine art. True, big name 'art' photographers such as Jeff Wall, Cindy Sherman and Craigie Horsfield, have never wanted for exhibitions, but it is significant that these are artists whose photography is conceived in dialogue with other media, particularly painting or film, which accounts for its relatively smooth assimilation into the space of the museum. Large, pictorial, limited in edition, this kind of photography

divergence. In Britain, the history of photography is rarely taught either alongside or as an integral part of the history of art, and photography has tended to be collected, exhibited, bought and sold within its own specialist arenas. Many British art critics display a lingering hesitancy about the medium's artistic credentials, even when the photographer has been enthusiastically embraced by the art establishment. Sarah Kent's recent evaluation of Wolfgang Tillmans' exhibition at Tate Britain in *Time Out*, for example, is revealing. It starts by pondering why the Tate has devoted the Linbury Galleries to the work not just of a photographer, but a 'straight' photographer at that, and concludes that while she deems the accompanying book full of gorgeous images, when gathered together *en masse* in the galleries, 'the work seems irredeemably trivial'. She's perplexed that she's seen many of the images before, a comment unlikely to be made of a contemporary painter or sculptor staging a large retrospective at the Tate.

THE STORY OF ART MISSING THE CHAPTER ON PHOTOGRAPHY IS A STORY HALF-TOLD.

has always looked and felt like art. It is photography's 'other' tradition, the tradition of rigorously observed, artistically ungarnished work, bequeathed from Eugène Atget and August Sander to Walker Evans, a photography which might be loosely dubbed, following Evans' definition, as 'documentary style', which has been curiously overlooked in this country, and whose history is finally, comprehensively – but still in separation from the wider history of art – reviewed in 'Cruel and Tender'.

Go abroad, particularly to a major American institution, and you are more likely to find the stories of art and photography narrated in terms of their convergence rather than their

The mechanical reproducibility of photography, famously celebrated by Walter Benjamin as the means for art to jettison its ritualistic past to become truly modern, democratic and political still poses the arbiters of art in a new century certain problems. Photography has always reached out into a wider visual culture outside the gallery to find a place for itself in books and the printed media, and it is this versatility that has been so at odds with modernist credo and its insistence on the artwork as a uniquely existing artefact. With 'Cruel and Tender', the opening of the museum to photography, and a wakening interest by curators and collectors in the medium's

Wolfgang Tillmans, *End of Land 1*, 2002. © the artist. Courtesy Maureen Paley Interim Art, London.

photographer's unique subjective vision, embedded in the formal aesthetics of the photograph, was paramount, and it informed the work of photographers as diverse as Edward Weston and Ansel Adams, Otto Steinert and Minor White. This kind of self-conscious 'art' photography though – significantly lacking from the 'Cruel and Tender' account – had by the 1960s become as formulaic and stylised as late Abstract Expressionism, and it was a different kind of photography that was to initiate the revolution. When in the early 1960s Robert Rauschenberg and Andy Warhol began to silkscreen photo-

rich and neglected histories, it would appear that the lines of separation drawn institutionally between photography and art in Britain, are finally being erased. Why is this important? Because the story of art missing the chapter on photography is a story half-told. Because the past always illuminates the present and much contemporary art is as rooted in photography as in fine art: can we imagine, to invoke a few examples, Richard Prince without Walker Evans' proto-Pop re-photographs of the American vernacular landscape? Gillian Wearing without Diane Arbus' dramatic depictions of social marginality? Wolfgang Tillmans without William Eggleston's lyric colourism, Richard Billingham without Larry Clark's personal immersion in the lives of his subjects, or Philip-Lorca diCorcia without Garry Winogrand's aggressively watchful street photography? And because, finally, at a moment when so many young artists turn increasingly towards photography and video as their preferred media, it's vital they do so with a knowledge of what has already been achieved in the past.

Most commentators define the 1960s as the moment that photography came of age as a modern art form. During modernism, photography was seen as too dependent on, too tied to the world it depicted, to achieve the level of autonomy and self-reflexivity so prerequisite for a modernist artwork – at least in Clement Greenberg's formulation which insisted that the essential formal characteristics of art should be prioritised over imagery, narrative or any reference to the actual world. Photography had along the way evolved its own kind of high modernism which in many ways shared the same thinking which sustained Abstract Expressionist painting. Here, the

(Top)
Walker Evans,
Subway Portrait,
1941 gelatin silver print 12 x 17.9 cm. The J. Paul Getty Museum, Los Angeles. © The Walker Evans Archive, The Metropolitan Museum of Art, New York.

(Below)
August Sander,
*Cretin,*1924. The Sprengel Museum, Hanover. © Die Photographische Sammlung/SK Stiftung Kultur – August Sander Archive, Cologne, VG BILD-KUNST, Bonn/DACS, London 2003

graphs onto their canvases they turned to the mass media for their source imagery, thereby grafting the 'real' world onto the hitherto self-sufficient surface of the painting. In so doing, according to Douglas Crimp's thesis in *On the Museum's Ruins,* photography came to 'pervert' modernism and to usher in the era of postmodernism. As the 60s unfolded, early conceptual artists turned increasingly to photography.

They can be loosely divided into those who utilised it as a tool to document actions or events or performances for the camera (such as Bruce Nauman or Richard London and later, at the end of the 70s, Cindy Sherman) and those who annexed photography, rather like a 'ready-made', for its inherent 'anti-artistry' – its widespread functional applications, its descriptive precision, its non-unique, serial nature, and its stylistic neutrality. Photography was recruited in a philosophical assault on the auratic and commodified artwork. As a pure instrument of reproduction, a 'dumb copying device' as Douglas Huebler termed it, photography could work to relieve the artist from aesthetic decision-making and leave him or her free to concentrate on pure idea. Photography could also potentially redeem art from the reificatory space of the art gallery by sharing its historical home in the de-material, democratically disseminated printed media, as Dan Graham in his magazine pieces (most famously 'Homes for America', 1966) and Ed Ruscha in his seventeen, cheaply produced photography books, such as *26 Gasoline Stations* (1963), discovered.

Paradoxically, although the conceptual artists were attracted to photography because it was potentially 'anti-artistic', this is also what created the conditions for 'straight' photography to be finally accepted as an art form in its own right. The influence of Walker Evans, for example, on the artistic community of the 1960s, is a significant but rarely acknowledged fact. Dan Graham elaborated in a 1991 interview: 'What is highly interesting about [Evans'] work is that it was published in magazines... It allowed certain things to work, like the idea of representation of the representation, which was crucial to Pop and conceptual art.' The retrospective publication of Evans' *Many Are Called* in 1966, in which he covertly photographed a predetermined number of strangers travelling on the subway over a fixed period of time, clearly presaged the radically impersonal procedures of late 1960s conceptual art. Bernt and Hilla Becher are pivotal figures here too, in that they represent a point where the two trajectories of art and photography converge. Influenced by the encylopaedic early-century documentary projects of Eugène Atget and August Sander, their photography systematically catalogues the world into types of object – here, types of industrial architecture. Rigorous observation and precise description take precedence over their subjective presence as authors of the image. With its deadpan look and bureaucratic methodology, the Bechers' work came to be situated within the context of conceptual art – but it could equally revert back to the photography tradition, as it did when they were included alongside photographers like Robert Adams and

Stephen Shore, *Ashland, Wisconsin, July 9 1973,* from the series 'Uncommon Places', c-print, 19 x 24 cm. Niedersächsische Sparkassenstiftung, Hanover. © Stephen Shore

Baltz and Robert Adams, and the colourists Stephen Shore and William Eggleston in the early 1970s, with Gursky, Ruff and Struth representing the 1980s and 1990s, and Philip-Lorca diCorcia, Rineke Dijkstra and Boris Mikhailov completing the genealogy into the present moment.

'Cruel and Tender' comes in the wake of a number of cultural events which have signalled a growing interest in documentary or realist modes, after the suppression of this type of image-making during late postmodernism (the powerful critiques of representational photography conducted by artists such as Victor Burgin, Martha Rosler and Jo Spence during the 1980s and early 1990s had a particular dominance in Britain and might help to account for the previously subdued interest in photography here). Catherine David's Documenta X in 1997, with its innovative juxtaposition of contemporary artists and the work of older photographers such Robert Adams, Walker Evans, Helen Levitt, Ed van der Elsken and Garry Winogrand, set the ball rolling, and five years later, by the time of Okwui Enwezor's Documenta XI, documentary style photography and video had become not just an inclusion, but arguably the dominant theme. 'Documentary' is a slippery word and Walker Evans coined the term 'documentary style' to distinguish his work both from the dramatic excess of social documentarians like Margaret Bourke White or Eugene

THE RECENT SPATE OF PHOTOGRAPHY EXHIBITIONS SUGGESTS THAT FINALLY THE MEDIUM IS BEING ACCEPTED AS A FINE ART.

Lewis Baltz in the exhibition 'New Topographics' at George Eastman House, Rochester, in 1975, a show which defined a new school of understated, unromantic landscape photography. The Bechers then handed on the baton to a new generation of German photographers under their tutelage at the Düsseldorf Kunstakademie from the late 1970s to the mid-1980s. With Andreas Gursky, Thomas Struth, Thomas Ruff and Candida Hofer photography finally and firmly establishes itself as a museum art – and an expensive commodity – to rival painting and sculpture.

'Cruel and Tender' traces a history of photography where the world, rather than the photographers' subjective vision, is the primary referent, and in which the image is conceived with maximum clarity and minimum artifice. The exhibition begins in the 1920s with August Sander and Albert Renger Patzch, following through to Walker Evans in the 1930s, Robert Frank in the 1950s, the American documentarists Diane Arbus, Lee Friedlander and Garry Winogrand in the 1960s, onto the black-and-white New Topographic landscapists Lewis

Smith, and literal, non-art documents such as police photographs. 'You see', he said in a 1971 interview, 'document has use whereas art is really useless. Therefore art is never a document, though it can certainly adopt that style.' 'Documentary style' is not simply synonymous with a 'straight' unmanipulated photograph though: it is much more than that. Great documentary photography articulates the world in complex ways rather than merely illustrating it. It resists simple statements and the reduction of its subjects to social facts, just as it resists the aestheticisation of its own style. As the 'look' of documentary becomes ever more ubiquitous in the work of contemporary artists, this is perhaps the greatest lesson the art of today can learn from photography's modern history. **MP**

'Cruel and Tender: The Real in the 20th Century', 5 June - 7 September, Tate Modern, London.
'WolfgangTillmans: If One thing Matters, Everything Matters', 6 June - 14 September, Tate Britain, London.
'Cindy Sherman', 3 June - 25 August, Serpentine Gallery, London.
'Philip-Lorca diCorcia: A Storybook Life', 7 June - 24 August, Whitechapel Art Gallery, London.

PHILIP ROTH

'One time, in Woodstock', Ross Feld said, 'I stood next to Guston in front of some of these canvases. I hadn't seen them before; I didn't really know what to say. For a time, then, there was silence. After a while, Guston took his thumbnail away from his teeth and said, "People, you know, complain that it's horrifying. As if it's a picnic for me, who has to come in here every day and see them first thing. But what's the alternative? I'm trying to see how much I can stand."'

From **Night Studio: A Memoir of Philip Guston** *by Musa Mayer*

Pictures of Guston

Philip Guston's soft spot for 'American crumminess' shaped in his painting a new landscape of terror.

N 1967, SICK OF LIFE IN THE NEW YORK ART WORLD, Philip Guston left his Manhattan studio forever and took up permanent residence with his wife, Musa, in their Woodstock house on Maverick Road, where they had been living off and on for some twenty years. Two years later, I turned my back on New York to hide out in a small furnished house in Woodstock, across town from Philip, whom I didn't know at the time. I was fleeing the publication of *Portnoy's Complaint*. My overnight notoriety as a sexual freak had become difficult to evade in Manhattan, and so I decided to clear out – first for Yaddo, the upstate artists' colony, and

then, beginning in the spring of 1969, for that small rented house tucked out of sight midway up a hillside meadow a couple of miles from Woodstock's main street. I lived there with a young woman who was finishing a PhD and who for several years had been renting a tiny cabin, heated by a wood stove, in the mountainside colony of Byrdcliffe, which some decades earlier had been a primitive hamlet of Woodstock artists. During the day I wrote on a table in the upstairs spare bedroom while she went off to the cabin to work on her dissertation.

Life in the country with a postgraduate student was anything but freakish, and it provided a combination of social seclusion

Philip Guston,
Head and Bottle,
1975, oil on canvas,
collection of Sally
Lilienthal.
Courtesy SFMoMA

and physical pleasure that, given the illogic of creation, led me to write, over a four-year period, a cluster of uncharacteristically freakish books. My new reputation as a crazed penis was what instigated the fantasy at the heart of *The Breast*, a book about a college professor who turns into a female breast; it had something to do as well with inspiring the farcical legend of homeless alienation in homespun America that evolved into *The Great American Novel*. The more simplehearted my Woodstock satisfactions, the more tempted I was in my work by the excesses of the Grand Guignol. I'd never felt more imaginatively polymorphous than when I would put two deck

chairs on the lawn at the end of the day and we'd stretch out to enjoy the twilight view of the southern foothills of the Catskills, for me unpassable Alps through which no disconcerting irrelevancy could pass. I felt refractory and unreachable and freewheeling, and I was dedicated – perversely overdedicated, probably – to shaking off the vast newfound audience whose collective fantasies were not without their own transforming power.

Guston's situation in 1969 – the year we met – was very different. At fifty-six, Philip was twenty years older than I and full of the doubt that can beset an artist of consequence in late middle age. He felt he'd exhausted the means that had unlocked him as an abstract painter, and he was bored and disgusted by the skills that had gained him renown. He didn't want to paint like that ever again; he tried to convince himself he shouldn't paint at all. But since nothing but painting could contain his emotional turbulence, let alone begin to deplete

in farce we know from what we ourselves dream and from what has been dreamed for us by Beckett and Kafka. Philip's discovery – akin to theirs, driven by a delight in mundane objects as boldly distended and bluntly depoeticised as theirs – was of the dread that emanates from the most commonplace appurtenances of the world of utter stupidity. The unexalted

NOTHING BUT PAINTING COULD CONTAIN HIS EMOTIONAL TURBULENCE, LET ALONE BEGIN TO DEPLETE HIS SELF-MYTHOLOGISING MONOMANIA.

his self-mythologising monomania, renouncing painting would have been tantamount to committing suicide. Although painting monopolised just enough of his despair and his seismic moodiness to make the anxiety of being himself something even he could sometimes laugh at, it never neutralised the nightmares entirely.

It wasn't supposed to. The nightmares were his not to dissipate with paint but, during the ten years before his death, to intensify with paint, to paint into nightmares that were imperishable and never before incarnated in such trashy props. That terror may be all the more bewildering when it is steeped

Philip Guston, *Sleeping*, 1977, oil on canvas, 215.9 x 177.8 cm, private collection. Courtesy SFMoMA

vision of everyday things that newspaper cartoon strips had impressed upon him when he was growing up in an immigrant Jewish family in California, the American crumminess for which, even in the heyday of his thoughtful lyricism, he always had an intellectual's soft spot, he came to contemplate – in an exercise familiar to lovers of *Molloy* and *The Castle* – as though his life, both as an artist and as a man, depended on it. This popular imagery of a shallow reality Philip imbued with such a weight of personal sorrow and artistic urgency as to shape in painting a new American landscape of terror. Cut off from New York and living apart from Woodstock's local artists, with whom he had little in common, Philip often felt out of it: isolated, resentful, uninfluential, misplaced. It wasn't the first time that his ruthless focus on his own imperatives had induced a black mood of alienation, nor was he the first American artist embittered by the syndrome. It was as common among the best as it was among the worst – only with the best it was not necessarily a puerile self-drama concocted out of egomaniacal delusion. In many ways it was a perfectly justified response for an artist like Guston, whose brooding, brainy, hypercritical scrutiny of every last aesthetic choice is routinely travestied by the misjudgements and simplifications that support a major reputation.

Philip and his gloom were not inseparable, however. In the company of the few friends he enjoyed and was willing to see, he could be a cordial, unharried host, exuding a captivating spiritual buoyancy unmarked by anguish. In his physical bearing, too, there was a nimble grace touchingly at variance with the bulky torso of the heavy-drinking, somewhat august-looking, white-haired personage into whom darkly, Jewishly, Don Juanishly handsome Guston had been transformed in his fifties. At dinner, wearing those baggy-bottomed, low-slung khaki trousers of his, with a white cotton shirt open over his burly chest and the sleeves still turned up from working in the studio, he looked like the Old Guard Israeli politicians in whom imperiousness and informality spring from an unassailable core of confidence. It was impossible around the Guston dining table, sharing the rich pasta that Philip had cooked up with a display of jovial expertise, to detect any sign of a self-flagellating component within his prodigious endowment of self-belief. Only in his eyes might you be able to gauge the toll of the wearing oscillation – from iron resolve through rapturous equilibrium to suicidal hopelessness – that underlay a day in the studio.

Philip Guston, *Boot*, 1968, acrylic on panel, 201.9 x 284.5 cm, private collection. Courtesy SFMoMA

Philip's illustrations of incidents in *The Breast*, drawn on ordinary typing paper, were presented to me one evening at dinner shortly after the book's publication. A couple of years earlier, while I was writing *Our Gang*, Philip had responded to the chapters that I showed him in manuscript with a series of caricatures of Nixon, Kissinger, Agnew, and John Mitchell. He worked on these caricatures with more concentration than he did on the drawings for *The Breast*, and he even toyed with the thought of publishing them as a collection under the title *Poor Richard*. The eight drawings inspired by *The Breast* were simply a spontaneous rejoinder to something he'd liked. The drawings were intended to do nothing other than please me – and did they! For me his blubbery cartoon rendering of the

WHAT CAUSED OUR FRIENDSHIP TO FLOURISH WAS, TO BEGIN WITH, A SHARED DELIGHT IN WHAT GUSTON CALLED 'CRAPOLA.'

What caused our friendship to flourish was, to begin with, a similar intellectual outlook, a love for many of the same books as well as a shared delight in what Guston called 'crapola', starting with billboards, garages, diners, burger joints, junk shops, auto body shops – all the roadside stuff that we occasionally set out to Kingston to enjoy – and extending from the flat-footed straight talk of the Catskill citizenry to the Uriah Heepisms of our perspiring president. What sealed the camaraderie was that we liked each other's new work. The dissimilarities in our personal lives and our professional fortunes did not obscure the coincidence of our having recently undertaken comparable self-critiques. Independently, impelled by very different dilemmas, each of us had begun to consider crapola not only as a curious subject with strong suggestive powers to which we had a native affinity but as potentially a tool in itself: a blunt aesthetic instrument providing access to a style of representation free of the complexity we were accustomed to valuing. What this self-subversion might be made to yield was anybody's guess, and premonitions of failure couldn't be entirely curbed by the liberating feeling that an artistic about-face usually inspires, at least in the early stages of not quite knowing what you are doing. At just about the time that I began not quite to know what I was doing exulting in Nixon's lies, or travelling up to Cooperstown's Hall of Fame to immerse myself in baseball lore, or taking seriously the idea of turning a man like myself into a breast – and reading up on endocrinology and mammary glands – Philip was beginning not quite to know what he was doing hanging cartoon light bulbs over the pointed hoods of slit-eyed, cigar-smoking Klansmen painting self-portraits in hideaways cluttered with shoes and clocks and steam irons of the sort that Mutt and Jeff would have been at home with.

Philip Guston, illustrations for *The Breast* by Philip Roth

breast into which Professor David Kepesh is inexplicably transformed – his vision of afflicted Kepesh as a beached mammary groping for contact through a nipple that is an unostentatious amalgam of lumpish, dumb penis and inquisitive nose – managed to encapsulate all the loneliness of Kepesh's humiliation while at the same time adhering to the mordantly comic perspective with which Kepesh tries to view his horrible metamorphosis. Though these drawings were no more than a pleasant diversion for Philip, his predilection for the self-satirisation of personal misery (the strategy for effacing the romance of self-pity that stuns us in Gogol's 'Diary of a Madman' and 'The Nose') as strongly determines the images here as it does in those paintings where his own tiresome addictions and sad renunciations are represented by whiskey bottles and cigarette butts and forlorn insomniacs epically cartoonised. He may only have been playing around, but what he was playing with was the point of view with which he had set about in his studio to overturn his history as a painter and to depict, without rhetorical hedging, the facts of his anxiety as a man. Coincidentally, Philip, who died in 1980 at the age of sixty-six, represents himself in his last paintings as someone who also endured a grotesque transformation – not into a thinking, dismembered sexual gland but into a bloated, cyclopsian, brutish head that has itself been cut loose from the body of its sex. ⓂⓅ

This piece first appeared in Vanity Fair *in 1989.*

'Philip Guston: Retrospective', 30 March - 8 June, Modern Art Museum of Forth Worth, Fort Worth; 28 June - 28 September, SFMoMA, San Francisco; 27 October - 4 January 2004, The Metropolitan Museum of Art, New York; 24 January 2004 - 12 April 2004, Royal Academy of Arts, London. Catalogue £35 hardback.

'Philip Guston', May - June 2004, Timothy Taylor Gallery, London.

Anya Gallaccio's exploration of the instability and transience of organic matter has produced installations of extraordinary power – and this year she has the Turner Prize nomination she deserves.

DARIAN LEADER

A Responsibility

I N A VERY FINE ESSAY IN THE CATALOGUE FOR ANYA Gallaccio's show 'Chasing Rainbows' in 1999, Ralph Rugoff suggested that the only appropriate way for a text about Gallaccio to behave would be to self-destruct after reading, like the message delivered at the start of *Mission Impossible*. The critic's text would slowly decompose, falling apart in one's hands and leaving perhaps only a few ink stains but no book to find shelf-space for and no document for the archive. After having read it, all that would be left would be no more nor less than what you could carry in your head.

Rugoff's prescription to the critic follows the logic of Anya Gallaccio's work. In some of her best-known pieces events are staged using organic substances which are then left to decay and

decompose in their own, unpredictable fashion. Gerberas, roses and apples dry, dissolve and putrefy in rhythms which no one could predict with the same precision that initially quantifies them. They follow their own course of dissolution, sometimes accelerated by the addition of glass panels that one would usually associate with the preservation of an object or its display for longevity.

Gallaccio's panels do quite the opposite, choking or stifling their inhabitants, gently fostering their decay. The flowers rot and collapse, generating ooze that drips off the glass, leaving odd shadows and stains on its surface.

Where contemporary culture is forever compelled to predict decay, Anya Gallaccio isn't. Industrial farming gives us

(Left)
Anya Gallaccio,
*As long as there were
any roads to amnesia
and anaesthesia still
to be explored, 7 felled
oak trees* from 'beat'
at Tate Britain,
16 September 2002 –
20 January 2003.
Courtesy Lehmann
Maupin, New York
© Anya Gallaccio
Photo: Steve White

(Right)
Anya Gallaccio in
her studio. Photo:
Jason Matthews

Towards Objects

sell-by dates, physics gives us the theory of carbon dating by radioactive decay, and in the United States a farm has been built where human bodies are left to rot outdoors so as to determine with exactitude rates of organic decomposition. In contrast, the only quantification present in Gallaccio's work concerns the initial ingredients: 10,000 roses, 800 gerberas, 8386 narcissi, 1500 apples, 200 pinecones... evoking not only the lists of an artist like Ann Hamilton but, with broader brushstroke, the gargantuan catalogues of the fairy tales and folklore of our childhoods.

These lists lyrically offset the other side to gathering and collecting, the beautiful and abject vicissitudes of decay that Gallaccio stages. Where culture tries to encompass

decomposition, her work responds by showing us both the unpredictable and contingent processes at play and also the renewed potentials of material that we consume so mechanically. If the numerical figures are associated with amassing and owning, the destiny of the material dispossesses us. And if we consume without giving things a chance to rot, now they have their own platform on which to disintegrate.

This aspect of Gallaccio's work has become, rightly or wrongly, something of a trademark. Her orchestrated decompositions have often been described as explorations of ephemerality, instability and transience. Like the vanitas to be found in the religious tincture of classical art, they evoke the spectre of our own demise, like that of all organic matter. We are witness to

the grubby and brilliant cycle of life and death, with its changing shapes, colours and odours. Like biographies, Gallaccio's works have two dates appended to them: the time of their birth and the time of their demise.

But these cycles of life and death are not entirely arbitrary. They have been engineered, framed by human hand. Gallaccio has made them and then let them run their course. As she says, 'I set up a situation and then try really hard not to interfere.' They have been called 'wonderfully unreliable experiments'. And they ask the question, 'What happens if you leave something?'

Waterloo, which appeared in the 1988 'Freeze' show in London, poses this question in a very particular way. It is generally described as consisting of a rectangular floor space covered in lead, yet Gallaccio included, against curatorial advice, the cast of a child's cardigan in one corner. This odd intrusion is essential to the work, as Gallaccio explains, and it represented, among other things, a gesture of her artistic independence. If the rectangle evoked the copper floor pieces of Carl Andre, the cardigan was there to show everyone that 'I wasn't an artist' in the sense of someone inserted in the whole game of labels which the reference to minimalism would involve.

Waterloo, indeed, is considered by the artist as her first true work, 'the first piece of work I made', and it is significant that a key moment in her trajectory was when Richard Wentworth told her in a tutorial to throw everything she'd

spatial parameters celebrated by much minimalist art. The familiar object, the orange, is first situated in this unfamiliar space and then left to decompose, and yet, as Gallaccio points out, in its decay it becomes more of an 'orange' since it smells more orangey, in the same way that her chocolate works become more 'chocolatey' as they age. Curiously, it becomes more of a concept the more it disappears as a recognised *object,* in a gesture that revives all the debates about essential qualities that once so fascinated the philosophers.

Forest Floor confounds simple oppositions in a similar way. An 8 square metre floral carpet is neatly laid down in a bluebell wood, with trees carefully accommodated as in any proper carpet-laying. This strange intrusion of a manufactured object associated with interiors looks marvellously and bizarrely at home on the forest floor. It reminds us of the manufactured, carefully cultivated concept of the forest itself, as well as our preconceptions about country outings, equally manufactured and conditioned. As Gallaccio says, despite our expectations, contemporary countryside dwellers aren't really too keen on going for walks and their habitat is no doubt just as artificial as everyone else's.

Although the artist had hoped to watch the carpet fabric decay and fade into the forest floor, culture played a cruel trick on her when it turned out that the carpet was synthetic and so refused to decompose. Just as Gallaccio has said 'I don't do nature,' here nature (or culture) replied, 'I don't do Anya.'

> WE ARE WITNESS TO THE GRUBBY AND BRILLIANT CYCLE OF
> LIFE AND DEATH, WITH ITS CHANGING SHAPES, COLOURS AND ODOURS.

done out of the window. After her anger had subsided, she says, 'I realised it was a generous thing to say,' and perhaps we can see here a moment of realising the idea that it was possible to lose something. Up until then, she had been working on bricks made of compressed clothing and structures formed from gluing together shells. These compressions, in contrast to the work that would follow, were 'about not losing', about making things that 'one could keep', about holding onto things. If the impulse that created them was about letting go, as Gallaccio explains, their physical stability and the fact that they could be kept belies this.

The subsequent work, in contrast, explores at all levels the theme of not keeping, of seeing what happens if something is left. Which is not simply to assume that it will return 'to nature'. In a work like *tense* (1990), for example, oranges are left to rot in a rectangular floor space, reminiscent of the

In another forest-based piece, pinecones were gathered and cast in bronze, then scattered in their original woodland location. Where other artists often investigate the resonances and properties of used and found objects, Gallaccio creates her own found objects, remainders and waste products that are the results of her own deliberate experiments and interventions. Rotten apples fall from a bronze tree onto a gallery floor, globs of wax spill over Plexiglas rings and blood drips through salt. Leftovers are given a new dignity in her work: rather than being equated with waste and hence removed from view, they are made to generate new spaces, new surfaces.

This creation of surfaces is a central preoccupation in Gallaccio's work. When she threads hundreds of gerberas to make a chain in a piece like *head over heals* (1995), she creates a surface through cutting and dividing the space of the gallery. The chain is an act of inscription, like a

'drawing in space'. In her wonderful piece *keep off the grass* (1997) shown at the Serpentine Gallery in London she sowed vegetable and flower seeds in the scars left on the gallery lawn by previous sculpture, and in *Glaschu* (1999) she planted seedlings in grooves cut into the concrete floor of a Glasgow law court to a carpet design contemporary with the building's construction.

Where we would associate a carpet with what covers up cracks, here the cracks constitute the carpet and invert the relations between what's covered and what covers. The floral patterns emerge in exactly the places where we would expect weeds to sprout up, to generate a gorgeous tension between what's inside and outside a given space. *repens* (2000) extends this motif, with the interior pattern of a carpet formed from wild flowers and weeds in the grounds of a country house. In each of these works, cutting into a space creates a new surface.

These new surfaces can either follow the contours of an earlier surface, as with the use of chocolate paint, or radically break with them, as with the gerbera and glass pieces. Gallaccio has described some of her flower works as 'paintings in space', and her choice of titles like red on green echoes this with their reference to Rothko. It is difficult, in fact, to avoid thinking of this latter artist when looking at the chocolate coatings Gallaccio has produced in different contexts. Their uneven and patchy surfaces are reminiscent of colour field painting, and the rough mixtures of opacity and transparency

created by the chocolate bring to mind the ghostly quality of the paint in Rothko's later works.

Never one to neglect a remainder, Gallaccio has worked not only with chocolate but with the foil wrappers of chocolate bars that most of us discard without a thought. In *chrematis* (1994), she used this gold foil to paper over the broken surface of a disused swimming pool in Tijuana. Like chocolate itself, the gold had painterly qualities, evoking among other things the use of gold leaf in pre- and early Renaissance painting, where it would often be used in combination with standard paints and precious stones to produce effects of light. Once again, she created a new surface from the holes in an old one.

These artistic acts are reparative. Gallaccio had initially intended to mend the swimming pool after its destruction by an earthquake. In the end, she worked not only with gold foil to cover the fractured points of the surface, but also with flowering pulmeria, which she planted in gashes left by the quake. Gallaccio has spoken of what she calls a 'responsibility towards objects', and it is no accident, perhaps, that in the Serpentine piece, her flowers and plants burgeon in the places left as scars. As in *chrematis*, she generates surfaces from wounds to the previous surface. She makes things grow in the places they have been damaged.   MP

Turner Prize 2003 Sponsored by Channel 4,
29 October 2003 - 18 January 2004

Anya Gallaccio, *repens,* 2000, mown green line, Compton Verney, Warwickshire. Courtesy the Artist and Lehmann Maupin Gallery, New York. Photo: John Kippin

Contained

Our craving for biographical detail not only gets in the way of looking at **Vuillard's** paintings – it's a betrayal of the artist.

JULIAN BARNES

Eloquence

A FEW MONTHS AGO I STOOD FOR THE FIRST TIME IN FRONT of Piero's *Flagellation* in Urbino. A great painting compels the viewer into verbal response, despite the awareness that any such articulations will be mere echoes of what others have already put more cogently and more knowledgeably. So words came into my head (and some out of my mouth) about the combination of solid structure and serene atmosphere, about lucidity and numinousness; a brief notion about the greatest art being that which combines beauty with mystery, which withholds (Vermeer, Giorgione) even as it luminously declares. Then, immediately, a counter-notion: what if what we call 'mystery' is mere subsequent ignorance or forgetting? Perhaps the *Flagellation*, or Giorgione's *Tempesta*, or a Vermeer of a waiting woman in front of a

Edouard Vuillard
La Nuque de Misia, 1897–9, oil on cardboard, 13.5 x 33 cm. Private collection.
© ADAGP 2003

readable to those who saw them fresh-painted? In which case, the radiant mystery we celebrate is just a bogus alloy mixed into our appreciation. With knowledge running out, assertion was called for: 'Well, it goes straight into my top ten,' I concluded.

Back home, I read Aldous Huxley's essay on Piero: 'Nothing is more futile than the occupation of those connoisseurs who spend their time compiling first and second elevens of the world's best painters, eights and fours of musicians, fifteens of poets, all-star troupes of architects and so on.' The sinner knows best the sin: Huxley admits by the very title of his essay – 'The Best Picture' – that he is as susceptible as anyone else to this futile, if harmless, game. For him The Best Picture is Piero's *Resurrection* at Borgo San Sepolcro. Best by personal taste, but also by the absolute standard of art, which is a moral one: 'whether a work of art is good or bad depends entirely on the character which expresses itself in the work.' Artistic virtue and integrity, as we know, are independent (sometimes startlingly so) from personal virtue and integrity. Bad art, the art which is a lie and a sham, may get away with it during the artist's lifetime. But 'in the end, lies are always found out'; the sham and the charlatan are exposed by time. Huxley is right (we hope), though the paradox must also be noted that while truth slowly triumphs, the ignorance of the subsequent viewer about what is actually going on in a picture may be on the increase.

I also wanted to know about Piero himself, so I looked up Vasari. There I read how the life of one whose art was so ordered and so trustingly serene had ended in misfortune and betrayal; how at sixty an attack of catarrh had left him blind for the last

Vuillard on a train in Spain, 1901, original silver print, 9.2 x 6.6 cm. Private Collection. © ADAGP, 2003

yet seemingly innocent vices which tempt us when faced with a few square feet of oil, tempera, pastel or watercolour that please us beyond any possible anticipation. The first time I visited the Phillips Collection in Washington I saw a painting which instantly entered my top ten and has remained there ever since. (In fact, I saw several others – a Courbet, a Degas and a Bonnard – but then I've never counted my top ten, which runs to well over a hundred by now.) This particular painting was more or less square, about eighteen inches per side, in hues of brown tending towards gold, and showing a plump woman in a stripey day-dress sweeping a room. There is an open door on the left which chimes with the other plainish flat space of a chest of drawers back centre. In the left foreground is the tumultuously patterned hump of a bed-cover; behind the chest of drawers, some answering wallpaper. The woman is sweeping stolidly with a fat-brushed broom. It is an intense organisation of space and colour, full of Huxleyan virtue and integrity. Beyond that, I decided, it was a deeply wise painting: the work of a painter in full maturity, or more likely old age, which reflects his knowledge of life, which has an autumnal, perhaps valedictory tenderness to it; the celebration of an ordinary, domestic, democratic moment, yet one filled with more understanding than many a mighty piece of public art. The measly black-and-white postcard, which was all that was available, told me that Vuillard – whom Huxley greatly admired – had painted *Woman Sweeping* in about 1892, when he would have been twenty-three or -four; while biography asserts that 'knowledge of life', as usually understood, was something Edouard Vuillard didn't have much of at the age of twenty-three or -four. Yet each time I see that painting I have the same reactions, and by now am convinced that I am right and biography is wrong. It is a wise painting, filled with the tenderness of age; it is just that Vuillard must have had these attributes preternaturally early.

Biography and Vuillard. At the front of the catalogue to the current Washington/Montreal/Paris/London show, there is a perfect photograph of the artist in his studio. Bearded and

VUILLARD'S FIRST PERIOD IS ONE OF THE MOST SUPREME AND COMPLETE EXPLOSIONS OF ART IN THE LAST TWO HUNDRED YEARS.

twenty-six years of his life; and how, after his death, his fame was stolen and his life almost annihilated by an envious pupil, Fra Luca del Borgo. These melancholy facts provoked the response they would in anyone – until I read the notes to my edition. Vasari hadn't just been embroidering; he'd made a whole tapestry. The story of the blindness was unfounded, while the pupil, far from stealing Piero's arithmetical and geometrical treatises, had merely published some routine workings-out of Euclid, which contained no original theorising by Piero. 'In the end, lies are always found out'? With biography, only sometimes.

Top-tennery and biography: these are the mild, distracting,

balding, with jacket tightly buttoned, Vuillard sits in a wicker chair with hands clasped between his knees, looking serious and faintly melancholy. He is also, thanks to the amateurishness (or perhaps super-subtlety) of the photographer, out of focus. The studio stove and iron coal-scuttle some six to eight feet behind the painter are crisply clear; so too are some of his paintings (including a portrait of the young Bonnard) tacked to the wall behind him; but Vuillard himself is a bit of a blur. This is, you suspect, exactly what he would have wanted. Look at what I see, not how I am.

For a century or so this stratagem, or tact, or modesty worked. Besides, the French have a fairly low regard for

Edouard Vuillard
*Intérieur, mère et
soeur de l'artiste*,
1893, oil on canvas,
46.3 x 56.5 cm.
The Museum of
Modern Art,
New York.
© ADAGP 2003

biography, especially of artists; while families tend to keep their secrets. Claude Roger-Marx's *Vuillard et son temps* – begun with the painter's approval, yet not published until 1945, five years after his death – opens with the conclusive words, 'Vuillard's life, like his work, is not anecdotal, and is marked by not a single external incident.' He was indeed shy, secretive and spectatorial; he lived with his mother until her death, by which time he was sixty. He was far from a hermit – he knew Valéry and Mallarmé (who wanted him to illustrate *Hérodiade*), Lautrec and Degas, Giraudoux, Proust and Léon Blum. He also travelled more widely than his paintings suggest; he came to London several times with Bonnard (and did set designs for *The Master Builder* here in 1895). But he glides through the interstices of social and artistic life; he leaves few traces in the journals and correspondence of others; his personal life seems to consist in being present in the drama of other people. In the early 1920s, for instance, he encountered Edith Wharton (via her great friend Walter Berry, whose portrait he had painted in

1918); but this potentially fascinating conjunction has come down to us as no more than his surname in a social jotting of hers.

In the same way, though he was acknowledged as a master, he was not the sort of master whom the next generation feels it useful or necessary to knock over in order to advance its cause. Picasso, for instance, was sufficiently threatened by Bonnard to dismiss his work violently: see Françoise Gilot. But in the same memoir Vuillard merits only a tiny side-swipe. Gilot recalls Picasso taking her to see Braque in his studio shortly after the war. Shown his host's latest work, the pathologically rivalrous Picasso commented, 'Well, I see you're returning to French painting. But you know, I never would have thought you would turn out to be the Vuillard of Cubism.' No compliment intended to either party.

But of course no one really has a life 'marked by not a single external incident', not even one who says of himself 'I have never been anything more than a spectator'; not even one whose

Edouard Vuillard
Les Jardins publics.
Les Deux écoliers,
1894, glue-based
distemper on canvas,
214 x 98 cm.
Musées royaux des
Beaux-Arts de
Belgique, Bruxelles.
© ADAGP 2003

women friends are discreet and protective. Misia Sert tells in her memoirs – and it is about the only anecdote ever attached to Vuillard's life – of walking through a beetroot field with him as the light was closing in, of her tripping on a root and nearly falling, of him helping her regain her balance, of their eyes meeting... whereupon Vuillard burst into sobs. Sert gives a separate paragraph to her next line: 'It was the most beautiful declaration of love ever made to me.' Beautiful, but also characteristic – of the man, and of the painting too. John

Russell, curator in 1971 of the last major Vuillard show, drew an astute comparison between Mallarmé's precepts about poetry and the young Vuillard's practice as a painter. Mallarmé's instruction was 'to paint not the thing itself, but the effect which it produces'; he also wrote, 'Somewhere in the creative act is the attempt to evoke an object by placing it deliberately in shadow and referring to it allusively and never by name.' Vuillard's painting is always less ethereal and less excluding than Mallarmé's poetry; but the incident in the beetfield is the Mallarméan aesthetic applied directly back to life. Vuillard's sobs are not a statement of love, but a display of the effect which it produces.

It is now clear that his relationship with Misia was the first true sexual passion of his life; while his decades-long attachment to her successor as social and artistic helpmeet, Lucy Hessel, was also not platonic. Further, his journal, which has become available to scholars since 1981, attests that the man Jacques-Emile Blanche described as a 'gourmand turned ascetic' wasn't all that ascetic. When I met Guy Cogeval, curator of the current show, and editor of the spectacular three-volume catalogue raisonné, he told me that the journal, written for the most part with the dryness of a sea-captain's log, contains coded entries indicating amorous adventures. I asked what code Vuillard used. 'He used to write *d'içi - passion*,' replied Cogeval. Yes, I thought, a strange code, but fairly crackable. In fact, I had simply misheard, and the code was uncoded: the word he wrote was dissipation.

So Vuillard, hitherto thought as monkish as Henry James, had a sex-life, and we can all be pleased or relieved (or indifferent) about that fact. Does it change in any way how we read the pictures? In the show there is a small, oblong, tender painting called *La Nuque de Misia*, Misia's Nape. In fact it is only a half-nape, with as much bare shoulder as back of the neck. Misia is seen slightly from above, with her head down, hair covering her face; she is wearing a white blouse. It is, indisputably, an intensely erotic work by a shy person. As I was looking at it in Montreal, a passing French journalist murmured, '*C'est une vraie declaration d'amour.*' Indeed; but the painting is still the same whether or not Vuillard and Misia were physical lovers when he painted it. We look at a religious painting of the fifteenth century and are distracted by our ignorance (who are those three blokes in the foreground?); we look at a secular painting of the twentieth century and are distracted by our knowledge (guess what they got up to).

Biography cannot be neutral, and some of Vuillard's early paintings are currently being subjected, however well-intendedly, however high-mindedly, to a sort of creeping anecdotalism. Facts about his life are becoming known; the pictures are in existence; conclusions are being drawn. The Montreal show was marketed with an alarmingly crass slogan: 'The experts call him Vuillard. You can call him Edouard.' But the attempt – at different levels – to make Vuillard into a regular sort of guy, a painter letting us in on his life in narrative form, is highly dubious.

For instance, it is an established truth (established by

HIS PERSONAL LIFE SEEMS TO CONSIST IN
BEING PRESENT IN THE DRAMA OF OTHER PEOPLE.

Cogeval) that Vuillard was the chief mover behind the marriage of his sister Marie to his close friend and fellow-Nabi Kerr-Xavier Roussel – a plan old Mme Vuillard thought misconceived since Roussel was an unstable womaniser. Around this time, Vuillard painted two of his best-known interiors: *Interior with Worktable*, which shows a figure like Roussel putting his head round the door of the dressmaking workshop to look at a figure like Marie; and *Interior with Red Bed*, which shows Marie standing with a tray in front of a yellow screen (her pose is apparently half-Japanese, half-Roman) while two women tidy the room behind her. They are typical Vuillard paintings of the time: interiors with figures bent upon tasks, in which the identity of the figures and the exact nature of the tasks are subsumed into the tonal and structural demands of the picture. The first is cool and playful in mood, all blue-grey and grey-brown; the latter hotter, with scarlet and orange and yellow (but also more black). When Jacques Salomon, the husband of Vuillard's niece Annette, saw *Interior with Worktable* at the Smith College of Art, he 'astutely' – according to the catalogue – assigned to it the title *The Suitor*,

and that is how it is principally referred to in the current exhibition. In the same way, *Interior with Red Bed* has been renamed *The Bridal Chamber*. Such rechristening is 'astute' only in the sense of commercial branding – Hey, don't be scared, you can call him Edouard. Artistically, it is far from astute. It's saying: oh, by the way, this is what he was really painting, it's just that he didn't like to tell us at the time. It's reductive, and while it couldn't make the pictures banal, it makes them seem more ordinary. It treats them as a narrative, as conversation piece, as domestic autobiography. It invites us to look for theme rather than composition and aesthetic. It is a small but significant betrayal of the artist.

Vuillard's first period is one of the most supreme and complete explosions of art in the last two hundred years. He barely has any juvenilia; by his late twenties he is master of oil, pastel, watercolour and pen; he finds, happily close to home, the perfect raw material (often literally so – the bolts and swathes of cloth used in his mother's dressmaking business). This he transforms into intense, jewel-like tonal meditations in which movement and links of colour and shape through

Edouard Vuillard
Yvonne Printemps et Sacha Guitry, 1919-21, oil on paper mounted on cardboard, 63 x 90 cm. Museu de Arte de São Paulo.
© ADAGP 2003

the painting override the 'facts' of the scene. They are not, of course, abstract; they are pictures of (mostly) interior spaces including the people who live and work in those spaces. Body positions – a hunch, a crouch, a turning-away – is key; Vuillard bears out Edouard Duranty's dictum that 'a man's back can reveal his temperament, his age and his social position.' (See, for instance, the trio of droll poses in what Vuillard called *The Conversation* and which has since been 'helpfully' redesignated *The Widow's Visit*.) But face is rarely key; the paintings may imply, even actively indicate, temperament or mood, but identity is irrelevant.

Thus *The Chat* may now be sub- or retitled *The Bride*, and we may be assured that it's 'about' a mother giving prenuptial advice to a daughter, but what it's really about is the relationship of the white-dressed daughter to the white flower-pot above and behind her, the relationship of the black-clad mother to the inchoate black item (counterpane? discarded cloak?) on the bed behind her, and the further relationship of this black and this white to the browns – ruddy, ochre, tawny, greenish – which occupy most of the rest of the space. As Gide put it, 'he never strives for brilliant effect; harmony of tone is his continual preoccupation; science and intuition play a double role in the disposition of his colours, and each one of them casts new light on its neighbour, and as it were extracts a confession from it.' Thus the extraordinary *Nude in an Armchair* (c. 1900), one of Vuillard's rare nudes, is an encounter between beigey-pink (the model's body, the wall behind) and chestnutty

leg and waist of Roussel's pants: it's as if he's reading the crotch of his own fancy two-tone trews.

In his Nabi phase, Vuillard was the clear leader of the group; Bonnard at his best seemed as if he was just trying to keep up with Vuillard. Early mastery comes at a price (though not so high a price as early incompetence does). Signac visited Vuillard in 1898 and his diary describes this 'highly strung, painter' with 'an unresting passion for art'. Despite finding too much fantasy in Vuillard and wishing him more realistic, Signac was very impressed by the work. He did, however, foresee a problem: 'So strong, in his work, is the element of fantasy that he has to keep to these little panels; it would be practically impossible for him to go further... His finished pictures are like sketches. If he had to work on a big scale he'd have to be more exact – and what would become of him then?'

What indeed? Signac seems unaware that Vuillard had already – since 1894, when he did *Les Jardins publics* for the Natansons – been painting on a big, indeed enormous, scale. But in any case, this is where the challenge of Vuillard begins. Bonnard, who has outstripped him in public recognition in the half-century or so since their deaths, is a painter whose artistic direction is easier to follow. After emerging from dark *intimisme* into bright colour, and sun, and the south, he works in a consistently recognisable way, knowing exactly the shape and nature of his own genius; he deepens, he extends, but he is manifestly the same painter. He is also – and this doesn't fail to help in terms of public response – painting a

'I DON'T PAINT PORTRAITS; I PAINT PEOPLE IN THEIR HOMES.'

brown (the model's hair, both head and pubic, the chair, the floor) with only a peacekeeping line of grey-blue to keep the shades apart.

The seriousness of gaze and high aesthetic creed are animated by a humane playfulness and visual wit. Fabric and textile, clothing and wallpaper ludicly leap their normal bounds, fuse and intertwine. In what is now called *Interior: The Artist's Mother and Sister* (though in 1909 its Bernheim-Jeune stock title was *La Robe Noire et la Robe Verte*) the younger woman, in a cross-striped dress, is backed up against wallpaper as vigorous as a flowering hedge, into which you feel she might at any moment just fall back and disappear, leaving only her boot-heels sticking out. In these luxuriant interiors there is little need for potted plants or hanging baskets when women like 'The Lady in Blue' are constantly wandering past with public gardens on their heads. Or take *Kerr-Xavier Roussel Reading the Newspaper* (1893), in which the subject sits on a low couch wearing a black morning jacket and a pair of billowing brownish zouave trousers. There is a preliminary drawing which resembles the final structure in all but one key detail. In the drawing, Roussel is sitting with his legs apart and the newspaper falls between them. In the final painting, Vuillard has wittily adjusted the tumbling newspaper to cover, and replace, the right trouser

life whose accoutrements seem very appealing. Wouldn't it be nice to be sitting at that window, eating that meal, using that rumpled bed, lazing in the sun on the terrace – why, if we could have all that, we could probably even put up with the bloody dachshund.

Vuillard is not like this: his interiors are too dark, or too hermetic, vaguely claustrophobic. However charmingly, they exclude: we are not especially wanted here. And then, suddenly, an immense gear change. Even if we know about them, the series of decorations he did in the 1890s and 1900s come as a towering surprise. They also surprise in their completeness: in 1971 John Russell lamented that the nine panels of *Les Jardins publics* 'can never be got together again'. They had last been shown in their entirety in 1906, at the Bernheim-Jeune Gallery: now, almost a century on, five separate owners have been persuaded to let us see them as intended. Standing before them, and the panels of the Place Vintimille, and looking forward to the Paris show when the fragile, tapestry-like Vaquez panels will be displayed, you can understand why Vuillard thought that large-scale decoration was a higher form of art than easel painting. ('Decoration' is perhaps a misleading term, suggesting idle diversion for the salon passer-by.) The stakes, like everything else, are simply bigger: for instance, in the matter of what happens between the pictures – the silence between the notes – and how the brain and eye are controlled and cajoled from one frame-edge to the next. These are paintings grouped with as much intensity and intent as any altar polyptych.

The gear change isn't just of scale, but also of style and subject matter. Vuillard got bigger – and bigger still; he became, as Signac had predicted, more exact in representation; and he began painting a different social stratum. In his youth, he had said, 'One can make a thing of beauty out of one's cook,' and turned his familiars and his mother's employees into intense arrangements of colour; by 1928, he was painting commissioned portraits of the Princesse de Polignac and other figures of the *haut monde*. Identity is now specific, indeed absolutely necessary, given who is paying the bill. For some, this was as if Debussy had gone to Hollywood and started writing scores for D W Griffith: a failure of nerve, or an acceptance of comfort; at any rate, a disappointment. In a large, 300–400 work show like this, and given the normal ocular fatigue that sets in after 90 minutes or so, many will joyfully linger in early Vuillard, admire the rarely seen decorations, and freewheel through the later work. But this in turn might be giving in to comfort – indeed, it might be a failure of nerve. If he could paint as he did at the start of his career, we owe him at least the duty of full attention thereafter. If ever there was a two-visit exhibition, this is it.

Vuillard's was a long, complicated, sometimes tortuous progress, constantly surprising, more varied than Bonnard's, high in ambition, producing some great triumphs and dismaying failures. Perhaps the best place to start is with technique. One unexpected side effect of Vuillard's work in the theatre in the early 1890s was his discovery of *peinture à la colle*, a glue-based distemper used for painting sets. As far as Cogeval knows, no regular painter had used it before (or since), though eighteenth-century decorative artists employed it for panels and screens. It was a cumbersome and tricky process that involved boiling up colours in copper pots, perhaps as many as thirty on the go at the same time; there was also a constant problem in matching the hues of yesterday's boiling

to today's. The advantages over oil were that large areas could be covered much more quickly; that the distemper dried fast and could be painted over much sooner; and that the paper on which you painted could be laid on the floor (and later attached to a more solid surface like canvas or wood). This was the technique Vuillard used for his large decorative panels; and it was gradually to replace oil in his favour.

Quite why remains undocumented; there is only a single reference to *peinture à la colle* in the journals. One abiding reason for its use in the theatre was that the surface absorbed any glare from the petrol-lamps which lit the stage rather than reflecting it back. John Russell exactly describes the *à la colle* pictures as having 'a subdued inner glow, a matt, felted contained eloquence'. But it's also quite possible to get a matt surface with oil: see, for instance, the *Ile-de-France Landscape* of 1895, which is also, confusingly, as vast as any of Vuillard's decorations. If he could get fairly similar effects with both oil and distemper, what guided his choice? The reasons may have been mainly psychological. He told Jacques Salomon that the attraction of *peinture à la colle* was its very laboriousness, which put a rein on his 'excessive facility' and allowed him to deliberate more fully, if only in the pauses while the colours were drying.

Edouard Vuillard
Jeanne Lanvin, 1933 glue-based distemper on canvas, 124.5 x 136.5 cm. Musée d'Orsay, Paris. © ADAGP 2003

Edouard Vuillard
Autoportrait octogonal, 1890,
oil on cardboard,
36 x 28 cm.
Private collection.
© ADAGP 2003

Could there also be an emotional linkage? Glowing oil for the domestic paintings involving his immediate family; distemper for the *beau monde* he went out into? Perhaps; but this in turn needs a certain qualification. There are two late pictures of Mme Vuillard in the show, one in oil, one in distemper, both wrong-footing. The oil, *Mme Vuillard Lighting the Fire* (1924), has the *intimiste* tonality of three decades previously (greys and browns), but also the matt finish and much more straightforward representationalism typical of his distemper pictures. The distemper portrait, *Sunlit Interior* (1920-21), is even more disconcerting. First, because the tonality is different from other maternal portrayals – yellow, grey-green and various creams predominate; second, because it is one of the two brightest pictures in the whole show (the other being the Munchish *Twilight at Le Poulignen*); third, because the source of such bright light is far from obvious. There is a pair of high windows at the end of her room, though they seem to give on to a heavily leafed tree which ought to screen off a fair amount of light. Of course one can be too pedantic when faced with what seems an illogicality of lighting or reflection (and there are plenty of illogical reflections in Vuillard). But the illogic raises a question which equal illogic might answer: could the real light source in the picture be Mme Vuillard herself, that tiny hunched-over figure in brown and black, who stands, head bowed, clutching a newspaper, at the back of the room? 'Maman is my muse,' Vuillard once famously remarked. Is this a painter's tribute to his symbolic source of light?

Peinture à la colle encouraged him to paint much larger. Like Bonnard, he began to depict the great outdoors as well as the great indoors – though Vuillard went outdoors in the north, and his palette therefore remains cooler. Finally, he began to move in rich and fashionable circles: first those revolving around Misia and Thadée Natanson, later those around Lucy and Jos Hessel. In the latter household he seems to have occupied a place similar to that of Turgenev chez Viardot: the acknowledged lover/ soulmate in a sophisticated and complaisant threesome. Hessel was much more concerned about the problems of handling Vuillard's work than what his wife got up to in bed; while the painter, for his part, was furious if anyone tried to disparage his mistress' husband in his presence.

The distance Vuillard travelled, both artistically and socially, can be exactly measured by one of his greatest late paintings – indeed, one of the great twentieth-century portraits. In the early 1890s he was doing small oils of the family corsetry- and dressmaking business in the rue de Miromesnil, which Mme Vuillard ran in a 'narrow, corridor-like space squeezed in between two storeys of an old-fashioned house'. Forty years later, he was at work on the large, commissioned distemper portrait of Jeanne Lanvin, head of one of the first modern fashion and luxury goods empires. Like Vuillard, she had risen in the world: from modest beginnings as a milliner to a position of power and influence – by 1925 the house of Lanvin employed 800 staff in twenty-three workshops. Lanvin's style attracted such customers as Mary Pickford and Yvonne Printemps; while her social ascent was confirmed when her daughter married Count Jean de Polignac.

Vuillard claimed: 'I don't paint portraits; I paint people in their homes.' And offices: here sits Mme Lanvin at her desk in the rue du Faubourg-Saint-Honoré, interrupted at her work, relaxed yet authoritative. On the right-hand side of the painting, picked out by the full light from the offstage window, are the simple tools of her trade: sharpened pencils standing in a pot and a laid-down pair of spectacles. On the opposite side, at about the same level, is an icon of the social outcome of these tools: a small plaster bust of Lanvin's daughter Marguerite, now aristocratic by marriage. (The bust stands in a glass case, which was doubtless representationally true, but perhaps more widely indicative.) This is a painting about work, skill, dedication, money, success and class. The traditional low-tech craft of pen and paper is displayed and meshed with the modern world of Art Deco furnishings and the telephone (Vuillard loved telephones, and especially their cords – in the *Portrait of Henry and Marcel Kapferer* a prominent multi-coloured flex romps all over the carpet like some Amazonian snake). It contrasts the disorder of creation – samples, fabrics, loose papers, and other items falling off the front right of the desk – with the absolute orderliness of money (the neat account books, the safe-like metallic drawers behind the sitter). The painting held together by colour: from bottom left to top right, the greens of the glass sculpture case, the sitter's jacket, and up into the grey-green shadows; from bottom right to top left, the reds of fabric samples, sitters lips, and book-spines. The two colours intersect cannily (and, no doubt, truly) in Mme Lanvin's jacket: there, on the green lapel, sits the scarlet ribbon of the Légion d'honneur.

It is a triumph of relevant detail. It is also a very long way from paintings of seamstresses in which there was minimal facial particularity and the figures indicated attitude rather than character. When Vuillard was on his way to paint Anna de Noailles, the sitter said to her maid, 'For heaven's sake put away that cold cream! You know how Monsieur Vuillard never leaves anything out.' Jeanne Lanvin is thus a very unMallarméan picture, full of the things themselves rather than the effects which they produce. It contains, nonetheless, some typical Vuillard ambiguities in the form of impossible reflections: try working out how the book spines in the bottom left-hand corner are compatible with the reflection of the plaster bust beside them; consider the implausibility of the reflection of Mme Lanvin's sleeve (or perhaps jacket). It is also, sadly, one of several pictures in a state of decline. Mme Lanvin's face seems at first full of unflattering wrinkles; in fact it is full of the consequences of *peinture à la colle*. Vuillard had normal difficulties with the face, and distemper allowed him a super-abundance of reworking; but these multiple layers are inherently unstable. Worse, according to Cogeval, the medium is virtually impossible to restore.

In 1910, writing in *The Art News*, Sickert, who was a great admirer of Vuillard, distinguished between 'artists who are masters of their customers' (among whom he numbered Vuillard) and those, like Jacques-Emile Blanche, whose every touch shows itself 'painted for the owners of the rooms'. Sickert goes on: 'Livery is an honourable wear, but liberty has a savour of its own.' Did Vuillard in later years slip from liberty to livery, just as two years before his death – having refused the Légion d'honneur along with Bonnard and Roussel in 1912 – he accepted election to the Académie des Beaux-Arts? Sometimes this is undeniable. The huge portrait of Marcelle Aron is yawningly empty: that of Mlle Jacqueline Fontaine embarrassingly kitsch. Here it looks as if – to return to Huxley's terms – artistic virtue has gone missing. The monumental *Les Surgeons* and the wartime *Interrogation* seem examples of a different kind of unsuccess: that of working against the grain of your natural genius, making the sort of art you think you ought to do. But against these we may rightly set the famous *Théodore Duret in His Study* or the wonderfully playful double portrait of Sacha Guitry and Yvonne Printemps.

The last major Vuillard show in Paris, at the Musée des Arts Décoratifs in 1938, was curated by Vuillard himself; and he deliberately emphasised his later work thinking it would be of more interest to the young. It was an implausible hope; the more so since by now he bore the curse of being hailed by conservative critics as the defender and upholder of 'authentic' French painting. But with time, the subject matter of art becomes less important; and just as subsequent generations can see past the fact that Proust is 'all about posh people', so we ought by now to be able to look at the later work more even-handedly.

In particular, since Vuillard was highly intelligent and deeply absorbed in the history of painting, we might look at seven late pictures whose subject is art itself. *The Self-Portrait in the Dressing-Room Mirror* is as bleak and unsparing as any of Bonnard's late self-portraits: the reflection of a white-bearded, Oedipal-eyed old man in a mirror surrounded by pictures, who thus seems himself on the verge of fading into the history of art. Next, the suite of four paintings called *The Anabaptists* (Bonnard, Roussel, Denis and Maillol), in which Vuillard's four colleagues – two of them by then dead – are seen dwarfed by the art they are creating. Denis gazes out from behind a barricade of vast paint-pots; Roussel sits behind a palette given four times the area of the painter's head; Maillol, a dumpy figure in striped suit and straw hat, is chipping away at the feet of an enormous marble goddess like some subservient pedicurist. As for Bonnard, he is given (perhaps rightly) the greatest physical presence; he is shown tall, full-length, centrally placed. But let the colours tell the story: the painter is managerially suited, with specs and grey hair,

THE ATTEMPT TO MAKE VUILLARD INTO A REGULAR SORT OF GUY, A PAINTER LETTING US IN ON HIS LIFE IN NARRATIVE FORM, IS HIGHLY DUBIOUS.

throwing a dark shadow, while on the wall in front of him blazes his own picture of *Le Cannet*, and behind his back, more subversively, blazes his open paint-box.

Finally, there is a suite of decorations Vuillard did in 1921–2 for Camille Bauer, depicting the art of museums: in particular, the two which celebrate the Salle des Cariatides and the Salle La Caze in the recently reopened Louvre. In the former, the vast Borghese Vase and other classical items occupy nine-tenths of the picture; at the very bottom are the faces of a handful of spectators – a woman in a blue hat (actually, Vuillard's niece Annette, but identity has once again shrunk to unimportance), a man in a homburg – are utterly and comically dwarfed by the art. In the latter, the living figures beneath the eighteenth-century French pictures are given somewhat more space; two of them are copyists bent over their tasks; another is reading the gallery guide; a fourth, in a fine hat and fur, is gazing out of shot. These paintings, according to the exhibition catalogue, are 'a celebration of the human gaze'. Up to a point; though significantly, only one of the nine figures represented is shown actively looking at any of the art objects around them. Vuillard may have described himself as nothing more than a spectator, but we who look at his pictures are even more spectatorish ourselves: sometimes mere copyists of the genius of others, sometimes attentive, sometimes mere idlers. We wander through the great galleries, appreciative or dismissive according to our temperament and according to the fashion of the times, putting this picture into our top ten, incorrigibly curious about that artist's private life. But the art itself goes on regardless, above our heads, massive and uncaring. **MP**

Edouard Vuillard, 19 January – 20 April 2003, National Gallery of Art, Washington; 15 May – 24 August, Museum of Fine Arts, Montreal; 23 September – 4 January 2004, Musée d'Orsay, Paris; 13 January – 18 May, Royal Academy of Arts, London. Catalogue available.

ROBERT ENRIGHT

Adventures in

Guy Maddin discusses how he convinced **Isabella Rossellini** to fill her legs with beer for his latest film, **The Saddest Music in the World**.

GUY MADDIN IS A FILMMAKER'S FILMMAKER. The Winnipeg *auteur* is so steeped in his medium that watching his films is like going into a dream chamber where every door that opens casts light upon the great achievements of cinematic history. Maddin describes his relationship with earlier filmmakers as 'reaching into the Titan's pockets for a second for a bit of grand larceny'. All of his films are acts of homage and all of his films are unique. You will recognise film styles – German Expressionism, Soviet montage, *film noir* – and you may recognise individual filmmakers – the Lumière Brothers, Georges Méliès, Abel Gance, Sergei

Eisenstein, Josef von Sternberg and Ernst Lubitsch. But even with all these visual echoes, you won't have seen anything quite like a Maddin film.

Almost all of the films he has made have received some international recognition. *The Heart of the World*, a five and a half minute film with 600 edits, is a miniature history of cinema. It won the National Society of Film Critics award for Best Experimental Film in 2000 (he had already won the same award in 1991 for his second feature *Archangel*). Last year he was awarded an International Emmy for his film version of a ballet by Montreal choreographer Mark Godden called *Dracula: Pages from a Virgin's Diary*. This year his most recent film, an autobiographical romp set in a beauty salon and a hockey rink called *Cowards Bend the Knee*, received a commendation from the Rotterdam Film Festival for 'its perversely witty fusing of the silent cinema tradition and contemporary installation art'. *Cowards* – the narrative of which contains sex, abortion, incest and murder – is divided into ten chapters which are viewed through peepholes, a relationship that turns the gallery-goer into a complicit voyeur. As early as 1995 Maddin was given the Telluride Medal for being 'a master of postmodern expressionism'. He was the youngest recipient ever to receive this prestigious award.

In March he finished shooting his most ambitious project to date, a three and a half million dollar musical called *The Saddest Music in the World*. Written by Maddin and his long-time collaborator George Toles, the film is a free adaptation of a ten-year-old screenplay by Kazuo Ishiguro that focuses on a competition to discover which country's music deserves the title of the saddest in the world. The contest gives the film licence to combine an unprecedented collection of musical styles: everything from klezmer, mariachi, classical cello, Romanian pan flute, sitar and bagpipes both compete with and play against one another through the course of the

Tell me how you acted differently as a director on the set of *The Saddest Music in the World* from the way you've been on other shoots.

This film was the calmest version of myself I've seen on a big set. I usually have the filmmaker's equivalent of road rage. It's like I have a horn on my camera and I'm always honking and swearing at people, 'Let's hurry up, let's fucking move.' Perhaps it was because Luc Montpellier, who was my DOP, was able to average 50 to 100 set-ups a day. One reason I didn't have road rage was that the traffic was moving fairly quickly.

The conditions were unusual – a huge unheated building and a set that reproduced Depression-era Winnipeg, in which parts of the city are buried in four feet of real snow and are seen through a lens with a slight German Expressionist twist.

The surprise bonus was the temperature. Not only was the building unheated, it was unheatable. It's the largest building in Winnipeg with 60ft ceilings and even when you get those flame-throwing turbo heaters, the heat goes straight up into

Maddinland

90-minute film. The tunes are often old classics – *Swing Low, Sweet Chariot, California Here I Come, The Song Is You* – the arrangements are not.

Like all of his films, *The Saddest Music in the World* contains excessive doses of his three As – amnesia, amputation and ardour. Maddin has a way of taking subject matter that in the hands of other filmmakers becomes abject, violent and horrible, and rendering it lyrical, enigmatic and irresistible. When I said earlier that he is steeped in his medium I probably should have said he is his medium. Maddin is a cinephile's Olympian: everything he touches turns to filmic gold.

the air. The renters promised us a 27-degrees Celsius working environment, but there were some days when it was minus 43 degrees on the set. Plus it had a concrete floor that literally sucked all the body heat out of your feet if you weren't wearing unbelievably clunky lunar exploration boots. It was like wearing coffins. The seasonal adjustment disorder that one normally gets in Winnipeg was raised to the power of twelve because not only were you in darkness and cold all day, but you were indoors on a fake set that didn't look very realistic. It was enchanting in a depressing and, eventually, euphoric way.

One of the other enchantments of the film is the cast.

You have both Isabella Rossellini and Maria de Medeiros in lead roles.

Normally I would worry that I'd repeated the mistake I made in *Archangel*, where I cast two women who were similar and therefore perceived to be just one woman – kind of an unintentional obscure object of desire. So while both Isabella and Maria have thick accents and they're both very beautiful

it was a simple matter of setting up Europe versus North America. Something in Ishiguro's original script led George Toles, my collaborator, and me to that. He had a lot of European sadness in his version and since we wanted an aggressive main character we thought, why not make it a little fable about brothers, one of them European and one of them American, and contrast how the two temperaments differ in the way they grieve? I also wanted the kind of twisted melodrama you get in films like *West of Zanzibar* or *The Unknown*, where Lon Chaney plays a vengeful armless circus performer. It has all the rigours of the human heart in love and it makes you laugh and cry at the same time. So I asked George if it was OK to chop the legs off one of the characters. He said OK and off they came, and that was Lady Port-Huntly, Isabella's character.

Lady Port-Huntly, the Baroness of Beer, has a pair of glass legs filled with the beer she so profitably produces. She sets up the competition to find the saddest music in the world that gives the film its name and much of its action and content. Where did you get the music in the film?

There's some stuff that had to be written especially for the movie, there's stuff played by various bands culled from Winnipeg's curious pool of talent and there's the score that acts as mortar to hold together all the pieces of the movie. Everyone keeps talking about America as a melting pot and it certainly has been a musical melting pot. I thought it would be fun to take all these people who had come to Winnipeg from around the world and have them, without realising it, turn the city into a frosty Petri dish in which jazz could be reinvented as if history

'I THOUGHT IT WOULD BE FUN TO TAKE SOMEONE'S HEART AND TWIST IT UNTIL IT ALMOST RIPS IN HALF.'

in unconventional ways, I think I'll leave it to viewers to make their own distinctions between the two characters. There was another thing, though, about the casting that gave me pause. My movies have always just starred themselves and the actors have been pretty anonymous. I was worried that introducing well-known people would start removing the spell I was trying to cast over the audience. Then I realised that a lot of the spells cast in the movies I love are because of the stars. And there's something about Isabella; in a word, she is the closest thing to a contemporary embodiment of film history that I can get my hands on. She can enter a room and start spraying off huge wafts of her distilled film history cologne. With Maria the explanation is simpler. She looks like she's been transported by a time machine from the 1920s. I couldn't think of anyone else who so thoroughly combined mischief, sexual indifference, beauty and ardour in one character.

Her character Narcissa is a nymphomaniac amnesiac who gets involved in a *ménage à trois* with a pair of feuding brothers. In suffering her malady, she becomes a standard Maddin-esque character.

I went into my dictionary of sadness, opened it on page one, and there was amnesia. I never seem to get past page one. Then

were repeating itself. So the pygmies and the klezmers and the Hispanic musicians in the film represent the three main ingredients of American pop music – African-American, Jewish traditional music and Mexican mariachi. They end up in a competition in which they're joined, nauseatingly enough, by an all-female Scottish Highlander pipe band. I was forcing musicians into unholy alliances. But the African drummers, some from the Sudan and some from Cameroon, really got along well with the Eastern Europeans. When Myron from the klezmer band suggested they play in a minor key everyone got goose bumps and tears welled up in their eyes. Then these bagpipers came on and people didn't know what to do other than duck. It sounded like a squadron of B-52s descending on the recording studio.

I can't imagine that anyone has ever mixed a sitar with bagpipes as you do in your version of *California Here I Come*. It must be one of the most unusual musical combinations in cinema history.

A number of people were excited to hear all this stuff played together. Some people were saying this could be the future of music and Myron blurted out before I could, 'No, this is the death of music.' I did feel like I was going to hell for forcing these groups to play together in a way that outraged their ethnicities. They had clung together tribally because of some kind of ethnic pride and here I was stomping all over their sombreros with my plaid booties. It felt all wrong. But then little did I suspect that these groups from around the world would jam spontaneously over Elvis' *Suspicious Minds*. It sounded amazing, a klezmer version with a mariachi string section. Even the dour Scots got into it for a couple of laments.

I know you're an admirer of Busby Berkeley and Flo Ziegfeld and I wonder if their production numbers play into your film. You do have one scene where everyone in the city lip-synchs the words to The Song Is You.

Berkeley's impossible to imitate because he's too great. It's like trying to imitate Einstein. The whole attitude of Ziegfeld, though, where you get a beautiful woman and stick her on top of a spectacular pile of garments, is one that I've always liked. It's just so politically anachronistic and hilarious. The number you're talking about is one where I moronically hired a bunch of extras and then expected them to be singers and dancers worthy of dinner theatre. The way that song was supposed to work came from an Ernst Lubitsch or Rouben Mamoulian style of musical or operetta where people just burst into song. I wanted to convey the contagion of song. It's not an original idea – it's appeared in *Love Me Tonight*, the Mamoulian movie with Maurice Chevalier and Jeanette MacDonald, and in another MacDonald movie, *Beyond the Blue Horizon*. I wanted to do my own twist on this idea of the contagious song. I wanted it to be like a rumour, so that every time it leaps from one pair of lips to another it becomes contorted and twisted until one person's most painful musical memory becomes perverted into a mockery of that man's grieving. I thought it would be fun, in a musical number, to take someone's heart and twist it until it almost rips in half.

Jerome Kern's The Song Is You is something like the anthem for the film, isn't it?

I've always loved that song. The lyric is a diamond-hard compression, in the simplest English words possible, of how a beloved can be linked to a piece of music. I would be hard-pressed to find a lyric that more simply and beautifully addresses the themes of the movie. If you gussy it up with over-orchestrations or foxtrot tempi you could easily conceal its power. All you have to do is strip it down to its simplest possible performance, the way Rodgers and Hart liked to record things. I think they even have a song called *Must You Bury the Tune?* and it's sung with a single voice and a piano. Once you peel away all the crud then you're in the territory of the unrepressed and I really like the song for that reason.

The movie is full of delights but is it ultimately a sad movie? Maybe all melodramas are necessarily sad.

Good melodramas are. I've certainly done everything I could to make the movie work as a weepy. But maybe there are too many storylines tying themselves up at just that moment when tears are flowing. I think the mind needs to be free of questions in order to weep. And tears come at the strangest times in movies. Sometimes they come from a simple look;

All stills from *The Saddest Music in the World* courtesy the film's producer, Rhombus Media

sometimes it's a storybook flashback of what could have been, or what was once and isn't anymore. If someone wants to feel melancholy or chortle out a laugh, or do those things at the same time, I'd be pleased.

Is the wash over the film an elegiac one? It sets a tone in which you seem to find considerable comfort.

I like it when there's a lot of aggression in a movie, say in *Sweet Smell of Success*, where Tony Curtis is always running away like a gingerbread man from the snapping jaws of the people he's screwed over, or where Burt Lancaster, through sheer brute verbal and muscular force, beats all of his foes into submission. But you've got to realise that you can't keep these forces at bay long enough and a feeling of rottenness just wells up, it backs up like a sewer in your basement. I want that threat to feel imminent. I want it to be fun along the way and then, like in *Macbeth* where his doom is predicted in the very first moments, you spend the rest of the movie detecting the gurgles from the sewer deep down below in the unlit basement while a party is going on upstairs. All the while you know that party isn't going to have a happy ending. I'm satisfied with just the faint aroma of doom or sadness while everything else is fun. It's a great tradition in comedy and in tragedy. I'm aspiring to something that is achieved in the oldest of dramas and it's a very ambitious aspiration. **MP**

The Saddest Music in the World received its world premiere at the Venice Film Festival in August and its North American premiere at the Toronto International Film Festival in September. It will be on general release in 2004.

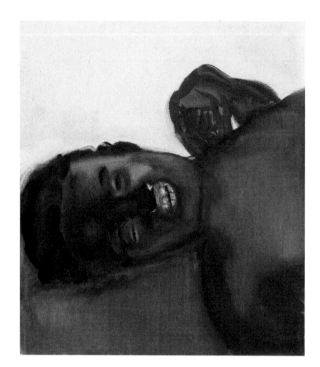

EMMA DEXTER

Painting Fear

Marlene Dumas' sensual and disturbing paintings look at how art and the big questions of life and death converge.

ONE OF THE GEMS OF THIS YEAR'S VENICE BIENNALE was Marlene Dumas' show 'Suspect' at the Palazetto Tito. Her first solo exhibition in an Italian museum, it consisted of a very precise selection of recent works, presented within a series of small elegant rooms, around the subject of death – a recurring theme in Dumas' work. Dumas, who was brought up in South Africa but now lives in Amsterdam, is one of a small number of painters, including the Flemish Luc Tuymans, responsible for the reinvigoration of European painting during the 1990s. Her sensual paintings, unflinchingly direct in their expression, give a fresh perspective on the human condition. She approaches all her human subjects with the same passion, whether babies, young children, men or women, and draws on material from a range of sources including her own photographs, newspaper cuttings and porno magazines. Through her fierce engagement both with aesthetics and with the world around her, Dumas achieves a transmogrification of imagery through the process of painting.

A list of Dumas' main themes – corpses lying in state, hanged schoolgirls, porno pictures – could appear crass or insensitive, yet it is a testament to her subtlety as a painter that by intermingling these themes she achieves nothing short

of a revelation. These paintings brought me out in goose bumps. Dumas deals with the very point at which art and the big questions of life and death converge, and she's not afraid to draw parallels between her timeless depictions of the poignancy and magnificence of death and the terrible political and human tragedies of our day. In the catalogue accompanying the exhibition, she introduces the different rooms and the themes examined in each. In the first, The Waiting Room, the morbid hanging theme, which occurs again later in the show, is immediately established with a grouse hanging by its neck. Also in this room is an exceedingly graphic painting of a female figure bent at the waist with the words 'measuring your own grave' looming over her from the top of the canvas. The hands of the figure stretch exactly from one side of the canvas to the other, suggesting a connection between the space of the canvas and the space of the grave.

The next small room, The Boys' Room, is dominated by two paintings of young Middle Eastern-looking men lying in open coffins. The viewer is not told that they are Palestinian martyrs, yet somehow it is evident. An open book, presumably the Koran, lies on the chest of one of them. Shrouded, almost swaddled, their faces emerge still beautiful, the

poignant object of a mother's grief. Despite the potentially disturbing aestheticisation of a real private, and political, trauma, the emotional engagement apparent in these paintings, and the sensuousness with which they are painted, evokes an intense feeling of anger at the loss of life and of the urgent need to find a solution.

In The Lovers' Room Dumas uses pornographic imagery as source material, yet always manages to translate the original, which might be sordid or exploitative, into a painting brimming with joy, pleasure and even symbolic power. She uses sensational colours – violet, mauve, aquamarine – and removes all specificity so that these images become a celebration of sexuality. But one magnificent work in this room behaves differently. In *Immaculate* (2003), a small painting measuring only 24 x 18 cm, the entire canvas is taken up with a female torso, her vulva at the centre, stomach and breasts beyond, and the nipples marking the top corners of the painting. Reminiscent of Courbet's *L'Origine du Monde*, the painting has the same sense of totality, as if nothing else matters or exists in the world – that this is it. This is not the plastic flesh of De Kooning; this is white smooth flesh, with pink highlights, the nipples and pudenda depicted in black; this is the painting of the absent mother who grieves for the Palestinian boys in the adjacent room; this is the same flesh that decays and gives birth to more flesh. This is not a picture of pleasure like the other porno pictures; this is a painting of inescapable fact.

In The Girls' Room we are confronted with four hanged schoolgirls, dressed demurely in old-fashioned smocks. There is surely nothing more grotesque and disturbing than the attitude of the human body when hanged, instantly recognisable even from a distance. Why is it so disturbing?

which are based on photographs, these pictures are of imaginary deaths and in that sense they are pictures of fear. As Dumas notes in the catalogue, 'I am not a visionary. I am not a witness. I am just afraid.'

In the last room, The Drawing Room, a series of works on paper, in ink, acrylic and watercolour, depict corpses on mortuary slabs, echoing Dürer's study of the dead Christ. Apparently life-size, these stretched-out corpses fill the paper, as if the paper itself has become the grave or coffin.

This exhibition is perhaps Dumas' most explicit display of what distinguishes her as a painter. Her work mirrors the natural passage of time from the living to the dead, as the living images of her source material metamorphose into dead

Marlene Dumas, *Measuring your own grave*, 2003, oil on canvas, 140 x 140 cm. Courtesy Galerie Paul Andriesse, Amsterdam

'I AM NOT A VISIONARY. I AM NOT A WITNESS. I AM JUST AFRAID.'

After all there is no visible disfigurement or dismemberment. Perhaps the mystery lies precisely in the proximity to life that this form of death possesses – the body is intact, upright as it should be, only the unnatural snap at the neck giving it all away. With their heads bowed these little girls look as if they are frozen in the moment of admonition. Yet we the viewers are admonished even by looking. Did these girls kill themselves or were they killed? At least two of the girls have their hands bound. Unlike so many of Dumas' images

images on canvas or paper. But, as Dumas asserts in the catalogue, 'a dead image is never as dead as a dead person.'

Careful to remind us of the circularity of the mortal process, she leaves us with a small drawing from 1992 in which two monkeys guard the entrance to a giant vulva, inscribed with words found at a Spanish Benedictine monastery: 'Death is a womb through which the soul is guided by Angels.' MP

'Marlene Dumas: Suspect', 12 June - 25 September, Fondazione Bevilaqua La Masa, Venice.

Edwin Dickinson, *Frazier's Path to the Beach*, 1940, oil on canvas, 35 x 57.5 cm. Courtesy Tibor de Nagy Gallery, New York

A Transcendental

'In the first place, he is a serious painter. We all say
we like serious painting – but do we?'

Henry McBride on Edwin Dickinson, **New York Sun**, 5 April 1941

LEARNING TO LOOK INVOLVES A SPECIAL KIND OF disinterestedness that can lead from objectivity to empathy, and ultimately, in an artist of strong sensibility, to a great projection of self. Painters naturally live by seeing; painting is a way of knowing what one feels, what really matters. Edwin Dickinson was the only American painter of his generation to develop a modern poetic expression by extending the plein air sketch until he could infuse the depiction of outer reality with an inner vision. In everything he did, perception was central to Dickinson's intelligence and sensibility.

The travelling retrospective, 'Edwin Dickinson: Dreams and Realities', is currently at the Sheldon Memorial Art Gallery and Sculpture Garden, part of the University of Nebraska in Lincoln, the final stop on a five-city tour. Douglas Dreishpoon, the show's curator, is to be applauded for producing both the exhibition and the first substantial monograph to explore the various aspects of Dickinson's life and work. In addition to his fine essay covering the life and career, there is an interpretive essay by Francis V O'Conner on the symbolical paintings and self-portraits. Both writers are indebted to the 1985 dissertation by gallerist, John P Driscoll, on the major symbolical paintings. There are a number of appreciations by critics, artists and poets, including John Ashbery, and Helen Dickinson Baldwin, the artist's daughter, has contributed a chronology of her father's life as well as an extensive bibliography. Despite the uneven quality of the colour reproductions, and a selection mixed with less than the best work, the book is essential reading.

Born into an old New England family in 1891, Edwin Dickinson was descended from clergymen; his father was the Reverend Edwin Henry Dickinson and his illustrious uncle, Charles Evans Hughes, was Chief Justice of the US Supreme

DAVID CARBONE

Vision

An influence on Kitaj, de Kooning and Rosenquist, **Edwin Dickinson's** images of loss and ruin mirror a life of constant sorrow.

told the interviewer Carol Gruber. The following year, 1914, Edwin's father remarried; his second wife was twenty-one years his junior. According to O'Conner, this stoked the coals of the 'family romance', creating in Edwin a resentment towards the new wife and an oedipal conflict with the father. On 1 November 1918 another tragedy occurred when his close friend, Herbert Groesbeck, was killed at Verdun. On 27 June 1935 Edwin's oldest brother Howard was murdered, a fact which both Dreishpoon and O'Conner fail to mention. In Baldwin's invaluable terse chronology we learn that Howard 'had been killed by a trio who had read about his arrival in Detroit to settle a large estate'. Undoubtedly this tragic event deepened Edwin's sense of loss and affected the development of his greatest symbolical lament, *Composition with Still Life*.

Dickinson's formative and lifelong pictorial influences were principally his teacher Hawthorne and Manet and Whistler. Dickinson was taught the plein air tradition which featured a direct response to nature through the painted sketch, also known as a *premier coup*. This process involves the construction of an image by juxtaposing spots of colour that interpret the appearance of light and colour. A way of describing forms in space, a *premier coup* involves a few hours of highly focused physical and mental activity where intuition spurs a spontaneous deployment of tone and touch. Working freely within a clearly defined format is a bit like jazz improvisation and it allows a painter to discover his or her sensibility without becoming self-conscious about it. Along the way, given the nature of his ambitions to produce complex subject pictures, Dickinson's profound dependence on this process was also to prove the measure of his limitations, as he himself acknowledged.

Court. Dickinson considered following his father into the clergy, but instead unsuccessfully attempted to enter the Naval Academy where he had hoped to become an officer. Yet Dickinson saw himself as a sailor and eventually spent two years, during the First World War, in the Coast Guard. However, his life was not one of a privileged career; rather, it was bohemian, eccentric and poor, spent in the pursuit of art. After studying painting with Charles W Hawthorne in Provincetown, Massachusetts, he stayed on as a resident from 1913 to 1944. At thirty-seven, he married a painter, Frances Foley, and raised two children. During the period of his greatest fame and late success, he would move between New York and Wellfleet – where he died in 1976 from Alzheimer's.

The chief revelation of the leading essays in the book is how several gothic events affected Dickinson and his work. Between the ages of four and twelve Edwin was a constant witness to his mother's protracted death from tuberculosis. After her death, the family was broken up. By 1913, Edwin was living in New York on Washington Square with his brother Burgess, a talented musician, nicknamed 'Beethoven' by his family and friends. It was Burgess who awakened Edwin to aesthetic experience. That year, Burgess, depressive and alcoholic, jumped to his death. Edwin discovered the body. 'Burgess was the chief influence in my entire life,' he

Edwin Dickinson, *Ruin At Daphne,* 1943-53, oil on canvas, 121.9 x 152.4 cm. Metropolitan Museum of Art, New York

THE EXHIBITION ITSELF WAS CONCEIVED AND INSTALLED along a pre-modern conception of segregating figurative genres: large figure compositions, the *premier coups*, small symbolic works developed out of *premier coups*, self-portraits and drawings. Given the biographical focus of the catalogue, it is a shame that the exhibition wasn't similarly organised; the integration of Dickinson's various formats and media would have demonstrated the essential unity of his vision and its diaristic aspect. Instead, the iconological focus of O'Conner's essay sets the large figure compositions at the show's centre, and Dreishpoon's installation has followed his lead. Unfortunately, this is not a room of masterpieces. The earliest pictures are a pale pastiche of the mannerisms of Hawthorne and others, but the room contains some successes too.

The Cello Player (1924-6) is Dickinson's breakthrough work and his first masterpiece. The mannerisms are gone. We look down over an old man playing a cello surrounded by a multitude of symbolically specific objects that sometimes shift position and re-appear elsewhere in the indigo grey space. O'Conner suggests that the old man represents Dickinson's father in love with his second wife Luty, rudely symbolised by the cello and, following Driscoll's analysis, surrounded by the wide range of the artist's preoccupations, perhaps interests also shared by his father.

Too little is given to us about the tight-lipped Yankee Reverend and his relation to Edwin; despite a conventional distance there seems to have been a richer and more complex relationship suggested in Dickinson's reminiscences and in his diaries. Strongly present in the paintings is Dickinson's sense of ethics and empathy for others, evidence of a spiritual idealism rarely encountered. This is also demonstrated equally in what he had to say as in what others had to say about him. His character has a distinctly Emersonian ring: he was anti-materialist and anti-careerist; his ambition was always for his work and the development of his individuality without egotism. Certainly the painting is about Dickinson's father but does it really convey an oedipal resentment? I'm more persuaded by Driscoll's argument that the implied theme of continuance between Mozart and Beethoven, symbolised by

certainly they talked to each other about their respective endeavours to produce an emotionally charged art. Just as O'Neill found an unconventional way to reveal the thoughts of his characters in *Strange Interlude*, Dickinson explored the conventions of naturalism and found a way to project the viewer into his head and eyes.

Another clue, remarked upon by Dreishspoon, immediately emerged for me when I first stood before *The Cello Player*, *An Anniversary* (1920-21), *The Fossil Hunters* (1926-8), *Woodland Scene* (1929-35), *Composition with Still Life* (1933-7) and *Stranded Brig* (1934). According to his diaries, Dickinson was an avid movie fan during the silent film era; he went to the movies several times a week. In these and other works, Dickinson made the radical gesture of adapting the hallucinatory aspects of the language of silent films into his perceptual practice; he

THE FEATURELESS FACES OF THE EARLY PAINTINGS BECOME
A PHOTOGRAPHIC BLUR THAT EVOKES THE VAGUENESS OF MEMORY.

sheet music, represents Dickinson's commitment to a continuing remembrance of his brother Burgess through his work.

Yet all this decoding of forms makes for a mean oedipal or sibling rebus; the use of biographical decoding of forms as a way of understanding works of art is a bit like opening an oyster and mistaking a pebble for a pearl. Such analysis closes down the painting's poetic richness and misses the picture's originality and achievement. What is really astonishing here is Dickinson's command of an emotionally charged and complex shifting space, which has no painted precedent. Or does it? Certainly one is inclined to think of Thomas Eakins' stilted realist portrait, *Mrs William D Trishmuth* (1900), where she is surrounded by a variety of ancient musical instruments strewn over the floor. Still, such a comparison shows more difference than similarity. Eakins' painting is a purely materialist vision of things, even the subject herself seems deprived of anything beyond physical existence. By contrast, *The Cello Player* is a revelation of a soul's mood; the old man does not seem to be playing the cello but appears collapsed about it, lost in the memory of all that we see. To me, this is more a sympathetic elegy than oedipal remonstrance.

One clue as to how Dickinson arrived at such a painting can be found in connection to the earlier failed tableaux, *Interior* (1916). As O'Conner indicates, the title refers to an 1894 one-act play by Maurice Maeterlinck, the symbolist writer. The play turns on a death in the family, an experience Dickinson certainly knew firsthand. Yet beyond the situation, Maeterlinck represents an anti-realist impulse where the theatrical emphasis shifts from action in the real world to intimations of unutterable feelings.

Dickinson was well read and seems to have arrived at a symbolist sensibility through literary sources instead of pictorial ones. During the Teens and Twenties, Provincetown was a tiny artist's colony. Among the writers Dickinson came to know there were John Dos Passos and Eugene O'Neill;

Edwin Dickinson,
An Anniversary,
1920-21, oil on canvas, 182.9 x 152.4 cm.
Albright-Knox Art
Gallery, Buffalo, NY

saw how the cinema could renew the visionary aspects of a baroque realism.

Few people today have had the privilege to see a silver nitrate film, as I did some years ago. It has a hypnogogic effect that can transform the most banal movie into a marvellous and phantasmagoric experience. Film and television have become so ubiquitous in our daily communications that the shock and magic of pictures moving is lost on us. Certainly a limited grey palette first appears in Dickinson's work as part of an admiration for Whistler, but by 1916 it also takes on an unnatural silvery remoteness that embodies the essence of loss, where even the closest things – a boy posing in the studio – are experienced as distant, elusive. This use of grey as 'symbolic colour' throws the world into a kind of limbo where everything becomes wraith-like, a built-in vanitas of sensual experience found on the silver screen for anyone who knew how to look. The colour tinting of early films are also a clue to the odd-coloured (pink-violet-indigo-blue) greys of many of Dickinson's works of the 1920s and 30s.

And this isn't all. The featureless faces of the early paintings may initially grow out of Hawthorne's admonition to paint in large colour-tone contrasts, but here they become a photographic blur that evokes the vagueness of memory. Closely aligned to this idea is Dickinson's use of steeply angled points of view, dissolving forms into shadow or light, the break with a coherent overall space in favour of fragments, even to the extent of wrenching the structure of the human body. These 'spots', as Dickinson called them, have a fairly direct correlation to cinematic montage. Such film techniques could be seen as early as 1916 in D W Griffith's *Intolerance* and in many films of the 1920s.

Of the filmmakers of that period, the French avant-garde director and theorist, Jean Epstein, seems to be the closest to Dickinson's expressive pursuits and is keenly alert to the originality of the new medium. Given Dickinson's love of Edgar Allen Poe, it is possible that he may have seen *La Chute de*

admired artist like Dickinson. In spite of that, Dickinson openly admitted to Carol Gruber that he used photographs when taking on portrait commissions, and a number of drawings are known to have been done from postcards.

The greatest painting of the symbolical pictures was the largest and the last, the oddly titled *Composition with Still Life* (1933-7). The subject is of a shipwreck and death by drowning. The picture's symbols seem to oscillate between private grief and a mythic scene; Dickinson wanted a painting of elegy and transcendence. It has the scale of a projected film and the presence of a great altarpiece. I am reminded of Dickinson's statement to Elaine de Kooning, 'When I saw the *Burial of Count Orgaz*, I knew where my aspirations lay.' In this work cinematic montage is substituted for pictorial

la Maison d'Usher, Epstein's acclaimed version of Poe's novel, a film popular among American cinema societies at the time. Epstein developed the concept of *flou,* or blur, the idea that film sees differently from the eye, creating 'an idea without awareness, a latent, secret but marvellous idea... The cinema is supernatural... All volumes are displaced and reach flashpoint... I am looking.'

Whether he did or not matters less than suggesting the kind of cinematic experience that must have quickened his studio experiments. Look at Dickinson's affecting *Self-Portrait* from 1941. He appears a disembodied chimera, his mouth open; his face yields up a mournful expression, not still, but rather, as if in slow motion, speaking. The stove pipe locates him in his studio, while the house with a dormer window echoes both his sojourn in France on the eve of the Second World War and the tubercular-cure cottages at Saranac Lake where he stayed with his mother.

If a cinematic reference never warranted a mention by Dickinson's contemporaries, it may have been owing to the prejudices of earlier writers who believed that it was cheating for an artist to use the fruits of photography as a source of any kind, blocking it out of their minds when thinking of an

Edwin Dickinson, *Self-Portrait,* 1949, oil on canvas, 58.4 x 51.1 cm. National Academy of Design, New York

conventions which convey emotion. At first, the painting seems to depict a view down into a sunken boat, a watery grave for two female figures. But the objects start to rush upwards towards us from the watery depths, expanding to a hallucinatory scale in a cinematic-mental space. Certainly one can intuit private meanings beneath what is shown, grasping at effects built by both readable Christian symbols (i.e., the fragment of mirror – suggesting the vanity of corporeal life, the Dantesque echo of the 'wood of suicides'– suggesting Burgess), and hermetic forms (i.e., the blue rose, the two vases and two figures) keeping their secrets. Nearest to us is a jack spewing forth water, creating a murmuring ripple in which the vases are mirrored – a metaphoric image signifying, perhaps, the artist himself. Through everything there is a listing roll and a vertiginous sense of movement.

Another sea picture, the compelling *Stranded Brig,* completed in 1943, grew out of his long interest in the arctic explorations of adventurers like Shackleton and Byrd. Here, everything seems to buckle and grind in a taut compressed space that functions like an El Greco, without using any of his mannerisms. The painting moves beyond the facts of history and is deeply engaged with the terrifying sublime.

From these pictures it is clear that Dickinson began to see himself as a sea and landscape painter. As a lifelong sailor, Dickinson loved the ocean, its grey vastness, its damp airs and dark tempests; he often walked the beaches and dunes for pleasure. In one of his best landscapes, *Frazier's Path to the Beach* (1940), the scene is not static but an imaginatively dynamic expression of space. We see through the blur of modulated forms, of sand dunes and grass, suggesting both the rush of space while walking, and the curvature of vision. Looking is made a heightened act of consciousness; drawn into the picture in this way we partake of a physical empathy that creates intimacy. The experience of landscape and 'in-scape' are one. Painted with the broad use of a palette knife and his little finger, signed with the wrong end of the brush, many of

Dickinson's *premiers coups* were painted at least a decade before the mature works of Willem de Kooning. And it is mostly these paintings that established his reputation among the yet-to-be members of the New York School during the 1940s.

Yet Dickinson is an imperfect perfectionist. Too often he fawns over an elegant smear that fails to be form, light or space. In some well-known pictures, tones placed back in space collapse into the surface or create holes where form should be; elsewhere hard edges of strong colour disrupt atmospheric continuity. Sometimes the painted performance simply fails to overcome the banality of various motifs. Such failures are part of the risk of following the provisory methods of Whistler and Manet; without them, we wouldn't have the successes. More consistently satisfying are Dickinson's mature drawings; they yield, in the subtlety of graphite greys, an illumination at once accurate and oneiric. Seen together his premiers coups and drawings may be read like his journals – a long tone poem to being.

Begun on 1 January 1943, during the height of the Second World War, *Ruin at Daphne* is Dickinson's most famous and admired painting. Baldwin informed me that it was abandoned in 1953 after a puncture repair left it varnished. In a disjunctive landscape Roman architectural forms are situated around a Syrian temple; the picture itself is a palimpsest of a pictorially imagined history. We are confronted by a paradoxical space seen from multiple points of view: its central section, painted in green-violet greys, floats against the nebulous lustre of a red-orange ground like a contemporary picture by Roberto Matta. The barren labyrinth of Piranesian geometry expresses a *terribilità* of spiritual anxiety, barely relieved by the spectral depiction of a cluster of doves in flight. Initially inspired by a visit to the Roman ruins at Arles, the painting began as a meditation on a long-lost Pax Romana. Dickinson said, 'I could see New York... in the light of Roman times – how the Romans must have looked at Rome, or how I look at New York, it seeming just like Rome... when Rome was pure in the Republic.'

Too much discussed as an eleven-year formal exercise in perspective and antiquarian interest, *Ruin at Daphne* ought to be seen as a complex monument to what was at risk during the Second World War. Still beneath this is a subtext discovered as one contemplates the confusion of architectural forms. This scene is disturbing, like viewing an ashen corpse. It is on such a personal level that Dickinson expressed his continuing sense of longing, abandonment and unfading agape – his desire to paint a tribute to Burgess, whose initials were kept at the top centre of the painting until it was sold to the Metropolitan Museum. When he removed them, he told his wife that 'it was not good enough for Burgess.'

ELAINE DE KOONING WROTE HER SEMINAL ARTICLE ON Dickinson's *Ruin at Daphne* for *Art News* in 1949. Willem de Kooning's response to this unfinished masterpiece may be

Edwin Dickinson, *Window and Oar,* 1955, oil on canvas, 30 x 45 cm. Whitney Museum, New York

seen in *Gansevoort Street* (1949). Beyond similar proportions, a red-orange field and architectural forms, these works share surprising variations on late cubist structure, kept in a constant state of flux, refashioned by the free play of imagination. Viewed this way, *Ruin at Daphne* could be seen as an alternate model to de Kooning's figuration. This is what caused so much excitement among painters in 1953 when Dickinson's work was featured in Dorothy Miller's 'Fifteen Americans' shows at the Museum of Modern Art in New York. Dickinson went on to have two successful major retrospectives in the 1960s and was the featured American artist at the XXXIV Venice Bienniale in 1968.

As an unacademic realist, Dickinson was *sui generis*. Yet there are parallels between his symbolical pictures and those of Felice Casorati and Fausto Pirandello. To a later generation, he was an inspiration to James McGarrell, Lennart Anderson, R B Kitaj, James Rosenquist and Chuck Close. Related uses of blur have been used by Gerhard Richter and by Francis Bacon, whose *Man with Dog* of 1953, was admired by Dickinson.

Yet today, Edwin Dickinson stands in the long shadow of Edward Hopper's fame. If he is not as widely appreciated as Hopper, it is partly because of the greater severity of his nature; as Henry McBride wrote, 'He is an ascetic.' In general, Dickinson's best work addresses the viewer in *sotto voce* with a silvery *sfumato*. Often it presents us with the starkest of motifs, images of loss and ruin in a transcendentalist vision. Everything depicted by Dickinson is experienced as if glimpsed through tremulous emotions; we are invited into a visceral intimacy. **MP**

'Edwin Dickinson: Dreams and Realities', 27 April – 14 July 2002, Albright-Knox Art Gallery, Buffalo; 14 September – 1 December 2002, The Pennsylvania Academy of Fine Arts, Philadelphia; 31 January – 13 April 2003, The National Academy of Design, New York; 9 May – 20 July 2003, Arkansas Art Center, Little Rock; 29 August – 9 November 2003, Sheldon Memorial Art Gallery and Sculpture Gallery, University of Nebraska, Lincoln. Catalogue published by Hudson Hills Ltd, $ 40.00

JOHN ASHBERY

How can a cult noir movie filmed thousands of miles away
capture New York's haunting and electrifying atmosphere?

The Seventh Victim

LIKE PARIS, NEW YORK IS ALWAYS READY FOR ITS CLOSE-
up. Somehow the city never fails to look good on the
screen, and quickens excitement the way the place
itself does. This is sometimes true even when the film is
obviously shot in a studio. The 'Riverside Drive' backdrop in
an early scene of everybody's favourite cheapo film noir,
Detour, adds a note of romance, though it is obviously a
photograph and a crude one at that. And at least two of Val
Lewton's low-budget programmers for RKO, *Cat People* and *The
Seventh Victim*, convey a haunting New York ambience,
though they were shot thousands of miles away.

Lewton's films, in a genre awkwardly labelled 'psychological
horror', are cult favourites today, but in their time (the early
1940s) they were considered B-movies. Though Lewton was
billed as producer, it was he who imposed a distinctive style
on his films. Besides the two mentioned above, *I Walked with
a Zombie* and *The Body Snatcher* have become classics of the
genre. My favourite, however, is *The Seventh Victim*.

I first heard of it when a fellow Harvard student, Edward Gorey,
recounted its plot in his unforgettable delivery, constantly interrupted by strangulated giggles and gasps, a few years after its
1943 release. In those pre-TV and VCR days, if you missed

seeing a B-movie when it first came out, you had pretty much
lost your chance of ever seeing it. Television, of course, would soon
arrive and begin recycling Hollywood's archives, so that children born after the 40s grew up with a cinema literacy that
those born in the 20s like me missed out on. It wasn't till the
mid-80s and my first VCR that I was able to buy a commercial
VHS cassette of *The Seventh Victim* and find out what Ted
Gorey had been gasping about all those years before.

Directed by neophyte Mark Robson (who would go on to commercial fame with the likes of *Peyton Place*, *Valley of the Dolls*
and *Von Ryan's Express*), it tells the eerie saga of young Mary
Gibson (the late Kim Hunter in her first role) as she leaves her
boarding school to go to New York in search of her older sister,
Jacqueline (the obscure Jean Brooks, sporting a dazed
expression and Morticia Addams hairdo). After the obliga-
tory, always electrifying logo of the RKO radio tower (accompanied by the opening notes of Beethoven's Fifth Symphony),
Roy Webb's angst-laden score (recently released on a CD)
surges forth to accompany a quotation from John Donne: 'I
runne to Death and Death greets me as fast/And all my
pleasures are like yesterday.' The opening shot is of a staircase
(borrowed from the set of *The Magnificent Ambersons*) at

Don't take the A Train:
Mary Gibson (Kim
Hunter) seeks help
from a puzzled NYC
subway cop (Kernan
Cripps) in Val Lewton's
The Seventh Victim.
© 1943 RKO Pictures.
Courtesy BFI Collections

Highcliffe, a boarding school. Mary is confronted by a tide of prattling schoolgirls as she makes her way up to the headmistress' office. The latter explains that Jacqueline is behind with Mary's tuition fees; Mary says she has been without news of Jacqueline and wants to go to New York to question her associate, Mrs Redi. The headmistress doubts that she'll learn anything from 'that woman', but gives Mary permission to go, offers to help her with her expenses and says she can always return to school as a teacher. After Mary leaves the office the headmistress' assistant, Gilchrist, follows her to the staircase and warns her not to come back, saying that she had once been in a similar situation and rued having returned to Highcliffe; she

is cut short by the headmistress' angry call of 'Gilchrist!'. Mary goes down the staircase and out the door, pausing to bestow an affectionate smile on the big grandfather clock in the hall.

This short scene contains a number of the small anomalies that finally make the film such a disorienting experience and contribute to the fascination it has held for its fans (including Carol Reed and Jacques Rivette, who reportedly screened it for the cast of his movie *Duelle*). The headmistress is actually being kind. But her appearance and tone are sinister. We wonder in passing what she knows about 'that woman,' Mrs Redi, and how she knows it, though we soon forget this detail as the story unwinds. Nor do we learn why Gilchrist urges Mary to leave, nor why the headmistress summons Gilchrist back with such urgency. (Neither actress appears in the film again.) Mary's affection for the grandfather clock is also unexplained.

We soon learn more about Jacqueline's disappearance and the satanic cult she has become involved with in Greenwich Village, but these mysteries tend to get side-tracked by small discrepancies of plot and motivation, and by erratic strands of dialogue. Tom Conway, the real-life alcoholic (and brother of George Sanders) who plays Dr Judd, at one point irrelevantly remarks to a receptionist that he doesn't treat alcoholics: 'Dipsomania can be rather sordid.' We hear nothing further of dipsomania or the receptionist's problem (her father drinks), but this odd exchange contributes to our sense throughout the film that people are saying anything that comes into their heads, and that the apparent mysteries of the plot are perhaps only a smokescreen for other, ill-defined ones. We gradually get the feeling that the ground under our feet is unstable.

pile up. (A curious one is a scene outside the 'Ivy Lane' theatre, obviously an allusion to the Village's still extant Cherry Lane theatre, above which Kim Hunter lived in later life!)

In the film's most famous scene, Mary is confronted in her bathroom shower by Mrs Redi (brilliantly played by an actress named Mary Newton), who has come to tell her to stop looking for her sister and return to school. While Mary listens naked under the dripping nozzle, Mrs Redi, wearing a hat and coat, looms as a menacing shadow against the shower curtain, her voice cold and ominous. (It has been said that Hitchcock, who knew Lewton, got the idea for the shower scene in *Psycho* from this episode.) Eventually Jacqueline is summoned before the assembled Palladists and told she must drink poison from a wineglass. Just as she is about to do so, young Frances, who is loyal to Jacqueline, smashes the glass and bursts into tears. (This cameo is magnificently acted by Isabel Jewell, the hard-boiled blonde in a

To make matters worse, the original film was cut clumsily to fit into its second-feature slot, adding to the narrative chaos. Some of these cuts are evident; others are not. Natalie (Evelyn Brent), leader and hostess of the sedate devil-worshipping cult that meets in her Greenwich Village duplex for tea and classical music (shades of *Rosemary's Baby*), has only one arm. It has been suggested that missing footage would reveal she was once a dancer who lost the arm in an accident, which drove her to satanism, but the story seems more engrossing when you don't know this detail.

After arriving in New York, Mary calls on Mrs Redi, a proper-seeming matron who has taken over Jacqueline's cosmetics factory, La Sagesse ('wisdom'; its trademark is a satanic emblem). Redi claims not to know Jacqueline's whereabouts, though the latter is in fact being kept prisoner in the factory for having revealed occult secrets to her psychiatrist Dr Judd and, it turns out, is facing execution: six other cult members have been similarly condemned and Jacqueline may well become the 'seventh victim.'

The spiralling complications of the plot take Mary on a scary trip through a studio-bound Manhattan which, as so often, seems more realistic than location filming would have produced. Particularly memorable is the 14th Street station of the IRT subway, where Mary boards a train at night and is soon fleeing from two formally dressed revellers who are supporting the corpse of a murdered man. She dines with a poet, Jason, and a lawyer, Gregory Ward (who turns out to be Jacqueline's husband; he is played by Hugh Beaumont, the future Ward Cleaver of the 60s sitcom, *Leave It to Beaver*) in a Perry Street Italian restaurant called the Dante, which features a mural copied from Henry Holiday's famous painting of Dante's first encounter with Beatrice along the Arno. Beatrice in the mural is a dead-ringer for Mary, but, as usual, this coincidence is left unexplored, while red herrings continue to

hundred forgotten and otherwise forgettable B-movies).

Jacqueline is allowed to leave, but told she will soon have to pay the price for her betrayal. A member of the group follows her through the oddly empty streets, at one point seizing her wrist and brandishing a knife. Jacqueline breaks free and makes it back to her room above the Dante. In the final moments of the film, Mary and Ward declare their love for each other, Mary insisting that it can never be consummated on account of Jacqueline. Jacqueline's neighbour Mimi (Elizabeth Russell, who produced a memorable frisson as Simone Simon's nemesis in Lewton's *Cat People*) emerges coughing from her room in evening dress, determined to go out for a last desperate night on the town, just as a thud from Jacqueline's room tells us that she has finally committed suicide with the noose she kept suspended for that eventuality. We hear a woman's voice intoning the Donne couplet that prefaced the film.

Muddled yet marvellous, *The Seventh Victim* is one of the great New York noir movies. (Though it is classified a horror film, the horror is kept under wraps; as in all the Lewton films, there is barely a splash of gore.) Even though the backgrounds are artificial they have a compelling authenticity. In his 1929 Surrealist novel *Hebdomeros*, de Chirico wrote: 'A false beard is always more real on the screen than a real beard, just as a wooden and cardboard set is always more real than a natural setting. But try telling that to your film directors, avid for beautiful locations and picturesque views; they won't know what you are talking about, alas!' Despite its second-tier cast and modest production values, *The Seventh Victim* captures the weird poetry of New York in a way that few films have ever done. MP

The Seventh Victim, Turner Classics, RKO Collection, VHS, 70 min.
This article will appear in the anthology **City Secrets: Movies** published by Little Bookworm in 2004.

INGENIOUS.
THE COBRA STORY, IN A BOTTLE.

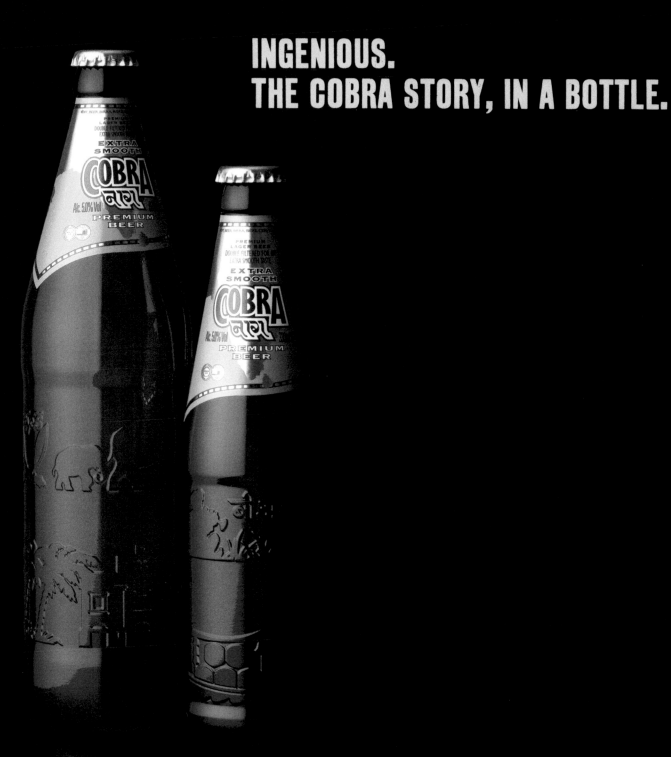

This is our ingenious new bottle. It's mould breaking. In fact, the mould got broken so often in the prototype stages that it's a little bit late. However, persistence is one of the Cobra values. The ingenious vision became reality. Phew, what a relief. A six-icon relief embossed on the bottle that ingeniously tells the story of Cobra beer. To cut a long story short; The General's Son, Learning Lessons in Lager, Charming Beer, Against All Odds, From Bangalore to Bedford, Around The World. If you'd like to know a little bit more of the story, visit the Cobra website and if you'd like to know where you can get your hands on some of Cobra's ingenious new bottles freephone 0800 146 944.

COBRA BOTTLED BEER. INGENIOUS BECAUSE LESS GASEOUS.

Cobra Beer Ltd. Alexander House, 14 - 16 Peterborough Road, London SW6 3BN Telephone: 020 7731 6200 Fax: 020 7731 6201 Email: cobrabeer@cobrabeer.com Website: www.cobrabeer.com

Paula Rego Studio Production

little Red Riding Hood

Cast of Characters:

little red riding hood , mother

the wolf , the grandmother

◉

1 – happy family – mother, red riding hood and grandmother

2 – little red riding hood on the edge

3 – the wolf

4 – the wolf chats up red riding hood

5 – mother takes revenge

6 – mother wears the wolf's pelt

Christian Title

oil on canvas   "Beach Picnic"   30" x 40"

Paintings & Graphics available for purchase
- inquire for details

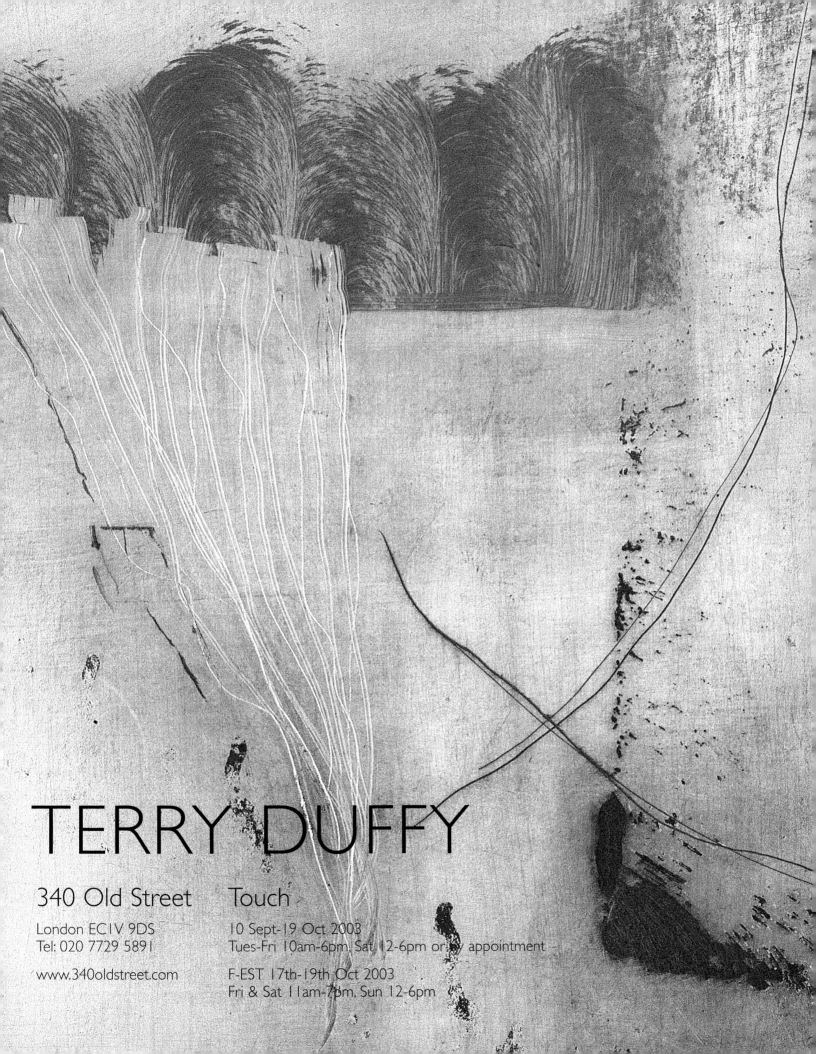

TERRY DUFFY

340 Old Street

London EC1V 9DS
Tel: 020 7729 5891

www.340oldstreet.com

Touch

10 Sept-19 Oct 2003
Tues-Fri 10am-6pm, Sat 12-6pm or by appointment

F-EST 17th-19th Oct 2003
Fri & Sat 11am-7pm, Sun 12-6pm

reviews

IN VIEW

PAUL NASH: MODERN ARTIST, ANCIENT LANDSCAPE
Tate, Liverpool
23 July – 19 October

PAUL NASH'S LATE WATERCOLOUR *Landscape of Ancient Country* must have prompted the exhibition's title. An instant poetic reflex is built into that word 'ancient': it evokes Blake's *Jerusalem:* 'And did those feet in ancient time/ Walk upon England's mountains green?' This poem, often sung at weddings and funerals, has become the trigger for a bracing, slightly weepy atavism. Yes, we want to reply, it was right here on the village green that those thundering feet went by, causing acorns to fall and sprout into mighty oaks which shade the beasts of the field and the fowls of the air. Apart from those synecdochic feet, for the human figure is pretty well absent, these associations – Blake, Englishness, pleasant greens, small birds, big trees (most especially the trees) – are seminal to Nash's art. He was much exercised as a painter in how to reconcile this ancient Englishness with the art movements of European modernity. In one 1932 article he asks 'whether it is possible to "go modern" and still "be British"'.

His own answer to this question is wavering and intermittent. He will often regroup into a Palmerish landscapism after forays into surrealism or abstraction. He feels an obligation to come to terms with the alien and progressive whilst being drawn back to the familiar and the conservative. It may be for this reason that, left to his own devices, his art has a tendency to stagnate. It's when he is not left but has his devices intruded upon, as was the case in the First World War, then the Second, that his most magnificent pictures come into being.

Although this generous exhibition devotes a whole room to the First World War, there are many crucial paintings of that period missing such as *Void, The Mule Track* (both 1918) and *A Night Bombardment* (1919–20). But *The Menin Road* (1919), which dominates this room, makes up for a lot of omissions. This painting, to use Nash's antithesis, is neither British nor modern, at least neither in any significant proportions, but epically his own work and subsequently one of the inescapable images of human history. To my mind, nothing in the rich archive of visual art from the First World War touches its bare and cluttered, devastated majesty – not C R W Nevinson's effective, muddy witnessing, not the Italian Futurists' festive and fragmented images.

The two pairs of dwarfed figures in the middle ground and the distance look like toppling toy soldiers – so much for the Slade's focus on figure drawing. But that doesn't seem to matter. As always with Nash the trees are the real human figures and the ultimate barometers of something easeful or amiss in the human sphere. And here the trees are splintered columns. Their only green is a

> Blake, Englishness, pleasant greens, small birds, big trees (most especially the trees) are seminal to Nash's art.

sickly stripe where the light should be. The foreground and the sky they imperfectly join are what dramatise the canvas. The sky is riven with searchlights and rent by the thick foliage of two explosions. The foreground is silvery-green deadwater in which float the reflected stumps, a German helmet and a ration tin. Crimson weeds grow on the mud islands. Blood-red wire and salmon-coloured corrugated iron mimic a listless, otherworldly vegetation. The metallic greens, tans, pinks and yellows of the foreground have a boldness and confidence unprecedented in any of his pre-war work. Indeed little of this work (the exhibition's first room) suggests the artist he would become. By 1912, the admittedly precocious Nevinson, born the year after Nash, had already painted several impressive canvases (and within a year would already be adopting a Futurist idiom) when Nash was content to paint *Vision at Evening* – an ineffectual landscape with a Pre-Raphaelitic woman's face draped in the clouds. Another

Paul Nash, *The Menin Road,* 1919, oil on canvas, 182.8 x 317.5 cm. Courtesy Imperial War Museum, London

case perhaps of Nash 'going Ancient' at an early age is a more unusual, more intense scene of the pyramids engulfed in stormy waves. A treatment of Wittenham Clumps signals a landscape he will frequently return to in his late works, but nothing anticipates the force of *The Menin Road* – a painting that describes an apocalyptic wound in nature and in consciousness.

That the wound was also internal became clear when he was diagnosed as suffering from 'war strain' after a prolonged unconsciousness. His recovery was slow and took place in Dymchurch, Kent, the site of many fine, bleak drawings, engravings, lithographs and paintings, culminating in one of his finest works *The Shore* (1923). Its colours are less than promising – sandy beige, orange, two shades of blue and an unappetising lilac for sky, sea and land. Its structure is bare and notional: some sketched breakwaters; the horizon with a hint of rondure. Yet the simplicity is part of its strength. Perhaps we see in the

concrete structure the shape of a bird's head and outspread wings or that of an aeroplane, but it's more likely that the picture owes its power to the starkness of its components and its eerie, restrained, inward quality.

The next decade was not a good one for his painting. He and his wife, Margaret, moved to Iden, where he painted, and tended, his garden. One spectacularly bad garden painting from this period is *Landscape at Iden* (1929). It has a folkloric woodpile flanked by an out-of-place, ancestral wicker-fence and what looks like a reed-screen. Behind are rows of leafless apple trees and a high horizon of English hills capped with banal, meringuish clouds – a sad idyll, part-Magritte, part-garden centre display. Perhaps with Nash, it's a question of trusting the trees not the teller: and so this neat pile of chopped wood is not to be read as a homely, Heideggerian metaphor of dwelling but as an image of nature as *mutilé de guerre*. And yet it's hard to believe this is the work of the same painter who created *The Menin*

Road or even *The Shore.*

In the 30s, he struggled to incorporate surrealist and abstract tendencies into his painting. Despite worsening health, with severe bronchial asthma, it was a time of greater engagement in the art world. The spirit of De Chirico, alongside other strands of surrealism, entered his work with a vengeance. The mid- to late 30s also saw Nash employed by Shell in a campaign to promote Britain's landmarks and motoring as a leisure pursuit. Though Nash himself never drove a car, the commission coincided with his growing interest in megaliths and planet-like spheres parked on ancient landscapes. *Event on the Downs* (1934) has a blasted oak weighed next to a huge tennis ball whose yin-yang seam is reworked as a split track over the next knoll. The background is a chalk cliff national monument brooded over by a chalky-looking cloud. The effect is paradoxically static and precipitant.

At the onset of the Second World War, Nash was for the second time commissioned as a

war artist. Two of Nash's large-scale oils of the Second World War – *Battle of Britain* and *Battle of Germany* (1944) – are among his most justly renowned works. They explore the sinister alchemy of war just as his paintings from the First World War did, but in a more detached fashion, almost with serenity. The first offers a dramatically dual perspective: an aerial view of the land and a terrestrial view of the air, whilst the second turns the explosions in the sky into a colouristic, almost abstract opportunity. Yet neither of these paintings so productively embody the tensions of his whole artistic career as does his *Totes Meer* (1940–41). Its unlikely wartime setting is Oxford: the Cowley dump for shot-down German aircraft. This dead sea of ripped metal and shattered wings employs much of the imagery of his surrealist ventures but with superb pictorial means and absolute conviction. The way, for example, the seamed moon's circle is picked up by the blue wheel below creates a strange planetary or gravitational axis in the picture. He makes use of the same doubling in *Pillar and Moon* (1932–42): there the Cotswold stone sphere atop the pillar is exactly the same dimension as, and mirrors, the moon. Though this picture has a haunting quality the double disc effect seems a coincidence, a painterly device. In *Totes Meer* the dynamic triangles combine to make the wheel and the moon, the flying and the finally grounded, the natural and the mechanical, into acrid antagonists and strange allies. The surrealist tropes of the last decade have finally found a place of residence where there is nothing forced about their idiom, where the nightmare of history has broken in on them with its own imperatives, and Nash was ready to record them.

Jamie McKendrick

BARBARA HEPWORTH CENTENARY

Tate St Ives

24 May – 12 October

IF ONLY WE COULD GET BARBARA Hepworth's biography into print and move on. Nearly forty years since her first major retrospective, we still don't really know what she was like. Feminists find a pioneering talent, who mapped the way for Tracey Emin and her sisters, an egotistical plagarist who alienated husbands, a son and the entire artistic community of Penwith, while a whole school of critics were influenced by Herbert Read to see only the inspired carver of hard substances whose transcendent modernism demands a pure, intellectual response. Meanwhile the prurient speculative fascination with her failings as a mother and lover, which is the handmaid to fame in the modern age, grows in the vacuum of our ignorance.

Certainly, Hepworth was a clever woman, determined to control and filter information about her image and her art. Apart from her personal manifestos which incorporate the latest modish thought in musical theory or psychology, her authorial coup was the fascinating *Pictorial Autobiography*, published in 1970, and still in print. Within its tightly edited pages of colourless schoolgirl prose, poised photographs and reproductions of honorary doctorates, two husbands glide on and off and babies arrive so politely that they might have been left by the storks under gooseberry bushes at the bottom of the garden. Since her death in 1975, leaving works then valued at £2.4 million, the Hepworth industry has been nursed by her son-in-law Sir Alan Bowness, appointed her executor and official biographer, her daughters and now her grandchildren

(one of them, the art historian Sophie Bowness, wrote the longest essay in the catalogue published for the Tate's current exhibition). In the Tate's archives, Hepworth's letters and papers have lain under the Bowness embargo for twenty-eight years. And even when his book does appear nearly all of the biography available will still be autobiography or family biography: the rather breathy, novelistic life published by Sally Festing in 1995 contains a few good insights weakened by the withholding of the archives, while others are deterred from attempting the

(Above) **Barbara Hepworth**, *Mother and Child*, 1934. © The Hepworth Estate

(Left) Installation shot of 'Barbara Hepworth Centenary', Tate St Ives

task altogether.

In this climate of censorship, critics continue to adopt partisan positions. Batting for the uniqueness of the female experience, the writer Jeanette Winterson entitles

her essay in the Tate catalogue 'The Hole of Life' (Bowness prefers a more gentlemanly 'exploration of the concavities'). She speculates, 'Perhaps Hepworth had a more complete sense of the hole than Moore. Perhaps that was because she was a woman.' Speaking for the dissenters, Henry Moore after her death rather vindictively opined that without his influence at Leeds School of Art she would have become a drawing teacher at a secondary school. The perennial argument as to whether Hepworth pierced her sculptures with a hole before or after Moore did is now rehearsed in terms of gender (but the desirably pierced ceramic table lamps peddled by Habitat and British Homes Stores are always credited to Hepworth's aesthetic, never Moore's). Others find a neat dichotomy between her work and that of Moore's in her avowed search for beauty, but see a masculinity in the solitary rigour of her working practices, her perfectionism in shaping some of the hardest stones and woods which nature has produced. She was frequently photographed alone, caressing her towering sculptures, perpetuating

the idea that her hands (often the focus of these images) were the sole instrument which had given them their forms. But one of the many studio assistants whom she employed attests to the camaraderie by which new recruits were advised to keep a chalk secreted in their pocket to retrace guide marks which Barbara obsessively made on her pieces, and which they frequently cut away in error (she never noticed).

The isolated seaside town of St Ives was the contained little world in which she chose to live and work, and which she increasingly came to dominate – her doll-sized studio house has become an outpost of the Tate's modernist gallery there, also founded upon her legacy ten years ago. Roughly half of the sculptures collected inside for her centenary exhibition are in wood, with paint and sometimes strings applied; in the curving seaward gallery they are superb, displayed in faultless, optimum conditions; we look through them and round them and see the sea and sky and curving headlands of Porthmeor beach. Their integral colours and volumes and the light within and without the gallery make sense of Hepworth's own belief, restated in Leeds in 1961, that the light in St Ives was the catalyst previously missing from her work, which could not have been accomplished without breaking away from 'the rigours and darkness of the north'. Perhaps the iron in her soul was also necessary to transform this hard-working, unpopular Wakefield schoolgirl into the intense, lonely, humourless mistress of wood, stone and bronze. But as to the censorship, while it might have been what she wanted, the dissenters must have been routed by now, and Barbara Hepworth, one of the greatest British artists of the twentieth century, deserves better than that.

Ruth Guilding

'BRIDGET RILEY'
Tate Britain
26 June – 28 September

BRIDGET RILEY'S NEW WALL-WORK, *Composition with Circles 3* (2003), included in her exhibition at Tate Britain, is an unashamedly retro statement. Its tricksy irregular grid of overlapping, rolling rings – like whizzing cue-balls seen in slow-motion – is painted black on white, a mode she hasn't employed since the late 1960s. It is predicated on after-images (gaze at any section for more than a couple of seconds and, when your eyeball shifts, a silvery neon spectre is briefly impressed on your retina), and seems chancy and free in a way that Riley's work hasn't for a long, long time. This is a strange opening, more like an envoi, to a career retrospective that is otherwise uncompromisingly forward-thinking.

As is clear from early works such as *Movement in Squares* (1961), in which the figured illusion of a pair of chequered wheels rolls together to create a singing, abyssal cleft where they meet, Riley began with the notion of painting as a generously vibrating optical structure. She has consistently worked outward from this idea. For the first half of the 1960s, Riley did all she could with figure/ground confusions, implied three-dimensionality and the destabilising of seemingly solid structures with fibrillating shoals of after-images. For example, in the work *Pause* (1964), a complicated variant of *Movement in Squares,* that uses a spectrum of grey dots, she plays all these angles at the same time. It is quite exhausting. What next? You can see colour coming by the time of *Arrest 2* (1965). There is a hint of blue in the steel-grey of its rippling, torqued diagonals. Weirdly, her early colour pieces

seem, at first, colder than their monochrome predecessors, which express more cleanly a yearning for painting to burst its boundaries, to be *more* than painting. When Riley revisits the same discombobulating iconography in colour, the shift seems almost mercenary.

Like many people's 1960s, hers seems to last longer than the next three decades. By the 1970s – the undervalued 'singing wallpaper' years – ripe, colourful stripes were bouncing off each other, breathing and expanding in an incense-laced fug. In *Veld* (1971) compressed cocktails of softly fizzing green, white, orange and blue diagonal lines seem to stretch languorously as you gaze and defocus. In the 1980s she increasingly focused on the interaction of colour and shape in a stream of works featuring dancing lozenges, whose echoes of glittering skyscraper windows preclude Sarah Morris but also have a halo of 'lobby art' about them that is going to take time to dissolve. Her work since, however, with its brightly toned inter-mingling of curves and slashing diagonals, has an increasingly arid and over-designed feel. Perhaps, as the un-monumental vibrancy of *Composition with Circles 3* suggests, Riley needs to go back-wards to go forwards. One feels, however, that it's not in her nature. For her the chase is all. *MH*

'GUY BOURDIN'
Victoria & Albert Museum
17 April – 17 August

THE FIRST TIME I SAW THIS exhibition, a retrospective of controversial French photographer Guy Bourdin (1928–91), I did so alone, relishing the dark pleasure of his ground-breaking commercial images for fashion houses and French *Vogue*. His work couldn't have a better setting than this angular, secretive, playful gallery, painted in sensuous aubergine and complete with peephole viewpoints

1. **Bridget Riley,** *Composition with Circles 3,* installation shot at Tate Britain, 2003, graphite, acrylic paint and permanent marker on plaster wall, 483 x 1760 cm. © 2003 Bridget Riley. Photo: Tate photography

2. **Guy Bourdin,** *Untitled,* c. 1978, © The Guy Bourdin Estate, 2003

and hidden rooms. Thrilling, dangerous, perverse and playing with representations of desire, Bourdin's aesthetic was way ahead of its time, and you can see how much contemporary fashion photography and advertising now derives from his photographs. I went back for a second look, this time with a male friend. He was bewildered: 'How can you like this stuff?' he asked. 'How can you, as a woman, bear to look at it?' He muttered something about it being the 'dodgiest soft porn'.

This is the crux of the issue regarding Bourdin's legacy. Nobody can doubt his visual flair and breathtaking confidence, but to some his invocation of murder-ous narratives, deadly desires and, yes, the borrowing of pornographic motifs (the supine, pliable female figure; women's legs spread open;

woman as perennial victim) means that whatever visual originality he may have had, Bourdin simply repeats a repugnant form of sexist objectification in his work.

The obvious response to this charge is lost in an exhibition setting, even one that includes fascinating, tender, unpublished photographs of landscapes and built environments familiar to Bourdin, which serve to counter much of what we know of him. Context, in his case, really is all. His slick images of mannequin-like women, sexualised and playing dead (or as good as) were aimed at a largely female audience, and that is a crucial detail. His images would have very different connotations if they had appeared, say, in *Playboy*.

Instead, they play with sexual play, flirt with the fetishisation of

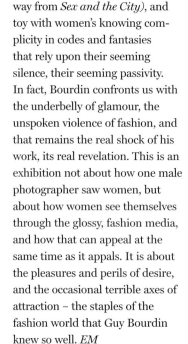

THE LABOUR PARTY ARE WEASELS AND VIPERS, FORKED TONGUED TURNCOATS WHO HAVE SPATTERED BRITISH PEOPLES FACES WITH BLOOD

1
2

1. **Bob & Roberta Smith,** *The Labour Party are weasels and vipers,* 2003, enamel paint on panel. Courtesy the artist

2. **Neal Tait,** *Boy and dog,* 2003, oil on linen, 117 x 101.5 cm. Courtesy Jay Jopling/ White Cube, London. Photo: Stephen White

3. **AK Dolven,** *The Meal,* 2003, 16 mm film on DVD, 8 min 23 sec, edition of 5 + 2 a/p. Courtesy Anthony Wilkinson Gallery

4. **Jonathan Meese,** *Pharao Meesegurke mit Tinten-fischauge,* 2003, oil on canvas, 60 x 50 cm. Courtesy Modern Art, London

3

4

fashion (in his celebration of foxy shoes, for example, we're not a long way from *Sex and the City*), and toy with women's knowing complicity in codes and fantasies that rely upon their seeming silence, their seeming passivity. In fact, Bourdin confronts us with the underbelly of glamour, the unspoken violence of fashion, and that remains the real shock of his work, its real revelation. This is an exhibition not about how one male photographer saw women, but about how women see themselves through the glossy, fashion media, and how that can appeal at the same time as it appals. It is about the pleasures and perils of desire, and the occasional terrible axes of attraction – the staples of the fashion world that Guy Bourdin knew so well. *EM*

'NEAL TAIT: THE BURNISHED RAMP'
White Cube
5 June – 5 July

IT'S THREE YEARS SINCE NEAL TAIT had his last solo show in London. Then, portrait heads in uniform rows were rendered schematically in greens, blues and deathly shades of grey and white. Ridged and mute with mask-like faces, some wore headscarves, as if this was a series of paintings of diminutive Eastern European peasant women.

If only superficially, they were reminiscent of the pale face of the mother in Arshile Gorky's painting *The Artist and His Mother*, and one may have ventured a guess that, in his own corpse-like figures, memory and loss are themes Tait wanted to carry on exploring. However, Tait has expanded his range and he is all the more interesting for it. While his earlier work could be described as sculptural, the paint is now looser, more gestural, and his subjects often look as if they are disappearing or fading away. *Mirror*, for instance, is a grey configuration of

flowers that have bled into a grey backdrop. Here, we could be reminded of Belgian painter Luc Tuymans, whose anaemic palette conveys a sense of a diseased and blighted world. Cropped and distorted, Tait's images trade on a similar vocabulary: a huge powder puff in livid, pinkish-greys occupies centre stage; a painted shape that looks like a climbing frame bleeds into its surroundings, near a closed parasol at a strange angle.

But the comparisons with Tuymans don't go that deep. Tait has a sense of humour for a start, which undercuts the occasional spooky strangeness. In *Boy and dog* a white ghost figure with a blanked-out face carries a large dog with bandaged forelegs. Tait appears to enjoy slipping into this realm of the absurd. In *Orange girl* he uses what feels like a childhood memory. A girl is hugging a weird dolphin-like creature in a cute and kooky kind of way. It looks like a tableau from a 1970s American sitcom, a programme that perhaps the thirtysomething Tait may have watched as a kid.

In the end, you feel that these paintings are not so much to do with personal memory after all, but self-conscious references to other paintings. However, the sense that these are snapshots of lost time ties the thematic threads together. His paintings could descend so easily into banal cliché, yet Tait's layered and elusive canvases offer more than we might initially expect to find. *FG*

'JONATHAN MEESE: FREIHEIT (THE EMPIRE PORTRAITS 1901)'
Modern Art
5 June – 13 July

THE HALF-GERMAN AND HALF-Welsh artist Jonathan Meese was born in Tokyo in 1970 and studied in Hamburg before gaining attention on the art scene in Berlin in 1998 with his performances and chaotic, large-scale installations. Cluttered obsessively with text, posters, photographs, photocopies, assemblages and other objects, his installations mix cultural references and icons from film, pop, literature and political history. Favourite faces include Diana Rigg, The Beastie Boys, Che Guevara, Stalin, Truman Capote, Clint Eastwood along with images from cult (and kitsch) 60s and 70s fantasy sci-fi films such as John Boorman's *Zardoz* and *Planet of the Apes*. One recent three-hour performance based on the 40s horror film, *Dr Cyclops,* had Meese acting out the role of the unhinged professor.

For his London debut Meese's contribution is more sedate. He has chosen to put his energy into a painting show. *The Empire Portraits 1901* are head-and-shoulders self-portraits in which Meese has made himself look like a series of expressionist nightmare visions. Some could be portraits of the Devil, some could be images of Christ. It is difficult to work it out. Others look like an uneasy hybrid – painterly 'don't knows'.

Red and black colours dominate. Using a combination of quick, loose strokes of thick paint, uneven washes and coloured dribbles, the features are aggressively sketched. In one canvas the eyes are blank voids. In another they are blue spotted with red. Small blobs of beige paint squeezed straight from the tube create a particularly weird row of teeth. Equally odd is the crown of thorns that appears on one head and the German cross that appears on many of the others.

The self-portraits are accompanied by a larger painting depicting the sexual antics of two hybrid animal creatures, the forked-tongued, dog-like female holding the large ejaculating member of her mate. Crude and naive this may seem at first but, like his other work, its lasting effect is far more complex and troubling. *HS*

'AK DOLVEN'
Anthony Wilkinson Gallery
29 May – 29 June

SOMETIMES THE DIFFICULTY IN intellectually unpacking a particular piece of work is down to some accidental ambiguity on behalf of the artist, at other times it is completely intentional. The trouble for the reviewer is working out which is which. AK Dolven's videos and painting seem to be wilfully obtuse. Their meaning is infuriatingly truant, yet there is a feeling that there are some grand issues at play. Such work can be easily dismissed as pretentious or simply bad, but it is this encounter with its reluctance to give up its meaning that matters. By removing distinct narrative, context or intention, the slightest formal inflections in Dolven's work seem exaggerated and, by degrees, assume a heightened importance.

The video *The Meal*, for example, is viewed through a hole just a couple of inches across. You peer into a scene in which a family are eating breakfast. A mother feeds a child, the cutlery clatters on the crockery. A simple scene. Then one of the young men starts feeding another his cereal. There is the barest of body language between them to explain their relationship. Dolven turns it into a freakish vignette using minimal means and makes us notice the most delicate of details that would otherwise go unnoticed in a racy narrative plot.

In the video installation *From Last Winter* a mundane occurrence is again perverted through slight means. A young woman stands beside an older man who is lying down. As the traffic files past in the background the man blinks and twitches. The woman's head, meanwhile, is enigmatically out of camera shot. Together they make up a cross, an architecture of bodies within the space of the film frame. With time, the falseness of the situation undermines any

initial assumptions we might have made about what is going on here. We start to question the relationship of the two. Are they father and daughter or are they lovers? The question is never answered.

Dolven switches from figurative video to abstract painting in the diptych *Can Women Think?* The two panels, with white on white biomorphic shapes painted in oil on aluminium, are a mirror image of one another. The effect is so über-white that it is dazzling, even painful, to look at. We start to see shoals of black squiggles floating across the surface of our eyeballs and this soon becomes the dominant imagery. In this case, Dolven's reductivism brings about an unpredictable source of animation, literally in the viewer's eye. *SO'R*

'INDEPENDENCE'
South London Gallery
3 June – 3 August

TO CELEBRATE ITS CHANGE FROM A space funded by Southwark Council to the more flexible status as a charitable trust, the South London Gallery staged the aptly named 'Independence', a group show bringing together 135 local, national and international artists who have all exhibited in the gallery over the last ten years. The artists have responded to the theme in many ways, ranging from the sexual to the political.

The first piece one comes across is Barbara Kruger's *Let Go* (2003), a billboard that hangs outside the building with an image of a bird ready to fly, cupped in a human hand. Kruger, best known for her hard-hitting, no nonsense one-liners, provides the neat message that seems to say: 'it is time, Southwark Council, to let them get on with it.' Meanwhile, in the courtyard the title of Thomas Kilpper's mobile home construction *Fuck Your Landlord* (2003) explores the problems associated with expensive London housing. It

consists of a converted hospital bed that had been turned into a self-contained living unit, with its own door and roof. An independence of sorts but, as any homeless person might tell you, not one borne out of choice.

A group show like this is bound to be a mixed bag but here the strongest was work that was overtly political. Ori Gersht's *Red Light, White City* (2003) shows a view of a Palestinian town from an Israeli hilltop. The red hues in the image are reminiscent of military night-sight vision technology; but, judging by the artist's previous work about Sarajevo, the image says more about the traces left on a landscape by conflict. As you imagine standing on the hill, you are aware that you are on some kind of frontier, but it is hard to know what is your role.

Mona Hatoum's *Set in Stone* (2002) makes a similar point about the despair of two cultures trying to understand each other. Two marble tumblers, one inscribed with the Arabic word for 'east' and the other 'west', and joined with a flimsy piece of string, make a communication device that will never work.

Bob and Roberta Smith's work is a more unequivocal statement. His painting *The Labour Party are weasels and vipers* is augmented by newspaper pictures of Baghdad casualties. A detail of bleeding feet looks like a modern-day *pietà;* the massacre of innocents pulls no punches. One leaves feeling that this is a genuinely shocking sight. *LG*

NEWLYN

'BREDA BEBAN: I CAN'T MAKE YOU LOVE ME'
Newlyn Art Gallery
16 June – 12 July

IF THERE'S ONE THING THAT MAKES watching video art different from cinema or television it's the fact that you hardly ever see the start of a video piece before you've seen the end. Usually this doesn't matter. Plot lines aren't that important. With Breda Beban's *Walk of Three Chairs*, however, you don't really get the point if you come in mid-loop. This is because it documents a performance that encodes a story – a love story of sorts.

Beban is a Croatian artist now working in England. As if a decade of butchery and political turmoil in her native (former) Yugoslavia weren't enough, she lost her partner and artistic collaborator, Hrvoje Horvatic, when he died of chickenpox contracted from a child after their arrival in this country. If you don't know these things when you see the show, you soon want to find out because Beban's three videos and eight suites of still photos convey a degree of intractable pain that's initially perplexing in work of such measured understatedness.

Walk of Three Chairs shows Beban as a neat ballet mistress-like figure in a dark skirt, floating on a barge through Belgrade, accompanied by a white-shirted folk band. As the band plays, she does a tricky routine of walking on chairs set on the barge as it travels along the Danube. She's also trying to learn a song, whose plangent middle European cadences don't need much translating ('Who doesn't know how to suffer / Doesn't know how to love' runs the chorus).

Beban's Danube is both life-river and death-river, and the artist's balancing act reflects this shaky duality. Upstairs, in Newlyn's main gallery space, *I Can't Make You Love Me* takes the two-way motion further as the focus physically swings from one large screen to another set at a right angle. Two people – a tearful Beban and a stony-faced stand-in for an ex-boyfriend – alternatively have their say about why the relationship crashed. Despite being scripted,

the emotional mess feels like it's spilling out at your feet against a background of blandly prosperous northern European suburbs.

Not for the first time in this show there's the sense of a bigger story trying to get out of this short film. Back downstairs, the photo pieces in *Arrivals* keep Beban's lens on loss and exile wide open – miscellaneous short-stay rooms with empty, rumpled beds, then the view through the window, then the view beyond the window. The final close-ups show banal details like a shop doorway or a man crossing a street, the kinds of things a prisoner or an assassin would spend hours looking out at. Small wonder the psychotherapist in the 90-minute DVD *Stories I Tell Myself* (described as a 'foot-note' to the show) often looks out of his depth. MB

SHEFFIELD

'STATES OF AMERICA: MICHAEL ORMEROD'
Graves Art Gallery
10 May – 9 August

IN THE INTRODUCTION TO ROBERT Frank's seminal book *The Americans,* published in 1955, Jack Kerouac described how the photographer 'sucked a sad poem right out of America onto film, taking rank among the tragic poets of the world'. This coming together of the strongest voice of the Beat generation and a new form of photo-journalism crystallised the American love affair with the open road and a way of documenting it which would prove hugely influential for generations of inter-national artists and filmmakers.

Among them was photographer Michael Ormerod who, though British-born, was fascinated by the United States and its ambiguous relationship between incredible landscapes and its relentless post-1950s commercialism. The country and its long highways was the

source and subject of almost all of his photography, so it is with a double sadness and irony that he met his untimely death in a road accident on one of his trips photographing the US in 1991.

Ormerod's images reflect a relationship with the US that contained mixed feelings, and for every image that champions America's power and glory, there is another that reflects its despair. A photograph of Houston that shows a gleaming office block is followed by a group of images that document a tackiness that is prevalent there, typified by *Sal's Barber Shop* in which two stuffed deer heads adorn a run-down shop window. Many of the images expose this throwaway culture. He shows the beauty of the desert interrupted by smashed televisions, discarded fridges and 'dead' cars abandoned by the roadside.

There are many unexpected interpretations of scenes. A building site becomes a strangely beautiful landscape. Photographs taken through a car window create an abstract world beyond the wind-screen wipers. He seemed to shy away from photographing people, preferring to document ghostly streets and empty high-ways, and in the few images where people do appear they are often lonely, somewhat hidden figures that reveal very little feeling. However, there is an exception here too, in an image that captures raw emotion from a Native American who stares impassively into the camera.

Although ostensibly creating documentary photography, Ormerod did not try to offer a definitive judgement on the country that gave him his subject matter. Nor did he seem to want to fix his images in any particular time or place. He leaves behind a body of work that reveals an outsider's complicated reactions to a place filled with contradictions – wealth

next to poverty, natural beauty coupled with human destruction, and technological progression mixed in with the crumbling remains of the past. *EW*

GRASMERE
CUMBRIA

'SIMON MORLEY: THE LIFE OF THINGS'
3°W @ Island View, The Wordsworth Trust
1 June – 25 September

WORKING IN ONE OF THE MOST beautiful and touristy parts of the country is fraught with seductive clichés. However, a six-month residence at the Wordsworth Trust has allowed Simon Morley to look beyond the picture-postcard beauty of the Lake District using photography and video. His exhibition cuts to the heart of the issue by dissecting the underlying and celebrated intertwining of this landscape with its long and distinguished links to poetry, typified in the work of the über-English poet William Wordsworth.

In Morley's video *Sweet Stream* we see the image of a rock bed of a local stream. It is a generic image of clear water flowing over pebbles and fills the gallery with the refreshing sound of gently running water. However, Morley interrupts this bucolic scene by floating along the current an abstract selection of printed words from the beginning of Wordsworth's *The Prelude*. This slightly surreal procession of words on paper in water literally inscribes the poetry into its landscape but also challenges the allegedly seamless, symbiotic relation between the two – how did nature inspire these words and how do words immortalise this nature?

His piece *An Elegy Wrote in an English Church Yard* juxtaposes photographs of lichen-mottled gravestones in the Grasmere churchyard with single, evocative words from nineteenth-century epitaphs. By encouraging the viewer to confront the arbitrariness of the pairing, these diptychs illustrate how the relationships between words and images are neither simple nor innocent. It is an idea that also features strongly in Morley's second video *Last Line: Wordsworth, 'The Prelude' (1805 version)*. It shows a group of anonymous lips, reciting the last line of the Wordsworth poem – silent, close-up and in slow motion. The effect of these oversized, mute but moving lips is sensuous and strange. The work frustrates the very mechanics of language by separating it from meaning. It confronts us with the ultimate distance between image and words and between landscape and poetry. The viewer is left to interpret and ascribe personal significance. It is a forceful ending for this project bound up with the much-interpreted identity of the Lake District. *SC*

SALISBURY

'GAVIN TURK: ET IN ARCADIA EGO'
New Art Centre Sculpture Park & Gallery, Roche Court
27 April – 13 July

GAVIN TURK MIGHT NEVER SHAKE off the instant association between his name and the blue plaque (*Cave*, 1991), which he made to commemorate his time as a student at the Royal College, but perhaps someday a real one will go up near his Charing Cross studio. It is this awareness, both of his place now in art and his eventual place in its history, that dominates his latest exhibition.

The centrepiece is an outdoor sculpture entitled *Her*, based on de Chirico's painted depictions of Ariadne. Here, instead of being swathed in classical drapery, the figure, made from marble dust and white cement, is sculpturally 'inserted' into a sleeping bag. Turk has crudely inscribed the words '

et in arcadia ego' on the base, the quotation lifted from a Poussin painting. On the wall behind, he has painted a colonnade, this too, based on de Chirico's imagery. Not only is Turk interested in his own place in art, but also in art's place in the physical world, within the bounds of a museum or gallery. In this work he plays with these boundaries, but the effect is academic and subtle, and will be lost on all but the most art-obsessed observers.

A mixture of smaller works is also on display, among them two finely detailed bronze cardboard boxes, both called *Box* (2003), which on first sight look as though they have been left there by a lazy gallery attendant. It's intentional for visitors almost to ignore them, but it is this twentieth-century conceptualist technique of creating value from objects that are essentially valueless which is perhaps most compelling about Turk's work. A few years ago he used this to great effect with *Nomad*, a full-size bronze figure in a sleeping bag which he displayed in Charing Cross Road. Creating a cardboard box costing £12,500, however, is nothing like as confrontational as creating a rough sleeper worth even more.

In the gallery there are also loaves of bread made of concrete, a spade carved in mahogany, and a brick wall painted on canvas in oil, but each of these works is so self-conscious it becomes difficult to see the everyday objects they are meant to be transforming. The most memorable work in the exhibition consists of three giant fibreglass eggs each a metre and a half tall and two metres long. Entitled *Oeuvre* (2000–2003), this is intended to suggest that the wholeness of an artist's work, his *oeuvre*, cannot be defined before the event of the artist's death, which, as the legend on the base of

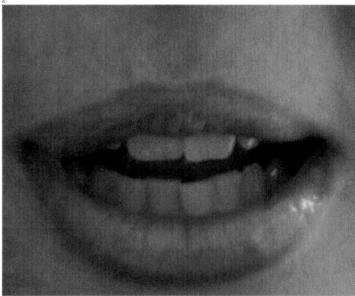

1. **Breda Beban,** *I Can't Make You Love Me*, 2003, video still. Courtesy Newlyn Art Gallery. © Breda Beban

2. **Simon Morley,** *Last Line: Wordsworth, 'The Prelude' (1805 version)*, 2003, video, 3 min. Courtesy The Wordsworth Trust

3. **Michael Ormerod,** from *States of America*, 1991

1. **Bernard Frize,** *Lucky V,*
2000, acrylic and resin
on canvas, 73 x 92 cm

2. **Wang Guangyi,** *Ardent
Face – A,* 2002, oil on
canvas, 200 x 200 cm.
Courtesy the artist © DR

3. **David Austen,** *Untitled,*
*(Dark grey figure in hat
and coat)* 2003,
watercolour on paper.
Courtesy Kettle's Yard
Gallery

4. **Gavin Turk,** *Oeuvre,*
2000, painted fibreglass.
Courtesy New Art Centre
Sculpture Park and
Gallery

Her reminds us, is an eventual certainty even in the peaceful gardens of the sculpture park.

What is most surprising about *Oeuvre* is that, sitting on the grass in its quiet surroundings, it looks as subdued as a Barbara Hepworth sculpture and as familiar as a Henry Moore, and suggests that, as this once rebellious YBA heads towards middle age, he has come to represent the art establishment many thought he set out to defy. *PS*

CAMBRIDGE

'EXODUS: BETWEEN PROMISE AND FULFILMENT'
Kettle's Yard Gallery
21 June – 3 August

IN 1869 ORDNANCE SURVEY TEAM member Sergeant James McDonald of the Royal Engineers lugged his cumbersome camera equipment across the mountainous desert of the Sinai Peninsula. He returned with 100 images that not only documented a harsh physical landscape but also embodied a spiritual one. In carrying out his work McDonald recorded the location where the Israelites were said to have rested on their flight from Egypt, and he stood at the foot of the mountain where it was believed Moses had received the Ten Commandments as well as at the possible location of the Burning Bush. With these associations in mind, artist and curator David Austen has exhibited McDonald's images alongside largely abstract sculptures, paintings and prints by eight contemporary artists. Similarities can undoubtedly be found between old and new, but as none of the works has been made in direct response to McDonald's photographs, Austen is on slightly shaky ground.

Helmut Federle's contribution has perhaps the most obvious visual connection to McDonald's landscapes. Taken at a time when photography was still a relatively new medium McDonald's detailed, high-contrast sepia prints highlight in great detail the sharp sun-baked rocks and the rough buildings hewn out of them. The black textures on layers of gold leaf and bronze in Federle's abstract screenprints look like rubbings from a similar landscape. Likewise, Vija Celmins' beautifully detailed wood engraving *Ocean Surface*, although depicting a choppy sea, has the same sense of a jagged, rocky landscape.

John McCracken's two large, minimalist, oblong sculptures, *Beacon* and *Fling*, lean upright against the walls. One is coloured black and one is coloured red. They are shiny resin and fibre-glass-covered sculptures, shiny enough to reflect the viewer. The shape of the sculptures is echoed too in McDonald's photographs of large, standing stones that hang nearby.

Austen's own contribution consists of panels of simple but engaging one-tone watercolour wash studies of single figures seen standing or squatting or leaning, isolated against white backgrounds and rendered in muted shades of reds, greys, browns and greens. As we find out in the catalogue essay, the link here is back to the Bedouin figures in McDonald's pictures, often seen sitting or standing almost unnoticed in the distance. Again there is a connection, but it feels like a flimsy one.

It may be hard to recapture the impact of first seeing photographs of such a harsh landscape that hold such strong spiritual associations but McDonald's images are still powerful. However, showing the contemporary works alongside them detracts from both. They would have worked better exhibited on their own. *HS*

'ALORS, LA CHINE?'
Centre Pompidou
25 June – 13 October

OVER 50 ARTISTS IN THIS LARGE show provide an eclectic, if not chaotic, skim through the past five years of Chinese culture, in the visual arts, music, cinema and architecture. Works run into one another in a huge open space. They include several ancient pieces – items of jade and a bronze mirror, which have been given iconic status in sealed glass cylinders. The projection of films within the exhibition and a substantial architectural section put the focus on the transformation of the city and the culture clash between the isolationism of the rural past and the global culture of modern urban life.

The centrepiece of the exhibition is Lu Hao's huge maquette *Beijing Welcomes You* (2000–2002). At first sight, it is a faithful representation of the Chinese capital, with its different districts and historic monuments, the Forbidden City and the Sky Temple, but there has been a subtle subversion of scale. The rundown, traditional *hutong* districts with their one- and two-storey courtyard homes, made from painted wood and card, are at a larger scale than the new Plexiglass skyscrapers and office blocks, reversing the relation between the rapidly disappearing, historic, vernacular housing and the imported modern architecture of outside.

More interesting are those artists who respond to Chinese tradition. In *Tonic*, Zhou Tiehai and Zhou Lin reproduce celebrated Chinese ink and wash paintings in acrylic on a long roll. Shi Hui's papier mâché *Artificial Mountain* creates the weird artificial rock formations that are part of the aesthetic of the Forbidden City and other historic Chinese gardens. Others react to a more recent past and the after-shocks of communism and the Cultural Revolution. The huge woodcut posters by Fang Lijun use the tools of popular propaganda. Meanwhile Wang Jianwei sets back to back, on either side of a screen, black and white footage of the communist taking of power in 1940, and colour films of the Red Army's appropriation of the Peking Opera during the Cultural Revolution. Mu Chen and Shao Yinong's *Assembly Halls* shows a series of colour photos that catalogue the transformation of Maoist assembly halls where mass meetings were held, now often abandoned or transformed into restaurants or theatres.

If there is no evident dominant style to the selection, there is a feeling of what there is not. There is neither kitsch, typified with mastery by the Liu brothers (recently seen at the Fondation Cartier), nor the urban buzz of artists as seen in *Zone of Urgency* at the Venice Bienniale. However, there is a rather bleak, cinematic vision of China at the crossroads. A sense of unease pervades, whether it is the film clips of migration to cities or the disquieting animal mutants by Xiao Yu that evokes with pessimism the alienation and implied violence of fast-changing Chinese society. *NE*

BERNARD FRIZE
Musée d'Art Moderne
de la Ville de Paris
6 June – 28 September

BERNARD FRIZE IS A HIGHLY regarded painter in his native France. This is his second large-scale, one-person exhibition at the Musée d'Art Moderne – the previous solo show was in 1988. This time he is showing over 100 paintings from a ten-year period – so this makes it his mid-career retrospective of sorts.

Frize's paintings are about the process of painting and the effect of brushstrokes, yet his abstract images are paradoxically perfectly smooth under their waxy surface, their transparent colours painted onto a resin-covered canvas placed flat on the ground. Each painting evolves from a set of predetermined rules that Frize lays out before he begins, whether working on a grid, using a particular size of brush, a pre-selected sequence of colours or working with assistants. While abstract, the lines that appear are loosely based on real objects, such as curtains, bars, even caterpillars. Frize demystifies the role of the artist in creating a work that obeys a mechanical principle, rejecting the idea of artist as genius for a Marxist-inspired theory of art as a form of production and system of labour. Despite his plurality of methods, using a limited vocabulary to produce a surprising variety of works, there is a style that is recognisably his own, whether it is the particular tones of purple and ochre or the grids and stripes or this deliberate flatness.

Frize espouses a form of neutrality, yet while there is a cerebral process, his paintings are remarkably sensual. If the different formulae and games that rule each painting remain deliberately obscure and not easily accessible, there is also an immediate visual impact of a masterly hanging, planned by the artist himself. Frize has not arranged his works chronologically but according to the visual affinities between the works. They can be barely perceptible evolutions, subtle nuances of colour, vertical or horizontal stripes or just wandering lines.

The show starts interestingly with the only works that are not paintings – three-dimensional painted forms based on Heawood's five-colour mathematical theorem. Most remarkable is the room of small canvases covered in meandering but bunched lines from the series *Lucky* and *Portable* (1999–2000), which were painted by Frize and his assistants – another of his methods. Each 'plait' is painted by six brushes, one for each colour, and interlaced until the paint runs out. Each canvas is an independent work, yet here they add up to create a rhythm all around the room. Here, Frize gives a very personal and contemporary lesson in the rules of abstraction. *NE*

'LARS NILSSON'
Palais de Tokyo
25 June – 13 October

THE CENTREPIECE OF SWEDISH artist Lars Nilsson's 'Game is Over', a retrospective of five installations conceived over the past eight years, looks like a window display one might see in an upmarket hunting shop. It comprises two male and two female mannequins dressed in masterfully cut and tailored Burberry checked wool. One of the women, wearing what looks like a fox-hunting catsuit, holds back a similarly clad man who strains at the end of a long leash, hands out like paws, lunging like a hound after the scent. Another tall male mannequin, derived from a cast of the artist's body, is wearing a Burberry neck scarf and frock coat on top of his full-on Burberry wrap. He strolls past the scene, head turned in curiosity. The second woman, also clad head to toe in Burberry, scales a wall, Batwoman-style, her body half-twisted to look down upon the scene. The figures are human, yet, like their game, there is something beastly about them: the women have long elfin ears sticking straight up; the men have long pig-like ears hanging down.

The tableau, like the other installations in 'Game is Over', is a cryptic exploration of gender roles and sexual tension. It is also a study in voyeurism. We observe these scenes while being observed. In one installation, a mannequin passer-by ogles a headless mannequin which is lying on the floor in a three-piece suit next to a giant, floor-to-ceiling chandelier of sixty-watt bulbs. In another, a man in a casual jacket and trousers watches the big, bodiless, leaping sculpture of a man, arms and legs wildly stretched apart and lit by a strobing light.

In the video component of the piece, *Midway In Our Life's Journey I Found Myself In Dark Woods*, a title borrowed from Dante, a gaunt woman lies half-naked in the ground foliage in a brightly lit wood. It is like stumbling across a corpse in the woods, until you notice that she is masturbating. It is a scene strongly reminiscent of Marcel Duchamp's *Etant Donnés* in which we view through a hole in a door the figure of a naked woman languishing in mock undergrowth, holding up a gas-lamp.

Nilsson's scenes are psychologically disturbing. They suggest a nightmarish dream world, laden with supernatural eeriness. Why else the animal ears, the sinister *Midsummer Night's Dream* feel of tree groves, man-beast creatures, foxhunts and leaping bogeymen? *CY*

'RICHARD ARTSCHWAGER: UP AND DOWN / BACK AND FORTH'
Deutsche Guggenheim
10 May – 6 July

MY FRIEND'S FATHER READ JOHN le Carré's novels from back to front. It was his way of getting around the idea of always knowing what would come next, his avoidance of a conventional complaint. Circumstances might have made him a great artist. Instead he funnelled his talents

into making brilliant miniature ships for his family.

Richard Artschwager also broke with many of life's quotidian formulas. Once a maker of solid wooden furniture, well-designed and sleek, he diverged from wood to make use of Formica. A fake wood, a picture of wood that is not wood. Before Artschwager, Formica spelt cheapness. It was a *faux pas* of real art, flimflamming the conceit of wood. After Artschwager, Formica metamorphosed into a material that basked proudly in its faux-ness, mocking wood's irregular blemishes and organic character. Artschwager's formica objects such as *Book* (1987), *Cross* (1986), *Door* (1987) and *Mirror* (1988) all on show at the Guggenheim, make a mockery of natural hardwood floor, like an Italian lady in stilettos snubbing a German *frau* in Birkenstocks. Unfortunately the Formica gems that made him famous are under-represented here. A few Celotex paintings make their way amongst the many simple charcoal drawings of chairs, landscapes and cat's eye views onto the requisites for seventeenth-century Dutch painted interiors: chair, basket, door, window.

This mild-mannered exhibition's saving grace is in its allowance of a generous appearance of that admirable, vowel-less, noun art-object Artschwager called the 'blp'. All black, their blurred edges make them appear out-of-focus and fuzzy. They pepper the gallery walls, up and down, high and low, in odd spots here and there, marking Artschwager's breakthrough in the making of this non-object object. In a way, he was the first to make graffiti a high art form. Far from the freestyle signature or bloated letters or spray-painted calligraphy scarring the landscape's surface, Artschwager's graffiti was a formal, minimal, repetitive interruption. The first blps were

painted wooden discs that he distributed out of a basket from the back of his Studebaker in 1967 in a roadtrip across the United States, like Hänsel and Gretel leaving behind their breadcrumbs, so that they might find their way back home.

Born of German-speaking parents, one can only wonder if his name is no accident. In German 'Schwager' means 'brother-in-law'. One could see the name 'Artschwager' as a genius compound noun marrying German to English, marrying art to art's brother-in-law, craft. Freeing his craft of function (reading a book backwards), his furniture slipped into the heady realm of art. *AL*

'DO-HO SUH'
Lehmann Maupin Gallery
30 May – 18 July

DO-HO SUH'S SECOND SOLO exhibition at Lehmann Maupin features *The Perfect House II*, a full-scale apartment interior hand-sewn from diaphanous nylon, complete with intricately detailed doorknobs, light fixtures and ceiling tiles. However, like the Korean-born artist's contribution to PS1's 2000 survey 'Greater New York', *Seoul Home/LA Home/New York Home/Baltimore Home, The Perfect House II* can in fact be packed into suitcases and transported from place to place. And each time it is shown it will have additional spaces. In this exhibition, Suh added a stairway. For the next, he will add the area immediately outside his ground-floor windows.

Crossbreeding Robert Irwin's translucent scrims, Claes Oldenberg's sagging sculptures and the portability of Duchamp's *Boite-en-valise*, Suh pinpoints one key aspect of recent art: what art historian Miwon Kwon has called the 'unhinging' of site specificity.

Rather than the art object itself, Kwon writes, 'it is now the *performative* aspect of an artist's characteristic mode of operation... that is repeated and circulated as a new art commodity, with the artist functioning as the primary vehicle for its verification, repetition and circulation.' Suh's unique contribution to this discussion – one succinctly encapsulated at Lehmann Maupin – is how he poses the conundrum, not just as a spatial disjunction between an immobile work and a mobile artist peregrinating from biennial to art fair to museum on the international exhibition circuit, but as a temporal disjunction as well.

Consider the infelicity of the work's title. While *The Perfect House II* replicates the artist's Chelsea apartment (and thus is premised on autobiographical fact and actuality of place), the insertion of the adjective 'perfect' intimates an ideal either projected into the future or retrospectively coloured through the lens of nostalgia. Indeed, entering *The Perfect House II* is akin to walking into an architect's blueprint. The economy of material as well as the use of colour-coding to designate function (blue for the kitchen and bathroom, green for the staircase, and rose for the bedroom and corridor) recall the schematic, if nonetheless, exacting austerity of a template. A model for a future house to be, Suh's rendition of architectural elements in near-immaterial cloth simultaneously evokes a trace of what once was. A sense of memory permeates the piece.

Suh once stated: 'My artistic inquiry doesn't only concern physical space, but... includes the history, culture, and memories we all carry with us.' Fittingly, even as *The Perfect House II* initially appears to possess a concern with space that has characterised much site-specific art since the 1970s, it further brings in the element of time. In so doing, Suh provides a unique and potentially invaluable contribution to contemporary art in the wake of site specificity. *CH*

'JEAN-LUC MYLANE: BLAZING RED'
Barbara Gladstone
5 June – 15 August

SO MUCH CURRENT ART IS predicated upon the 'urban condition'. It is made in cities about such cities, and for consumption almost exclusively within them. Any *oeuvre* devoted to the country can often appear incongruous in the smart white cube context. Thus the photography of Jean-Luc Mylane has always maintained an ambiguous relation to the mainstream, the fashionable canon of contemporary practice, precisely because it has been so resolutely concerned with the quieter side of the countryside.

Jean-Luc Mylane, born in Marquise, France, in 1946 is a self-taught photographer who lives a reclusive and partly nomadic life dedicated to photographing birds. He operates not unlike a nineteenth-century field naturalist, spending weeks, even months tracking down his subject. He waits, he looks and he studies. He has been known to sleep in his car in order to get the best shot. However, his photographs are far from being in the realms of natural history photography. They do not capture every feather and bill with clarity and precision. Mylane's birds usually only subtley feature in the picture, almost hidden out of view or partly obscured by foliage. You have to look for them.

And there is a passivity to Mylane's approach. Even though the exhibition has a fiery title, he titles each image dispassionately: *No. 63 January – February 1987, No. 83 November – December 2000–2001.* Perhaps he keeps a logbook to record his meticulous activity.

In this show many of the photographs have been taken from the perspective of indoors looking out. At first glance the images look like a very ordinary snapshot of what may be Mylane's living room. (Perhaps he was sitting in his favourite chair when he took these shots?) Then, after closer inspection, there is a bird, often a fairly ordinary bird – a robin, for example, appearing as a small, unassuming presence in a corner of the image. The birds appear as one might see them looking out of a window – sitting on a piece of garden furniture or on a part of agricultural machinery. They are not photographed close up as majestic beasts roaming their territory, but as everyday birds going about their everyday business.

There is a strange mixed sensibility to Mylane's art. On the one hand, he can give the impression that he is not the obsessive twitcher as his biography tells us – these images can look impersonal and detached. On the other, underneath this, there is a tender, empathetic side at work here. Mylane wants to get to know these birds. *AD*

HOUSTON

'FRED WILSON: OBJECTS AND INSTALLATIONS 1979–2000'
The Blaffer Gallery, University of Texas
3 May – 20 July

FRED WILSON, THE US REPRESENT-ative at the 2003 Venice Biennale, is the subject of an in-depth, mid-career retrospective, organised by the Center for Art and Visual Culture at the University of Maryland and now travelling through the US. An African-American artist of Caribbean descent, Fred Wilson helped usher in a revelatory era of multicultural revisionist history through

1. **Lars Nilsson,** *Game is Over,* 2000. Courtesy DAKS Simpson
2. **Richard Artschwager,** *Two Dinners,* 1986, charcoal on paper, 47.8 x 63.7 cm. Photo: Nolan/Eckman Gallery NY, © VG Bild
3. **Do-Ho Suh,** *The Perfect Home II,* 2003, translucent nylon, 279.4 x 609.6 x 1310.6 cm. Courtesy the artist and Lehmann Maupin Gallery

1. **Jean-Luc Mylayne,**
*No. 63 January –
February 1987,*
1987, c-print,
185.4 x 185.4 cm
Courtesy Barbara
Gladstone

2. **Fred Wilson,**
Guarded View, 1991,
four mannequins
with museum guard
uniforms. Photo:
Benjamin Blackwell,
Whitney Museum of
American Art

3. **Allan Sekula,**
*Volunteer's Soup
(Isla de Ons,
12/19/02),* 2002-3,
cibachrome diptych,
Edition of 5,
162.56 x 111.76cm.
Courtesy Christopher
Grimes Gallery

4. **RB Kitaj,**
Los Angeles No. 21,
2003, oil on canvas,
91.4 x 91.4 cm.
Courtesy LA Louver
Gallery and
Marlborough,
London

contemporary art practice and discourse during the 80s and 90s in the US. He, and other artists such as Jimmie Durham and James Luna, aim their institutional critique directly at museums and at curatorial practice by uncovering implicit racist beliefs, colonialist behaviour and prejudiced assumptions within the very mechanisms of museum display, collection, preservation and interpretation.

Wilson's 'mock collections', such as the memorable 'Mining the Museum', which took place in 1992 at the Maryland Historical Society, consisted of shifting objects within museums, unleashing their racist and colonialist underpinnings through each juxtaposition. His aesthetic commentaries reach across a wide art historical and museological expanse – from Egyptian, classical Greek and Roman sculpture to African masks and African-American memorabilia. Having once been an educator at the Metropolitan Museum of Art and a curator at the Longwood Gallery in the Bronx, Wilson has been in a unique position to question the practice from within.

In this show we have groundbreaking works such as *Guarded View* (1991), an installation of four headless mannequins, all African-American, wearing museum guard uniforms and a nametag with the museum's name. Lined up in a row, each anonymous figure stands to attention facing the viewer, ready to serve. Context labels presented next to the work provide historical information on where the work had been shown or where it had once 'intervened'.

The installations and text panels serve to recreate each original scenario, and lead us to question the current work's continued agency. A particularly challenging dilemma for this exhibition becomes: how does work engaging in 'institutional critique' fare with

distance and relative absence from that institution? Once intended as a sharp critique of the manipulative and authoritative powers of display and conservation within museums, the works here tend to become relics themselves, cushioned as they are in the safety of the white cube gallery, their potency deactivated, their activism retired. Though the inevitable reversal may be more a curatorial issue than it is Fred Wilson's concern, it is an issue that plagues most performative art and activist exhibitions when the attempt to represent accurately a political position is made. If context is everything, then perhaps the context and intentions of each of the exhibiting institutions need to be addressed as well, in order to resist actively the same calcification that Wilson's work so fervently fought to dissolve. *RB*

LOS ANGELES

'RB KITAJ'
LA Louver
21 May – 5 July

A RARE SOLO EXHIBITION BY LA resident (and British expatriate) RB Kitaj is a disappointment. Kitaj's paintings are barely more than sketches with bright swathes of garish colour; line drawings which are stiff when they are not clumsy. The only drawings that go beyond cursory outlines are the half-laboured renderings of the artist's own face.

The theme of the show appears to be the pleasures of the flesh (or, more accurately, straight-from-the-tube flesh-tone paint). We are treated to all sorts of semi-clothed pictorial encounters between the bearded septuagenarian artist and a younger badly drawn girl. As far from erotic and arousing as perhaps is humanly possible, many of these literal illustrations of bold-faced groping would border on studies of mistress-humiliation if they were at all cogently rendered.

But the fault may not lie in the art star. At some point an exhibition space must, surely, take on the role of editor and curator, neither of which occurs in the jampacked main room, as a jumble of framed charcoal sketches incongruously hang amidst the selection of brightly coloured works on canvas.

But among the rubble, one brilliant painting stares out, quietly suggesting that these rudimentary scrawls are simply warm-ups for greater investigations. In *Los Angeles No. 21* Kitaj fills the canvas with an expressive, full frontal self-portrait. The wild colour combinations that sink his other paintings here suddenly blend and balance with the precision and harmony of a good orchestra. The slender and gawky figure of the mistress is placed at the extreme left of the picture. She is naked and looks detached. The centre of the image is filled with the artist. His hair is a deep crimson and he has a bright turquoise beard. He stares at the viewer through a pair of darkened glasses. Down by his left cheek is the shape of what looks like a cannonball, with thick black marks rising from it, as if it was in mid-explosion. In its entirety, it is illogically perfect in expressing the complexity of looking into one's own image and drawing out the truths from within the illusion of paint.

If the exhibition seeks to strengthen the ageing master's reputation, they should empty the gallery save for this canvas, potentially resplendent in solemn solitude. *MG*

'ALLAN SEKULA: BLACK TIDE/ MAREA NEGRA'
Christopher Grimes Gallery
7 June – 12 July

IN DECEMBER 2002 ALLAN SEKULA accepted an invitation from a Barcelona newspaper to go to Galicia, an area on the northwest coast of Spain, where a tanker carrying 20 million gallons of oil had recently run aground, split open and had emptied much of its toxic contents, devastating the ecology of the area. His job was to document the clean-up process.

The resulting photographs showed more than the usual journalistic imagery of soaked seagulls and clogged seashores. Sekula focused on the people who volunteered to clear this precious coastline. In one picture we see an anorak-clad man covered up to his elbows in shiny black oil, working with determined concentration on a huge oily rock. In another, he shows the physical effect of this kind of back-breaking work: a sleeping couple in the vibrant bright orange uniform of sea-rescue related activities lie exhausted, slumped on each other. In a third image a distressed young girl standing on the deck of a ship stares forlornly into the distance. Not all the photographs show glum faces, however. One shows a man wolfing down some suspicious-looking seafood while grinning into the camera. Another – a self-portrait – stares cheekily out at us. Triumph in the face of adversity could be a theme that comes through here, a way of articulating the near Sisyphean task that faces those involved in the operation.

These photographs are expressive and beautifully composed but Sekula's main talent is his ability to combine multi-layered themes within his work. Yes, this is a photographic record of a man-made disaster but Sekula tries to illustrate the social divisions in the community he was working within. He shows a glamorous and uncomfortably windswept group delicately picking its way through the puddles of a promenade, a far cry from the up-to-the-elbows involvement of the local people whose very livelihood is threatened by the slick. He continues this theme of contrasts between rich and poor with his accompanying text for the show, *Fragments for an Opera*, an imaginary restaging of the event thirty years in the future. Here 'the people of the sea' – in other words, those who are getting their hands dirty – are pitted against the comings and goings and shady antics of the incumbent right-wing political party.

In the back room the industrial sea-theme continues in work from Sekula's past. There is an image of a rusty, abandoned blue Citroën 2CV resting at an angle on the grey sand. There is the grimy exit of Dover's railway station, and there is a gargantuan tanker docked in a French port. These photographs show the impact of man on the coastal environment, and it's a bleak vision, a soiled scene of industrialisation. *LS*

CHRISTIAN MARCLAY
UCLA Hammer Museum
1 June – 31 August

UNIQUE AMONG THE RECENT RASH of artist-musicians, Christian Marclay not only conflates the conditions of music and visual art, but articulates the issues involved in that conflation. And by doing so, ironically enough, he begins to re-distinguish between art and music, ultimately employing one as the representation of the other. Marclay engages himself with the range of objects and materials associated with music in the eyes of Western (and Westernised) audiences. He recognises that the traditional 'artifacture' of sonic production (instruments and scores) has been augmented with the 'artifacture' of sonic re-production (audio recording and performance documentation) to determine a vast array of things that signal or symbolise 'music'. Perhaps because of music's ability to transcend its packaging without having to discard it, music's consumers are wont to ritualise, even fetishise, its consumption as well as its production. Some enthusiasts become walking record catalogues, while others become experts on various kinds of instruments and still others wax nostalgic over obsolete recording and playback technologies. Marclay deeply appreciates this sonic idolatry and pays wry homage to it with series of works ranging from photographs taken of musical references in everyday life (from record-sale signs to stylised references to notations and instruments) to elaborations on real instruments fantastical enough to seem to have originated from a Magritte painting (e.g. an accordion with a fourteen-foot-wide bellows, a tuba and a pocket trumpet joined at their mouthpieces). Marclay's most consistently addressed medium is the 12-inch long-playing record. An accomplished and innovative DJ, he admits to a love of vinyl LPs. His largest and most varied body of work engages the LP and its packaging in clever, even startling ways, radically transforming disc and jacket alike into an aesthetic object. Among the earliest objects in Marclay's retrospective, for instance, are the *Recycled Records* (1980–86), expansions on the affectionate insults visited on the LP by artists such as Milan Knizak in which dotty looking (and sounding) LPs are assembled from others. Elsewhere, the show includes a number of the objects Marclay has fashioned from partially melted records. Clearly, records for him are sculptures or canvases. The artworks they comprise are invested with their associative power, which is a power to be reckoned with, given the ubiquity of the vinyl disc in recent popular culture. Indeed, when Marclay fashions objects and installations

1. **Christian Marclay,** *Guitar Drag,* 2000, video still. Courtesy the artist and Paula Cooper Gallery, New York

2. **Marc Chagall,** *Above the Town,* 1914–18, oil on canvas, 137 x 195.5 cm. Collection The State Tretiakov Gallery, Moscow. © DACS, London/ ADAGP, Paris, 2003

temporary shifts. After the Russian Revolution of 1917 he was appointed Fine Arts Commissar for his home province of Vitebsk, where he founded and ran an art school. However, the authorities, who demanded traditional realism with a social message, disliked his fantastical works. Consequently, he moved to Moscow where he designed for the newly founded Jewish Theatre. It wasn't long before he was back in Paris, this time at the invitation of the artist Vollard. He settled in France in 1948, where he painted landscapes, and illustrated texts - in particular, the Bible - until his death in 1985.

Chagall was a prolific painter and illustrator as well as a book, set and costume designer. He had a lifelong interest in depicting personal memories of his Jewish upbringing, and the Bible was a key source for his work. A deeply religious man, Chagall conceived his Bible paintings as an ensemble, and in this exhibition they are grouped together in the gallery's final room, in stark contrast to the 'terrestrial' world of the artist's other work. The predominately Old Testament scenes, from *Abraham Mourning Sarah* (1930) to *The Crossing of the Red Sea* (1952), were regarded as reactionary by the artist's contemporaries, but these works have a new poignancy in the context of current events in the Middle East.

And beyond the religious messages, even at its most surreal, Chagall's universe has an internal logic. Flying fish and floating brides co-exist with angels and Russian peasants in recurring patterns, implying a hidden meaning within individual paintings. And the pleasure of a Chagall painting is that it always hints at an untold story, whether spiritual, allegorical, personal, or some cryptic fusion of all three. *JT*

out of CDs, he seems to regard the newer medium as visually inferior, glossy and superficial as well as too small to come in visually adequate packaging.

The retrospective culminates not in an orgiastic cascade of LPs, as one might expect, but in a room-filling four-channel video consisting of excerpts from commercial films. Every one of these excerpts features people producing music. With deft artistry, Marclay has woven together these excerpts into a sonic and visual composition of unstinting coherency. *Video Quartet* (2002) is a veritable symphony, entirely bricolaged from the movies. The visual representation of music has become music, and by

distinguishing between music and art, Christian Marclay has made both at once. *PF*

SAN FRANCISCO

'MARC CHAGALL'
San Francisco Museum of Modern Art
26 July – 4 November

A FLYING FISH, CHRIST CRUCIFIED, a Russian acrobat. It is surrealism, but not as you think you know it. Chagall had a visual language that blended allegory with surreal juxtapositions, humour and a sublimely luminous palette. His paintings are joyful dreamscapes and intensely personal prayers made manifest in harlequin colour.

This is the first comprehensive retrospective of Marc Chagall's work in the US since 1985, with 153 works covering the years from 1907 to 1970. The show does a skilful job at emphasising the artist's image as both storyteller and spiritual messenger, as well as convincing us that he was a distinctive voice within the twentieth-century avant-garde. What stands out, however, is that while Chagall engaged with the significant movements of European modernism, he never embraced them entirely, always believing in his own idiosyncratic style.

The show – curated by Jean-Michel Foray, the director of the Musée National Message Biblique Marc Chagall – begins with early works of family and village life drawn from his childhood experiences in rural Russia. It then charts a period in Paris where he counted the avant-garde artists Léger and Delaunay among his friends. As a result, Chagall's style shifts to include hints of cubism and futurism in his scenes of Jewish folklore, but they are

PREVIEWS

CRAIG BURNETT

POLKE DOTS

SIGMAR POLKE'S PAINTINGS ARE playfully put together with found imagery and the artist's own smears, washes and sketches, and the results usually end up both hilarious and cerebral – no easy balance to achieve. 'History of Everything' is a show of recent paintings that feature imagery found in magazines and newspapers – graphic surveillance diagrams from the Iraq war, for instance, or a photo from the annual Ernest Hemingway lookalike contest in Key West, Florida – that look both sinister and banal. The paintings usually waver somewhere between abstraction and a chronicle of current events. Polke's playful vision even extends to his titles: *I Live in My Own World, but its OK, They Know Me Here.* Get to know Sigmar Polke at Tate Modern, London, 2 October – 4 January 2004.

SPRING IN SEPTEMBER

'GESTURES' IS THE THEME OF THIS year's *'Printemps de Septembre',* a 'Festival of Contemporary Images' that features photography, video, drawing and painting in various venues throughout the city of Toulouse, 26 September – 19 October. The artists, including Paul Noble, Sylvie Blocher, Kutlug Ataman, Adrian Paci, Liu Wei and Leandro Erlich, among many others, are relatively young and come from every corner of the globe, lending a festive and dynamic atmosphere to what might have been just another annual art circus. In fact, I heard that last year's festival showcased superb young artists and that the Fondation Cartier, the festival sponsor, provided the resources to present the work beautifully.

Mette Tronvoll, *Isortoq Unartoq #24,* 1999, c-print, 73.7 x 89.9 cm. From 'Happiness'

HAPPINESS

ARCADIA, NIRVANA, DESIRE AND Harmony: these are the elements of bliss that the Mori Art Museum, a new space atop a Tokyo skyscraper, will present in 'Happiness: A Survival Guide for Art and Life', its inaugural exhibition. The group show features work by an unlikely blend of new and old, from Constable and Monet to Twombly, Murakami and Beuys. It's an ambitious idea for a show that could end up as a gimmicky farce. But you have to admire the gumption of curators David Elliot, director of the museum, and Pier Luigi Tazzi, for trying to make a splash. 18 October – 18 January 2004, Mori Art Museum, Tokyo.

CONFUCIUS SAYS

'WE TAKE GREATER PAINS', SAID Confucius, 'to persuade others that we are happy than in endeavouring to think so ourselves.' Did he really? It would be interesting to know how many epigrams have been attributed to the Chinese philosopher (b. 551BC) that are, in fact, latter-day platitudes in awkward syntax to give the patina of wisdom. Despite his silly sayings, Confucius remains one of the most influential thinkers in history, and his thoughts about bureaucracy and family roles cemented into a pseudo-religion that still shapes South Korean and Japanese society. 'Confucius: Spring and Autumn', will offer a chance to see, through the objects and documents of Confucius' era, the brilliance of ancient Chinese culture. As Confucius so sagely advised: 'Study the past if you would divine the future.' 28 October – 9 February 2004, Musée National des Arts Asiatique-Guimet; 25 May – 29 August 2004, CaixaForum, Barcelona.

BOUCHER'S DOODLES

I DOUBT IF BOUCHER HAD TO persuade any of his Rococo contemporaries that he was happy. Jarring artificiality and sentimentality aside, even flesh and vegetation look damp and edible in his effortlessly sensual paintings. This exhibition features his lesser-known but equally graceful drawings, a format he took more seriously than most of his peers, producing over 10, 000 drawings in his lifetime and cultivating collectors, too, at a time when most artists considered drawing an academic exercise. 'The Drawings of François Boucher', 8 October – 14 December, Frick Collection, New York; 17 January – 18 April 2004, Kimbell Art Museum, Fort Worth, Texas.

REMBRANDT'S JOURNEY

REMBRANDT'S EMINENCE AS A master of gestural painting has somewhat overshadowed his draughtsmanship, and his amazing spontaneity and accuracy of touch may be most palpable in his etchings. 'Rembrandt's Journey: Painter, Draftsman, Etcher' will feature over 200 works, with loans from all over the world, and aims to show how his small yet powerful prints informed his paintings. 26 October – 18 January, Museum of Fine Arts, Boston; 14 February – 9 May 2004, Art Institute of Chicago.

EL GRECO'S ADVENTURES

WE KNOW VERY LITTLE ABOUT El Greco's life, but I like to imagine him as a kind of ancient hero on an exhilarating Mediterranean adventure, leaving a trail of stories and brilliant paintings in his wake. Born on Crete, he moved to Venice as an ambitious neophyte (he purportedly worked in Titian's studio), before stopping briefly in Rome, where he offered to repaint Michelangelo's *Last Judgement,* and finally to Toledo, where he produced his most extraordinary work. This major retrospective will feature about 80 paintings, focusing on his portraits of saints, with their delicate lips and eyes like shucked oysters. 'El Greco', 7 October – 11 January 2004, Metropolitan Museum of Art, New York; 11 February – 23 May 2004, National Gallery, London.

DOIG IN FRANCE

PETER DOIG'S WORK ELICITS extreme responses, from swoons of delight to snorts of derision. Perhaps inconsistency is to blame. At his most recent Victoria Miro show, a few superb paintings – atmospheric landscapes in saturated colour – hung alongside bathetic stabs at mystery. But it is safe to say that he is one of contemporary art's most popular figurative painters, drawing huge crowds to his shows and big money from collectors. This show of 15 large canvases and 8 drawings traces his development over the past 14 years. 'Peter Doig: Charley's Space', 3 October – 4 June, Musée d'Art Contemporain de Nîmes, Nîmes.

I love Bedlington terriers and no one paints them better than veteran colourist **CRAIGIE AITCHISON**. Check out paintings such as *Dog in Red Painting* (1975) at the Sackler Gallery, Royal Academy, London, where the Scottish artist is having a long overdue retrospective, 9 October – 9 November.

HELAINE BLUMENFELD, PETER NEWSOME and **JOHANNES VON STUMM** are three established sculptors showing in 'light, vision and transformation', an exhibition at the Royal British Society of Sculptors, London, until 11 October. Helaine Blumenfeld translates the spiritual into the physical by trapping light in marble works such as the appropriately titled *Esprit*.

One of the most popular exhibits of this year's Venice Biennale was **OLAFUR ELIASSON**'s installation at the Danish Pavilion. Inside you got the very strange sensation that someone was observing you from the eyehole of a large kaleidoscope. Eliasson turns his inventive way with space to the Turbine Hall at Tate Modern, London, following in the big footsteps of Anish Kapoor, Juan Muñoz and Louise Bourgeois in the popular Unilever Series, 16 October – 21 March. Here is the lovely and terribly cool *Ice Pavilion*, Reykjavik, 1998.

PAULA REGO shows paintings and prints that make up this masterful artist's interpretation of Jane Eyre and other stories at Marlborough, London, 15 October – 22 November. Bunnies have never looked so sinister as they do in Rego's *War*. Please go to p.109 for a special Paula Rego reader's offer.

Timothy Taylor Gallery, London, will show recent paintings by **FIONA RAE** in a show marvellously titled 'Hong Kong Garden', 14 October – 15 November. The work reflects Rae's recent use of computer graphics and how she has gracefully 'fused' them with a more traditional painterly vocabulary. Don't miss stunning paintings such as *Moonlite Bunny Ranch*.

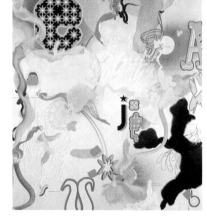

The lucky person who bought **DAMIEN HIRST**'s picture at last year's RCA Secret for £35 got a bargain. Where else could you buy a genuine and signed (albeit postcard-sized) drawing by a famous artist for such a low price? None of the postcards for sale at RCA Secret (in aid of the Royal College of Art, London) is signed or identified, so only those of you with sharp eyes should hasten down to this perennially popular exhibition at the Royal College, 21 – 27 November, for viewing. Then the bidders will have to sharpen their elbows for the sale days on 27 and 28 November.

Victoria Miro shows **ISAAC JULIEN**'s latest work until 11 October. Julien will exhibit two ambitious film installations, *Baltimore* and *Paradise Omeros*, as well as large photographs. *Baltimore* is a three-screen installation that stars veteran artist and director Melvin Van Peebles, to whom the film is a tribute.

RICHARD PRINCE told me that he decided to start his nurse paintings after his interview with MODERN PAINTERS – when he was just joking about doing them. So two points to MODERN PAINTERS for inspiring a great body of work, including the paintings recently on show at Sadie Coles HQ, London, and *Man Crazy Nurse*, shown here, plus other new paintings at Barbara Gladstone, New York, 20 September – 18 October.

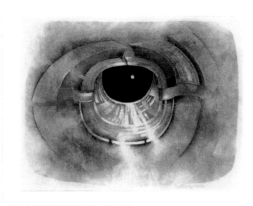

LEE BONTECOU was one of the few recognisable woman sculptors of the 60s. Despite her success, she opted out of the New York art scene and moved to Pennsylvania with her artist husband, where she still lives and works. While one can see elements of her colleague Eva Hesse in her work, she has her own distinctive language. The most comprehensive exhibition of her work, including this wonderful *Untitled* soot on paper drawing, will be at the UCLA Hammer Museum, Los Angeles, 5 October – 11 January 2004 before it travels to Museum of Contemporary Art, Chicago, and MoMA, QNS.

HANNAH COLLINS shows at CAC Malaga, Spain, 20 September – 4 January 2004. This one-time Turner Prize nominee shows photographs and videos that invite the viewer to enter a different and sometimes harrowing world – here is *In the Course of Time (The Hunter's Space – The Road to Auschwitz)*, 1995.

JOSEPH BEUYS was undoubtedly one of the most influential artists of the twentieth century, so he's a smart choice for Gagosian, London, to kick off its autumn season with a bang. The show features work drawn from the Speck Collection – Dr Rainer Speck is a Cologne-based physician who met Beuys in the 60s and continued to buy his work throughout the artist's lifetime – until 15 November. Pictured here is *Mensch*.

RALPH T COE collected over 200 Native American objects during a 50-year period after starting his collection with a totem-pole he bought in the unlikely location of Third Avenue, New York City. The collection goes on show at the Metropolitan Museum, New York, until 14 December. Here is a colourful button blanket from Kagani Haida, Prince of Wales Island, Alaska, c. 1880.

JIM LAMBIE's floor was one of the few hits at 'Days Like These', the recent Tate Britain Triennial. Lambie has been given the upper floor of Modern Art Oxford to make over, 13 September – 9 November. In the words of the press release, 'Lambie transforms discarded belongings gleaned from junk shops into shamanistic objects of power that embrace the hedonism of popular culture.' Here is a piece from the Scottish Pavilion at the Venice Biennale.

While spoilt for choice this autumn, I will make sure I see recent work by the innovative video/installation artist **TONY OURSLER** at Lisson Gallery, London, until 1 November. Who says aliens don't exist? Just come to see *Drip* and more of Oursler's extraterrestrial-style creatures.

Viennese artist **FRANZ WEST** always produces thought-provoking and even – dare I say it? – beautiful shows, so hasten down to the Whitechapel Art Gallery, London, until 9 November to see a big retrospective called 'Franz West-ite'. Pictured is Otto Kobalek wearing the first 'Adaptive', circa 1973. It looks like he's wearing a plaster tutu. Other interpretations welcome!

books

IN VIEW

FLOWERS
Jo Self
and Howard Sooley
(photographs)

Frances Lincoln, £30.00

J O SELF SAYS SHE IS NOT LIKE other artists. She sees the finished image on the canvas before she paints it. Her six-foot square *Morning Glory* is a classic example of this process. Self sits at a Herne Hill café table texting a friend as she explains her working psyche: 'I saw this morning glory in my garden one morning in a perfect state. People call me a drama queen but

I am a nuclear reactor. My first language is pictures not words. In that moment I saw what was in my imagination. The flower, its vibrancy. I've been thinking about this explosive image. See it. Think about it. See it think about it. Obsessionally... and then it explodes into a nuclear reactor and I have to paint it immediately. I'm sentient, sexual and emotional. My

sexuality is the driving force not the image. Not like Georgia O'Keeffe whose image is the driving force. I paint it with different layers of colours reacting together – opposites – then leave the image till the next year to finish it. I wait till the painting and the flower dies in my eyes.'

How does she finish it? 'I re-look at it and it appears in my mind's eye. My paintings are off centre. Never geometric. The focus is the centre. The centre is detailed and drawn. Music is quite important because I don't draw with my hand but with my shoulder. I paint because my ten-year-old, Felix, who is a brilliant guitarist, plays next to me. I hummed the theme tune to *Paris, Texas* while I painted *Morning Glory*.'

The ultramarine blue flower on a cadmium red background has to be seen in all its glory to be believed. On seeing a planted morning glory it has the effect of making us say, 'Oh look, a Jo Self.' As people can look at a sky and say, 'Oh look at that Turner.' While humming the music from *Paris, Texas* helped Jo paint *Morning Glory*, singing Jimi Hendrix's *Purple Haze* fired her imagination for another six-foot square painting, *Purple Orchid*. The flower is cobalt violet on cobalt green.

'Orchids are strange flowers. The flower looks like a beating heart. It's like going on a strange journey. The orchid grows in my kitchen. I'd been looking at it a lot and the whole painting appeared while I was having sex. It could almost be called *Deep Purple*. Saying that, it's not a very sexy picture. It's a cerebral picture. The front of it looks like hands, open palms, and you travel up through it. It's a spiritual journey, bringing you to a lovely place, like going to Nirvana. I got up at six, painted it for eight hours in the heat and resolved the painting. The painting became itself. To resolve it took eight hours

but the whole painting took six months. The flower bloomed twice when I started it, then again in my kitchen and that's when I resolved the painting.'

Her corrugated-iron walled garden is a masterpiece of urban exotica. Jo Self created it out of a derelict builder's yard in 1999. Neighbours are skip people and scaffolders with tattoos. The lawn is shingle. A winding blue astroturf path leads into a 60s brick building called 'home'. The lollipop lady from Dulwich Road visits the koi pond regularly. These fish inspired a five-foot square painting in which a leaping koi in profile stares at the viewer with a Goyaesque single eye. One eye in profile was Goya's revolutionary symbol. Many of Self's paintings are a Goyaesque red. She sometimes turns poppies, geraniums, and camellias into prints.

A leaping koi in profile stares at the viewer with a Goyaesque single eye.

A scaffolding tower by the garden door compliments the concrete tower blocks opposite. Her bespoke tower has a platform on which beech trees stand in containers. Between the trees two leather hairdresser's chairs await guests for cocktails on a balmy evening. The building has been converted into an upstairs flat of small box rooms. These living quarters feel similar to being below deck on a sloop yacht. The back extension is an ingenious Perspex domed studio. In it she produces prints as well as paintings. There is a small charcoal of her pug Dudley called *What no Bentley?*, a title taken from a line in a film spoken by the late comic actor Terry-Thomas. From her studio is another large room, which leads into the garden through double

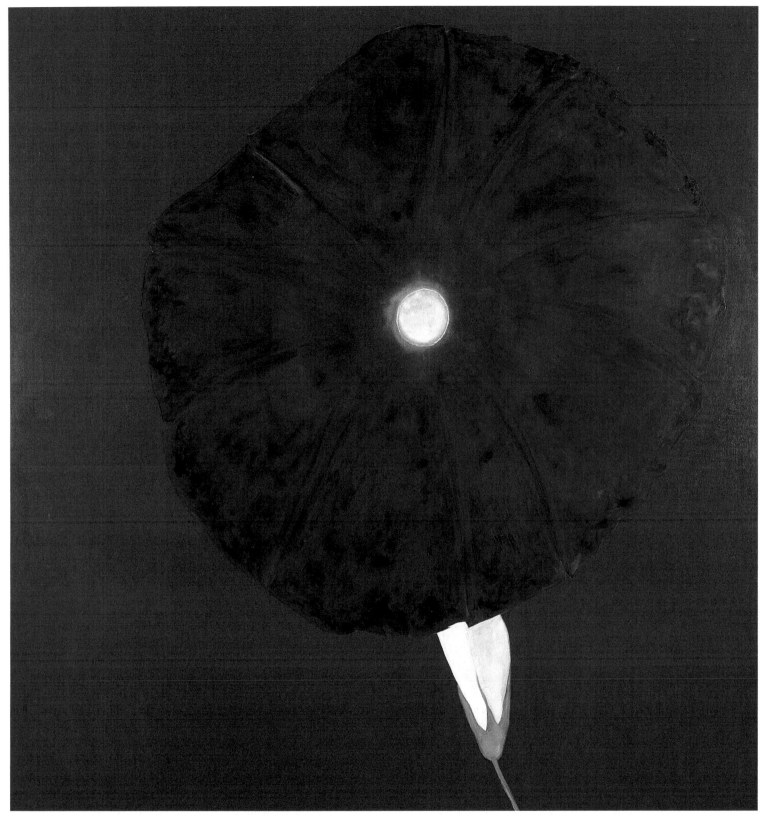

Jo Self, *Morning Glory*, 2003, oil on canvas, 198 x 182.9 cm. Courtesy Redfern Gallery

doors, formerly the official entrance for JCBs, and perhaps one day a Bentley for Self. Flanking this grand entrance is a monkey-puzzle tree. Clematis climb the corrugated-iron walls. Roses, dahlias and orchids sit in pots like characters on stage waiting to speak. In their case they await their cues to be exploded onto canvas, then take a bow at the applause.

But applause for Jo Self has been intermittent. After several shows at the Flowers East Gallery between 1994 and 1998, and a stint as 'painter-in-residence' at Kew Gardens, Self, who was trained at the Chelsea School of Art, has found a new home at the Redfern Gallery. This solo show is her first since her Kew Gardens show in 2001.

Flowers is the first book about Jo Self and her achievement. The book, with numerous colour prints, contains detailed interviews with the artist by Sarah Kent and Cathy Courtney, photographs of Self's Brixton garden, and childhood family snaps. It becomes clear that this 'easel painter', as she likes to

Jo Self, *Purple Orchid,* 2003, oil on canvas, 152.4 x 152.4 cm. Courtesy Redfern Gallery

describe herself, is no botanist painter. There is a tiny Dürer-inspired *A Patch of Grass* (1995); wispy fronds stretch out against an unearthly blue-bronze background. And a near political *Petunia* (1999) which suggests markedly the Bikini Atoll explosion. Jo Self is neither Georgia O'Keeffe nor Rachel Ruysch, but now emerges as an angry-spirit colourist who approaches nature with the modern discipline of Andy Goldsworthy. Her giant magenta eclipses and burning vermilion do not present us with predictable sexual analogies.

Instead, when Self paints an orchid she conjures up the surface of raw bacon. There is no easy journey into her paintings.

Self's father was an ITV camera-man and astronomer, her mother a nurse. She and her two brothers were brought up in a council house in Essex. Self has two sons, one from an early marriage, the younger son from a long-term partnership. But what happened to Jo Self when she left art school? It may sound trivial to repeat how in the absence of proper work she applied to be a bunny girl in a nightclub. But look again at the work and see how many paintings of suppressed blooms try to break out in the dark kingdom of night.

And is it too private an anecdote to recall her mother dying? How the features drained of blood, and a kind of Naples yellow spread across the face. It remains a colour which will always make Self angry.

From early days, how did Self get past the obvious artistic icebergs, Rothko or Redon? Did this self-proclaimed 'outsider' become a leper in some critical quarters like Bomberg? Did she just wait for movements like Dada and Expressionism to have their last day in Britain? For Self, there were other influences: certain middle period Picassos struck her 'like holes made in my chest'. And the impact of Dürer's

unimpeachable fine line forced her to create an act of homage – *A Patch of Grass* (not the best colour reproduction in this book). After this painting, which was completed in 1995, her canvases get much larger. *Luminous Jasmine* (2002) and *Morning Glory* (2003) show that she is no longer just a witness to botanical marvels; she has in her own words 'stepped through the picture plane'.

When Self paints an orchid she conjures up the surface of raw bacon.

Jo Self's most recent pictures defy us to allow them borders. The flower in *Morning Glory* is noticeably not placed in the centre of the canvas, so that the painting begins to dictate its own geography of the eye. It's as if we are being told by the artist to take her on trust and accept an unlimited scale. Her impatience with the past is evident; she cannot go back to the decorativeness of Redon or the controlled landscapes of Nolde. If she is now in her 'plateau phase', then we have misinterpreted Self as an easel botanist. Now 48, she has pushed her character through her canvases with a singular driven nature.

And yet, not all is large-scale emotion. In one painting, a mouse has climbed a blade of grass. The mouse is heading hopelessly for a fall. The blade of grass cannot take the weight. Fear. Pandemonium. Comic dismay in the light of an impossible balancing act. The mouse attests to the dangerous art of implacable nature without borders.

*Michael Hastings
and Victoria Hardie*

REAL SPACES: WORLD ART HISTORY AND THE RISE OF WESTERN MODERNISM
by David Summers

Phaidon Press, £49.95

THE MODERN WORLD DOESN'T really have a lot of time for people who practise human sacrifice. We say it's barbaric and had better stop, and don't waste time pondering the lives of those who indulge in it. But *Real Spaces*, the new book by American art historian David Summers, was inspired by contact with just such a culture. Teotihaucan, the extraordinary city in central Mexico, was, at the height of its power in 600 CE, the sixth largest on earth. Its leaders were hidden but ruthless; its religious belief systems were an industrial-strength social glue of the kind that regularly called for blood sacrifice; and yet its culture was richly accomplished. Now the city lies as a grassy patchwork of ruins, avenues and pyramids; a magnet for tourists, and a puzzle for the likes of Summers.

When he originally visited Teotihaucan in the 1960s it was as a graduate student of Pre-Columbian art. Being a fearsome swot, he no doubt arrived with a good sense of what to expect, and yet he still felt utterly lost. Summers had the sensitivity and insight to perceive that the terms which Western art history provided for the student to assimilate this culture – even its basic descriptive terms – misrepresented it entirely. The discipline operated, un-consciously perhaps, with the imperialistic hubris of the age during which it had been forged.

If all the world's art was ever to be understood properly, and from a common perspective, the only solution, Summers concluded, was to shred the old lexicon of art historical terminology and write it

Mask (ngon-tang), nineteenth century, wood and kaolin, height of faces: 21, 34.3, 29.2 and 21.5 cm. Detroit Institute of Art

anew. *Real Spaces* is the culmination of that labour: it is humungous, compendious and staggeringly erudite. Summers wants to be remembered for this book, and he probably will be.

In it he begins by explaining why discussion of form, iconography and linguistic signs has blinkered art historians throughout the twentieth century. Even umbrella notions like 'art' and 'visual culture' are, he says, too narrow to encompass a field which should rightfully include artefacts,

architecture and the symbolism of places. In fact, the visual arts should be considered under a new, expanded heading termed the 'spatial arts', encompassing all those arts that are manifested in space and are oriented to the space around them – hence the emphasis of the book's title. Summers rarely discards art history's traditional terms entirely, however; rather, he refreshes our sense of them, delving into etymology for sign-posts before placing them back before us with new purpose. A handful of ideas take centre stage (terms like planarity, virtuality and metaopticality), while a host of subsidiaries assemble in the wings.

Soon he has a sizeable glossary to hand and goes to work employing it on all manner of problems, from Prehistoric axes (why are some tools different from others?) to pagodas (why are they so tall?) to Impressionism (why are its images so hazy?) to Jerusalem (why is it fought over?).

For instance, he argues that notions of planarity and alignment are present in civilisations across the world. They are fundamental because they are the basic conceptual tools with which we order terrain around us; different peoples simply have different understandings of the notions that follow from this process. In order to illuminate this he discusses a nineteenth-century African helmet-mask that was used in a ritual invoking the dead, and which has four oval faces pointing in opposing directions. Artefacts or architecture that bear several faces, he argues, suggest qualities of power and mystery in all cultures (think of the Christian Trinity, or of Janus, the Roman god of gates and beginnings). The character of these qualities is locally determined,

however, and in the case of the mask, Summers speculates, the different alignment of the faces may have related to the practice of associating villages upstream and downstream with different ancestors. How might this help us understand Western art? Well, just as many-sidedness suggests mystery, qualities of frontality suggest acknowledgement and knowing: the stress on one-point perspective in Western art being entirely of a piece with its ambition to make the world known and understood.

Having first been inspired by Pre-Columbian art, it is no surprise that Summers' art history takes an anthropological turn. While for the modern West an object's uselessness is probably its highest qualification as art, for him it is use and the context of use that matters most. Never leaping to overarching interpreta-tions, his interpretations always grow from fieldwork observations of the most basic kind; conse-quently they have a powerfully commonsensical persuasiveness

> While for the modern West an object's use-lessness is probably its highest qualification as art – for him it is use and the context of use that matters most.

which serves to make light of the extraordinary range of his learning. This is an imposing work of scholarship which makes great demands of its readers, but ultimately Summers sees it as having a wider purpose in attempting to make right a few of the world imbalances. They all say that, of course, but Summers may just well be good enough to make that difference.

Morgan Falconer

PHOTOGRAPHY

CANDIDA HOFER
Michael Kruger

Thames and Hudson, £48

CANDIDA HOFER, ALONGSIDE Martin Kippenberger, is Germany's co-representative at this year's Venice Biennale and the least known of a number of successful photographer artists from Düsseldorf. These, in a fabulous oxymoron, seem to have become known as the 'New Objectivity Tradition', their work imbued with the example of their Academy of Art teachers, Bernd and Hilla Becher. The school includes Thomas Struth, Thomas Ruff and Andreas Gursky, and they are enjoying a market dominance in fine art photography.

The Bechers created an influential project in the 60s through their systematic photographic documentation of water towers. The apparently dispassionate, elegantly minimalist approach taken to these unselfconscious architectural forms was conceptually pure and gently amusing. Their followers continue this interest in the human relationship to mundane architectural systems, now given searing extremes of scale and colour, made possible by improvements to photo technology. This kind of work is characterised by vast prints of specialised building interiors such as libraries, offices and shops, in which people are revealed as controlled or significantly absent, and the prosaic, apparently 'boring' evidences of their institutional processing are exposed. There is a particular interest in repetitive systemisation, such as shelving displays, library books and office files; or of stacked chairs or neatly arranged consumer products and building

construction forms, where modular systems predominate. An intellectual brow-furrowing of sorts is present in these depictions, as the defeats of architectural and social idealism within global homogenisation are in correspondence with many notions of postmodern theory.

Hofer, for whatever reason, comes late to this particular party, which is not exclusive. It also includes Rut Blees Luxemburg, Jane and Louise Wilson, Mike Nelson, and Langlands and Bell, who all explore architecture, ambiguous presence and absence, and power. Hofer's take on architectural interiors is, maybe, as Rineka Dijkstra's is to people. It's a bit disassociated, pure, with a preponderance of the muted colours of northern light, and characterised by endless, agonisingly exposed compositional peripheries. Huge expanses of floor area or wall detail the sad human scuffings and stainings that soil architectural vision – the architectural equivalent of bad skin.

It's powerful stuff, given plenty of space in this elegant and desirable book. What compromises Hofer's work, though, are the occasional lapses into an over-celebrating of the retro-ironies of design and style – the 'aren't-we-a-slightly-superior-elite' form of awareness that will date her work in the future more than any amount of 'objectivity'. *NB*

CONTEMPORARY

VEIL: VEILING, REPRESENTATION AND CONTEMPORARY ART
edited by David A Bailey and Gilane Tawadros

inIVA in association with Modern Art Oxford, £17.50

'HOW ODD', WRITES AHDAF SOUEIF, 'that we don't have one word in

Arabic equivalent to "the veil". But perhaps not odd at all, for doesn't English have bowler hats, top hats, trilbies, cloth caps, boaters and stetsons, while Arabic only has *qubba'ah*, "hat"?' Soueif's article 'The Language of the Veil' was first published in the *Guardian* in December 2001, as the US was trying to come to terms with (or flatly refusing to acknowledge) the reasons behind the passionate loathing of its values and symbols that grips much of the Arab–Islamic world. It is illustrated in *Veil*, an essay collection about this prodigiously multi-valent piece of clothing, by a photo of a Saudi woman wearing a veil sporting the Yves Saint Laurent logo.

Unfortunately, for those who want to see the wearing of the Islamic veil (or any of its many national, regional and social varieties) as a political badge or a sign of women's oppression or a mechanism that provides women with a welcome degree of protection, there are no simple routes to the meaning of the veil – 'differenced meanings', I should say, since *Veil* contains its share of sententious cultural studies cud-chewing.

As Reina Lewis intones in her preface: 'Negotiating with local, national or diasporic community gender systems is never an isolated event when the figure of the veiled woman is fought over as emblematic of whole societies.'

Whether you find it subtly differenced or baggily inconclusive,

Veil's liveliest moments are when the 'figure of the veiled woman' as cultural studies construct or Islamist Jeanne d'Arc gives way to the irreducible specificities of experience. Franz Fanon's 'Algeria Unveiled', dating from 1959, is a powerful analysis of the politics of the veil during the Algerian struggle for independence, when the French colonial administration adopted a policy of 'unveiling', based on the doctrine that 'to destroy the structure of Algerian society... we must first of all conquer the women; we must go and find them behind the veil.'

Marc Garanger's portraits of Algerian women, whom he was assigned by the military to unveil and photograph – a double rape – for ID purposes, are the book's strongest images.

The visuals are otherwise disappointing: poorly tied to the text, often grey and grainy, they help create an impression of uniformly low-res seriousness that does little justice to the more thought-provoking stuff here, like Fanon's piece or the historiographic introduction by editors David A Bailey and Gilane Tawadros.

It's unfair, of course, to review *Veil* as a stand-alone book. It accompanies the touring exhibition staged by inIVA (Institute of International Visual Arts) this year, intended to 'open up a space for dialogue and exchange... through the prism of contemporary visual arts practice'. A great idea, though some contributors raise the question of whether women in 'veiling societies' need this exchange more than other, more prosaic dialogues about healthcare or education, say, in which facial covering isn't really the main issue.

The exhibition will be on at Modern Art Oxford from 22 November to 26 January 2004. *MB*

ROAM: A READER IN THE AESTHETICS OF MOBILITY
Edited by Anthony Hoete
Black Dog, £19.95

THIS BOOK IS TRYING DESPERATELY hard to be trendy. This is pseudo-academia for the MTV generation and none the worse for it. Although the headache-inducing font is a trial and the lack of original work irritating, this is a worthwhile publication on a subject that has become a great concern to parts of the architecture world: how to deal with the communications explosion. What does it mean for the most static of art forms to inhabit a world increasingly defined by our ability to commune with the wider world through mobile telephony, internet, car ownership and proliferate air travel?

Earlier this year, the first Rotterdam architecture biennale opened and its subject was mobility. *ROAM* will have a problem competing with the catalogue for that exhibition, which is called *A Room With a View*. That publication is nearly twice the length and provides solid and completely original research on the subject. *ROAM's* strength, however, is its big tent approach. The contributors are architects, academics, artists, musicians, photographers and illustrators.

There are bits of *ROAM* which are totally throwaway, and particularly frustrating are the things we have seen a hundred times before such as Mother's cut-away line drawings of cars, and Mecanoo's roundabout diagrams of the Randstad in the Netherlands. Even the longest essay in the book, Paul Virilio's eerily prescient 'The Overexposed City', was first

published in 1986 and is now outdated. However, some of the newer work is more provocative. Eyal Weizman's essay 'From a cross to a nought' proposes a giant cross-Thames roundabout in London's Vauxhall as a way of dealing with the area's traffic problems. A photography project by Weizman and photographer Christian Nicolas is the subject of an essay by Mark Cousins. Weizman and Nicolas took pictures of people walking across London Bridge with an adapted camera lens aperture. The pictures look unremarkable until you realise that, depending on the speed of the walker relative to the speed of the film moving behind the lens, the portraits are elongated or compressed, making every walker look as if he is travelling in the same direction. Cousins' essay beautifully explores the ideas behind the project and, though on the short side, stays in the mind.

The book is successful with these provocations, but less successful with its information. Jane England's survey of the use of maps in art is pedestrian and the essay by Andreas Schafer and David Victor attempts to do in a few pages what the Rotterdam book takes over 400 pages to do: presenting facts and figures about global mobility and making predictions about future trends. Overall the book is worth it if you want an introduction to the subject, otherwise it reads as yesterday's news. *KL*

DESIGNED BY PETER SAVILLE
Rick Poyner et al
Frieze, £19.95

WHETHER PETER SAVILLE WOULD be satisfied by being called an

artist is not entirely clear. His latest book, published to coincide with his retrospective exhibition at the Design Museum, tackles this question by ignoring it almost totally. If graphic design can be described as 'art with a client', Saville has remained subject to clients only because he needed to pay the bills. However, his periodic flirtations with bankruptcy and his cuckoo-like living habits have necessitated a certain compromise from time to time.

There is a sense of disappointment that pervades Saville now. Rather unfairly, many consider that it has been broadly downhill for the Mancunian since he did his era-defining work in his twenties when he was the co-founder of Factory Records in Manchester. The cover of Joy Division's *Unknown Pleasures* (an image reworked for the cover of this book) and the famous 12 inch of New Order's *Blue Monday* are pieces of graphic art that inspired a generation, despite the latter costing so much to produce that Factory lost money on the sales of the record, the biggest ever selling 12-inch single.

There is something endearingly homespun about the poise of Saville's work for Factory. A poster dating from 1978, reproduced in the book, advertises a series of gigs by Factory artists. Despite the conscious references to Swiss modernist Jan Tschichold's Neue Typographie and the immaculate, almost tectonic command of the spaces between the sans serif lettering and the thick black lines that run across the page, there is a spelling mistake in the name of one of the bands.

This shows that whilst this work was epoch-making it was also very much the product of a cottage industry.

Saville talks about his attitude to graphics as 'post-pun'. This is design for the design-literate. The

semiotics of that 1978 poster, its pseudo-industrial logo, its process colours, even the spelling mistake, tell the Factory Records listener all he or she needs to know about the music.

Saville's later career has been a mixed bag. An ill-fated period working for the design consultancy Pentagram is skirted around in this book which jumps to his later work for Yohji Yamamoto and his more recent album covers for Pulp and Suede. Saville is an outsider, realising an inexorable truth about graphic design – it is basically about selling products. In a fascinating interview in this book, Saville describes one of the dilemmas he's found himself in since his Pentagram days: 'I didn't want to be in the corporate communications industry. It's boring and unsexy.'

One can't help but feel that Saville's constant self-promotion, the Design Museum exhibition (which he has claimed was a disappointing greatest hits collection)

and this largely hagiographic book are all intended to place Saville in a prime position in the world of graphics so that as he gets older he can do the work he wants to. However, his is such an engaging story and the images are so compelling that one forgives him. There are better artists than Saville, but none so fashionable. There are better designers, too, but barely one with such an ability to take the temperature of a moment and distil it into a record cover or magazine advert. *KL*

ART HISTORY

WHISTLER'S MOTHER: AN AMERICAN ICON

Edited by Margaret MacDonald

Lund Humphries, £16.95

AS THE WHISTLER CENTENARY glides towards its conclusion sans a large London exhibition or a major media fanfare, it's a good time to ask why his *Arrangement in Grey and Black*, better known to the world as *Whistler's Mother*, ever became an icon in the first place. After all, here's a painting that, on the face of it, has little to recommend it to the popular imagination. The subject is an old-age pensioner who exudes neither glamour nor excitement. She sits there, seemingly resigned, staring at something outside the frame. The colours are low key, verging on monochrome, while the composition has the wilful oddity of a harshly cropped Polaroid. Yet by all accounts this is one of the most famous paintings in the world. Why?

Whistler's Mother: An American Icon does a decent job of coming up with an explanation, though as a compendium of essays it suffers from the usual drawbacks of its form: needless repetition and unevenness of tone. It also suffers from some sloppy editing: 'focused' is spelled 'focussed' throughout and, in a surrealist moment, we're asked to imagine Whistler 'as he poured over press clippings'. On the whole, though, it's an informative and timely book.

It also approaches the artist from many disciplinary angles, including art history, biography, social history, psychoanalysis and popular culture.

Oddly, perhaps, the biographical element turns out to be the dullest. Georgia Toutziari's research into the life of Anna Matilda Whistler reveals nothing more thrilling than the fact that she was a nice old bird who quoted the Bible at every opportunity to her thoroughly bohemian son, while acting as his business manager. More interesting is Margaret MacDonald's almost brushstroke-by-brushstroke description of the painting itself. Starting with the genesis of the work, MacDonald goes on to consider the curious detail that the *Mother* is actually painted on the back of a canvas (Whistler preferred its rougher texture), as well as the painting's once-controversial title, which prefigures the twentieth-century obsession with the teasing moniker.

Most fascinating of all is Kevin Sharp's history of the painting's American tour, organised by MoMA in 1932–4. Sharp shows how a slack-jawed fascination with the painting's insurance value, along with cheesy interpretations of its subject, rapidly supplanted the work's rigorously aesthetic origins – exactly the same anti-intellectual process that has transformed any number of other popular 'masterpieces', from Van Gogh's *Sunflowers* to the *Mona Lisa*.

What this book makes apparent is that much of the *Mother*'s allure resides precisely in what it, at first glance, lacks. Its subject's apparent indifference to the viewer, its narrow tonal range, its abruptly cropped edges (so reminiscent of Degas), all function as cleverly controlled invitations for us to supply the missing details – something that, on the evidence of these essays, we happily continue to do. *CS*

THE MUSEUM OF THE MIND: ART AND MEMORY IN WORLD CULTURES

John Mack

British Museum, £19.99

THIS YEAR MARKS THE 250TH anniversary of the British Museum's foundation. The astonishing range of its collections was fully exploited in a recent exhibition, accompanied by John Mack's idiosyncratic and illuminating book. The theme, however, was not merely one of celebration. Instead Mack analysed the cultural phenomenon on which the very existence of a museum depends – society's use of images and other artefacts to aid, encourage and interpret its memories.

It is, of course, unfashionable to see the museum merely as a neutral space in which works of art are objectively classified and displayed. Inevitably, it is selective in preserving memories of the cultures that it represents. Moreover, it is also an organisation with its own history – a point evocatively made by nineteenth-century photographs of the British Museum's staff, as well as by the war memorial and bust of a former director, to which Mack refers in his introductory chapter.

Having established the role of the museum as a 'theatre of memory', Mack then goes on to relate the individual exhibits to this overarching theme of remembrance. Perhaps surprisingly, there is little discussion of the objects' acquisitions and subsequent histories within the institution. Instead the analysis concentrates on the role of memory in the production of the

artefacts and in their original functions, which ranged from 'mnemonic devices' to 'remembering and forgetting events'.

Mack's approach is demonstrated by his perceptive account of a *Malanggan* from New Ireland – a carved figure enclosed in a lattice of elaborate animal forms – which was designed to be placed above a grave for only one night, before being destroyed (or sold to a museum). Despite its ephemeral nature, its remembered design was 'owned' by specific individuals who passed it on to successive generations.

The *Malanggan*'s creation depended on the operation of memory, while numerous other artefacts, ranging from English calendar coins to Micronesian navigational charts, relied on the recalling of codes and complex data in order to work successfully. In general Mack's emphasis is on how memories are aroused or used rather than on their actual content. The final chapter, 'Holy Relics and Memorabilia', brings together pilgrim tokens, antiquities bought on the Grand Tour and photograph albums – an uneasy association of disparate experiences whose essential differences are perhaps more significant than the objects' shared qualities as souvenirs.

When, in 1911, the Futurist Umberto Boccioni represented the feelings of those left behind by a departing train, he regarded memory as intensely personal, to be expressed through appropriate colours and abstract forms. Yet such individual, subjective sensations have little place in Mack's analysis – and not simply because Boccioni's painting is not part of the British Museum's collections. *The Museum of the Mind* is, fundamentally, an exercise in classification rather than empathy, with the relationships between art and memory sorted into half a dozen neatly labelled categories.

Perhaps the museum's traditional taxonomical role still has some mileage after all. *CM*

BERNARD LEACH
Emmanuel Cooper
Yale University Press, £29.95

GIVEN THE ALREADY SUBSTANTIAL number of books available both about and by Bernard Leach, it's perhaps surprising that this biography, written by one of the genre's most devoted chroniclers, is the first to examine comprehensively his personal life as the inspiration for his art. Leach's quest to marry the unique aesthetic and spiritual temperaments of the East with the modernism of the West in high-art pottery is well known. He conversed, wrote and lectured extensively around the world about balancing progress while guarding tradition, but the private inspiration behind his philosophies has been somewhat more enigmatic.

Cooper, himself a successful potter, quickly establishes Leach's primary motivation: his spiritual yearning, beginning, perhaps, with his mother's death during childbirth in 1887 in Hong Kong. A busy British colonial Judge, his father sent Bernard to live with his grandparents who had recently moved to Japan. At age 10 he was sent to boarding school in England, thus establishing a lifelong pattern of unrest and movement between these countries. Strong, life-long friendships became the keystones of Leach's development. Among those he bonded with were Reggie

Turvey, who he met at the Slade School of Art, Yanagi Soetsu, the leader of the Japanese Folkcraft Movement, Hamada, a Japanese potter who eventually moved to England with Leach to help found his famous pottery in St Ives in Cornwall and at Dartington Hall in Devon, where he met Mark Tobey, an American painter who introduced him to the Baha'i faith, which became an important part of his life in later years.

His relationships with women, however, were more tumultuous. His first marriage to his cousin Muriel lasted for 34 years and produced several children, but was blemished by Leach's desire to find 'spiritual and creative inspiration' in extra-marital sexual adventures. With his second wife Laurie, assistant and secretary to the Leach pottery in St Ives, he had a closer artistic bond, but soon found he needed more space to explore his Baha'i beliefs. His third marriage to American potter Janet Darnell lasted until his death, but for much of the time the two lived apart.

Solace was found in his work. Selling his pots primarily through art gallery exhibitions, Leach was close to the artistic community in Cornwall that included Patrick Heron and Barbara Hepworth. He decried the proliferation of mass-produced wares, but as such was, on several occasions, forced to rely on the financial buffering of patrons until his son David instigated new production methods for standard tablewares in the 30s. Nonetheless his pursuit of truth and beauty was rewarding – especially in the face of his personal anxieties – and he received numerous honours at home and abroad, travelled, exhibited and wrote extensively well into old age, and was regarded as something of a sage before passing away at age 92.

Spread over nearly 400 pages, the generously recorded detail of this book flirts at times with being

didactically repetitive, even taking into account the motifs Leach returned to time and again throughout his life. Nonetheless, given Leach's own long-held tenet that the pot reveals the man, the comparisons of his philosophies with the more intimate realities of his personal life impart welcome and long overdue revelations. *PH*

MAGAZINE
Mike Nelson
Bookworks/Matt's Gallery, £25

WHAT YOU SEE IS WHAT YOU GET. A textless book containing over 300 pages of photographs, showing seedily soiled rooms, dingy corridors and dispirited, unclean waiting areas. This is unless (as the artist and publishers presumably assumed) noble reviewers provide the expositional analysis that allows the elusive 'hidden key' to be revealed. Although they might seem real, these rooms and corridors are actually installation photographs of vast artworks in vast art galleries. The dirty, sad rooms and endless corridors are in fact highly skilled facsimiles cleverly fabricated by the artist in Matt's Gallery, the ICA and elsewhere, and are not, as might otherwise appear, 'reality'.

Maybe the reviewer is ignoble, though. If it looks just like a book of documentary photography and quacks just like a book of documentary photography, then maybe it should be reviewed just like a book of documentary photography. Not least the merit of this is that Nelson can then be considered as part of mainstream photographic practice, thus allowing the Candida Hofer book review (see above) a lazy re-use. Like her, Nelson's photographs are exclusively of unpopulated architectural interiors and there is a great deal about 'unselfconscious architectural forms' and the 'human

relationship to mundane architectural systems', as well as some 'searing extremes of scale' and much 'ambiguous presence and absence'. And so it goes on.

The book is a remorseless, disjunctive narrative, whose emotional tone is one of loss; principally loss of self through various disorientations. According to the details of Nelson's evidence, these include the literal loss of way caused by maze-like architectural physicality, the losing of identity status through immigration, and the loss of control through being victim to workplace exploitation. There are also losses of personal power to the Kafkas of officialdom and ticket sellers of commerce, as well as weirdo drug use and wacko religion. For the middle-class art goer the effect is like coming out of blackout in South London at 3am where you have been trying to score, and finding yourself lost in the corridors of what seems, at best, a dodgy minicab office, your friends having all disappeared. With the money.

For many people, these kinds of interiors are their true and actual reality, of course. For the £25 art book-buying public it's like purchasing the recreational rights to

the night sweats of a classic anxiety dream. Doors open only to reveal other closed doors. Dirty corridors, mazes and dead ends are trudged and despaired. Keys, bolts and padlocks remain inviolate and Freudian. And all is lit by bare, existential light bulbs, those mockers of the human soul. *NB*

BOOK

Christian Marclay
Russell Ferguson (editor)
Steidl, £20.00

CHRISTIAN MARCLAY, LIKE A market-wise pop musician, is currently touring the world at the height of his renown, and this superb catalogue makes the perfect concert T-shirt if you can't make the show (UCLA Hammer Museum, 1 June – 31 August; the Center for Curatorial Studies Department, Bard College, Annandale-on-Hudson, New York, 28 September – 19 December; the Seattle Art Museum, 5 February – 2 May 2004; Kunstmuseum, Thun, 12 June – 6 September 2004). Russell Ferguson's introductory essay is informative (I was surprised to learn that most of Marclay's work is, in fact, silent) and full of fun anecdotes. For instance, Marclay stumbled upon the idea of a loop while browsing a record store and accidentally spotting an album of Batman music that skipped and played a repetitive rhythmic fragment of the score. *Voilà* – he recorded the fragment and it became part of one his performances. One of the few artists so playfully engaged with sound and music.

Bliss: Postcards of Couples and Families
Collected by Martin Parr
Chris Boot, £14.95 / $24.95

AS AN ICEBREAKER, BLISS WOULD beat any party game. After flipping through the pages of this Martin Parr collection of postcards, you might ask: why do 70s couples like

to cuddle under the light of post-apocalyptic sunsets? The most inscrutable photo in the collection shows an interior with, naturally, a young couple. But wait. The man appears to be dressed in a Romanian peasant outfit and he's holding a huge plate of what looks like cooked bacon and rabbit legs. His partner, wearing shorts so tight she probably left the photo shoot with varicose veins, is reaching over her man to pinch a piece of meat, a large bowl of white sauce in the other hand. In the background, ashes smoulder in the fireplace. Bliss indeed. My only complaint is the lack of information about the postcards – where and when they were taken – but the publishers claim they don't know themselves. More visual treats abound in this astonishingly odd book, another thing for which we should be thankful for Martin Parr's kaleidoscopic eye.

The Contingent Object of Art
Martha Buskirk
The MIT Press, £24.95 / $39.95

IN 1990, DONALD JUDD PUT AN ad in *Art in America* withdrawing his authorship of a work attributed to him in a show at the Ace Gallery, Los Angeles, in 1989. The piece was, in fact, a freshly manufactured copy of a 1974 piece that was 'authorised' by Giuseppe Panza, the collector who owned the original, because it would be easier to recreate the work than ship it from Panza's villa in Italy. Buskirk begins her book with this

example to raise questions about how the artist's hand guarantees the authenticity of a work of art. Her thesis that 'the removal of the artist's hand... makes the connection between work and artist that more significant' sounds convincing in a contemporary climate that favours intentions and ideas more than objects, but it may place too much emphasis on the institutional model, ignoring the more slippery market. Yet this book helps to explain how, over the past forty years, most of us have come to accept that art can be anything as long as an artist gives it a name.

Alberto Giacometti: Myth, Magic, and the Man
Laurie Wilson
Yale, £27.50

GIACOMETTI SPENT WHAT MUST have been a blissful childhood in the Swiss Alps amid a loving family, and yet, after witnessing the death of an old man, he said, 'I have never been able to sleep without a lamp, nor go to bed without thinking I might never wake up.' According to a friend, a sense of terror accompanied him everywhere but his studio, and 'only by uncovering the source of his suffering', writes author Laurie Wilson, 'can we fully understand Giacometti's goals as an artist.' Wilson explains how an obsession with death inspired the frizzy-haired, gaunt denizen of Montparnasse to make some of the most haunting sculptures of the twentieth century. Wilson is a psychoanalyst, and some readers might

M A R K

find her discussions about erotic feelings for his sister while posing nude for her father (for whom he may have had homoerotic feelings) off the mark; nevertheless, this is a comprehensive look at the life of an amazing artist.

Luc Tuymans
Ulrich Loock, Juan Vicente Aliaga, Nancy Spector, Hans Rudolf Reust
Phaidon, £24.95 / $39.95

A HUNDRED PAGES HAVE BEEN added to the original Phaidon monograph to include the artist's recent work for this new, expanded edition. Tuymans once said in an interview that he has to start and finish a painting in a day, so even if he worked, say, 3 months a year, that's about one hundred paintings per year, a startling figure that makes this a welcome update. Besides, Tuymans rarely repeats himself and with every surprise his work seems to get stronger.

Paul McCarthy at Tate Modern
Frances Morris, Sarah Glennie, David Thorp
Tate Publishing, £24.99

PAUL MCCARTHY'S WORK IS LURID, mesmerising, strange, a carnival of palpable neuroses. My kind of stuff. His *Blockhead* is a lumbering Pinocchio in front of the Tate, with a phallus of a nose that points straight across the Thames to St Paul's until 26 October. So you might think this book would make a good souvenir of a great piece of public art. Well, not really. Open it

and you get endless doodles, snapshots, models, diagrams, photomontages, sketches – 170 pages of claustrophobic process fetish. Although a book of images might be a good way of showing how an artist conceives of his work (and may in fact be the artist's idea), it still feels like a cop-out. And once you get to the articles, the print is in a barely readable grey. I couldn't help but think – come on, Tate, surely you could do better!

Handbooks of Korean Art
Youngsook Pak, Roderick Whitfield, Yeol-su Yoon, Jae-yeol Kim
Laurence King, £11.95 – 13.95

KOREAN ART TENDS TO GET overlooked because the culture has always resided between the two giants of East Asia, China and Japan, but it has its own artistic tradition, and Japanese pottery, so famous in the West, is almost unthinkable without Korea's example. The handbooks are separated into four categories: *Buddhist Sculpture*, *White Porcelain and Punch'ong Ware*, *Earthenware and Celadon*, and *Folk Painting*. The *Buddhist Sculpture* handbook offers a useful glossary to help you keep track of terms such as *dhyana mudra* (gesture of meditation), and in the *Folk Painting* volume you can learn why you will almost always see a magpie in a pine tree in pictures of tigers. This quartet of handbooks is a thorough introduction to an oft-ignored cultural heritage.

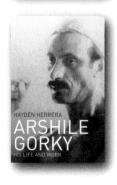

This is not it
Lynne Tillman
Distributed Art Publishers, £19.99

A DARKLY HILARIOUS TAKE ON alienation from yourself and the rest of the world, the title story of *This is not it* begins, 'Whenever I arrive, it's the wrong time.' Most of these stories by Lynne Tillman are Manhattan hurtin' tunes, all sung to the accompaniment of pictures by Kiki Smith, Jessica Stockholder, Roni Horn, Barbara Kruger, Vik Muniz and many others. Each piece of art – mostly photographs, with a couple of sculptures and paintings – is used to design a 'cover' to each story, and it is a beautiful way to pace a book. A great project.

Arshile Gorky: His Life and Work
Hayden Herrera
Bloomsbury, £35

VOSDANIK ADOIAN ESCAPED the Armenian massacres of 1915, went to America in 1920, renamed himself Arshile Gorky and became an artist who influenced de Kooning and the course of Abstract Expressionism. Despite his intrepid nature, Herrera writes, he was 'dark, remote and saturnine'. After he committed suicide, a note was found among his things and the first line read, 'in this world there is no place for me'. But as this vivid biography demonstrates, he carved himself a place as one of the great artists of the twentieth century.

Art | Basel | Miami Beach | 4–7 | Dec | 03
Art | 35 | Basel | 16–21 | June | 04

✳ UBS

The International Art Show – La Exposición Internacional de Arte
Art Basel Miami Beach, PO Box, CH-4005 Basel
Fax +41/58-206 31 32, MiamiBeach@ArtBasel.com, www.ArtBasel.com
mch
messe schweiz

Celebrating 10 Years of Partnership with

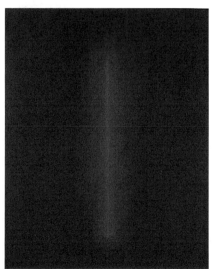

1301 PE, Los Angeles
303 Gallery, New York
ACME., Los Angeles
Air de Paris, Paris
The Approach, London
Art: Concept, Paris
asprey jacques, London
Blum & Poe, Los Angeles
Tanya Bonakdar Gallery, New York
BQ, Cologne
The Breeder Projects, Athens
Gavin Brown's enterprise, Corp., New York
Galerie Daniel Buchholz, Cologne
Cabinet, London
Luis Campaña Galerie, Cologne
Galerie Gisela Capitain, Cologne
carlier | gebauer, Berlin
China Art Objects Galleries, Los Angeles
Sadie Coles HQ, London
Contemporary Fine Arts, Berlin
Corvi-Mora, London
Counter, London
CRG Gallery, New York
Galerie Chantal Crousel, Paris
doggerfisher, Edinburgh
Galerie EIGEN + ART, Berlin
Entwistle, London
Foksal Gallery Foundation, Warsaw
Galeria Fortes Vilaça, San Paulo
Marc Foxx, Los Angeles
Stephen Friedman Gallery, London

Frith Street Gallery, London
Gagosian Gallery, New York
Galerie Gebr. Lehmann, Dresden
Gimpel Fils, London
Marian Goodman Gallery, New York
Greene Naftali, New York
greengrassi, London
Galerie Karin Guenther, Hamburg
Hales Gallery, London
Galerie Hammelehle und Ahrens, Cologne
Jack Hanley Gallery, San Francisco
Haunch of Venison, London
Galerie Hauser & Wirth, Zurich
Galerie Hauser & Wirth & Presenhuber, Zurich
Galerie Ghislaine Hussenot, Paris
Taka Ishii Gallery, Tokyo
Jablonka Galerie Linn Lühn, Cologne
Galerie Martin Janda, Vienna
Galerie Rodolphe Janssen, Brussels
Annely Juda Fine Art, London
Georg Kargl, Vienna
galleria francesca kaufmann, Milan
Kerlin Gallery, Dublin
Klosterfelde, Berlin
Johann König, Berlin
Leo Koenig Inc., New York
Michael Kohn Gallery, Los Angeles
Tomio Koyama Gallery, Tokyo

Andrew Kreps Gallery, New York
Galerie Krinzinger, Vienna
kurimanzutto, Mexico City
Yvon Lambert, Paris
Lisson Gallery, London
Luhring Augustine, New York
Maccarone Inc., New York
Kate MacGarry, London
Magnani, London
Mai 36 Galerie, Zurich
Giò Marconi, Milan
Matthew Marks Gallery, New York
Galerie Meyer Kainer, Vienna
Meyer Riegger, Karlsruhe
Milton Keynes Gallery, Bucks
Victoria Miro Gallery, London
Mizuma Art Gallery, Tokyo
Modern Art, London
The Modern Institute, Glasgow
MW projects, London
Galerie Christian Nagel, Cologne
Galerie Michael Neff, Frankfurt
Galerie Neu, Berlin
neugerriemschneider, Berlin
Galleria Franco Noero, Turin
Galerie Nordenhake, Berlin
Galerie Giti Nourbakhsch, Berlin
Galerie Nathalie Obadia, Paris
Patrick Painter Inc., Santa Monica
Maureen Paley Interim Art, London
Paragon Press, London
Parkett Editions, Zurich
Galerie Francesca Pia, Bern

Galerie Praz-Delavallade, Paris
The Project, New York
Galerie Almine Rech, Paris
Anthony Reynolds Gallery, London
Ridinghouse, London
Galerie Thaddaeus Ropac, Salzburg
Galleria Sonia Rosso, Turin
Salon 94, New York
Galerie Aurel Scheibler, Cologne
Schipper & Krome, Berlin
Gallery Side 2, Tokyo
Brent Sikkema, New York
Sommer Contemporary Art, Tel Aviv
Sprovieri, London
Sprüth Magers Lee, London
Paul Stolper, London
Galerie Micheline Szwajcer, Antwerp
Timothy Taylor Gallery, London
Galerie Barbara Thumm, Berlin
Transmission Gallery, Glasgow
Emily Tsingou Gallery, London
Two Palms Press, New York
Vilma Gold, London
Waddington Galleries, London
Galleri Nicolai Wallner, Copenhagen
Barbara Weiss, Berlin
Galerie Barbara Wien, Berlin
White Cube, London
Wilkinson Gallery, London
The Wrong Gallery, New York
David Zwirner, New York

Supported by

CiTYINN
contemporary hotels

Media partners

THE INDEPENDENT   THE INDEPENDENT
ON SUNDAY

Time Out
London

Frieze Art Fair
Regent's Park, London
17—20 October 2003
Ticket hotline 0870 060 1789 (24 hrs)
For more information:–
Telephone +44 (0)20 7692 0000
Email info@friezeartfair.com
www.friezeartfair.com

FRIEZE
ART
FAIR

ANDREW HOLMES
GAS TANK CITY

Ex - pencil on paper, 53x79cm

WEDNESDAY 10TH SEPTEMBER - SATURDAY 4TH OCTOBER 2003
Exhibition catalogue available on request.

Plus One Plus Two Galleries
161/163 Seymour Place, London W1H 4PJ
Tel: 020 7724 7304   Fax: 020 7724 5032
info@plusonegallery.com
www.plusonegallery.com

Plus

Opening Times
Monday-Friday: 10.30am - 6.30pm
Saturday: 11.00am - 3.00pm

Interior (w. 98), 2003, (detail) 92 x 132 cm / 36 x 52 in, mixed media

Marlborough

Daniela Gullotta
Interiors

10 September – 11 October 2003

Fully illustrated catalogue available

Marlborough Fine Art (London) Ltd.
6 Albemarle Street, London W1S 4BY
Tel: 020 7629 5161   Fax: 020 7629 6338
mfa@marlboroughfineart.com
www.marlboroughfineart.com

barbican art

17 September
– 24 October 2003

14 Wharf Road
London
N1 7RW

opening times:
Tuesday – Saturday 11.00-6.00pm
Sunday 12noon-4.00pm

Bloomberg
newcontemporaries
2003

Selectors
JJ Charlesworth
Cerith Wyn Evans
Hayley Newman
Rebecca Warren

Bloomberg New Contemporaries 2003 is organised in collaboration with Barbican Art

Sponsored by
Bloomberg

ARTS COUNCIL ENGLAND

afoundation

Peter Griffen

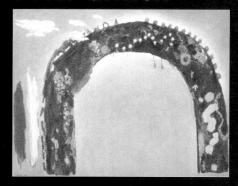

Red Hill. 2003: Oil on canvas, 138 x 183cm

Land and Sky 1
James Colman. 23 Sept - 14 Oct 2003
Wed - Fri 10am - 6pm Sat 10am - 2pm or by app
41 Coronet St, Hoxton N1 6HD London UK
tel. 44 (0)20 7729 5553   e. gallery@jamescolman.com

Land and Sky 2
Dagmar Art Gallery. 14 Nov - 5 Dec 2003
Tues - Fri 11am - 6pm or by app
554 Queensbury St, Nth Melbourne 3051 VIC Australia
tel/fax. 61 (0)3 9329 4220   e. dagmarcyrulla@aol.com

Mediterranean Field Studies
Rencontres Internationales du Cinema des Antipodes.
13 Oct - 19 Oct 2003   St Tropez, France
tel/fax. 66 (0)2 9564 5828   e. bbories@hotmail.com

JOSEPH SOLMAN

Studio Interior, 1950, oil on canvas, 28 x 38 ins. Private collection

*Seventy Years
of Painting*

4 – 28 October 2003

Six Chapel Row Contemporary Art
6 Chapel Row, Bath, BA1 1HN
T: 01225 337900
E: sixchapelrow@btinternet.com
W: www.sixchapelrow.com

LAST WORDS

IN THE STARS

Within 5 minutes of meeting Dan Graham I knew that his birth sign is Aries and that he was born on 31 March. So what, you ask? But he can also tell you the birth sign of every artist he has ever met. Leaving aside Graham's own obsession, the stars have been propitious for Hayward director Susan Brades, who quickly raised the £1.8 million needed for the long overdue refurbishment of the gallery. Due to reopen in October with a purpose-built café and transparent façade, it will boast a Dan Graham pavilion featuring touch screens loaded with cartoons and Sister Wendy videos. Finally the rubber-neckers on the top of double-decker buses crossing Waterloo Bridge will be able to see that something really does happen in the castle-keep precinct of the South Bank centre.

MORE COLOUR

For those of you who missed *Colour* in the *Guardian* in July you will soon be able to purchase copies in your nearest bookshop as well as bid on many of the drawings in the colouring book. MODERN PAINTERS will be conducting an auction in London before Christmas so for more information on this and on the publication date of *Colour* check out our website – www.modernpainters.co.uk. Royalties go to Unicef to help children in need.

VENICE IN DRAG

MODERN PAINTERS launched its music and art issue at the Venice Biennale in the fantastic Henry Moore Foundation space on the Guidecca. Lucky party-goers sipped delicious bellinis and prosecco, and admired the art of Richard Woods, Hilary Lloyd and Graham Gussin to the non-dulcet strains of the wonderfully talented Kieran Hebden, aka Four Tet. Perhaps the star moment was observing Turner Prize-nominated artist Grayson Perry chatting to a 94-year-old toothless Venetian

widow. It was not good to be in drag in 90 degrees heat and Grayson's make-up seemed to be literally melting in the heat but the granny was in seventh heaven.

HOT PURCHASE

The heat wave was the main topic of conversation at the Venice Biennale. Indeed 12 unlucky punters allegedly died as a result of its intensity. Carpeting is the last thing you need in such climes, as David Adjaye, who designed the British Pavilion, should have known. Despite the sweltering atmosphere one of Chris Ofili's paintings sold to Peter Simon to add to his colourful Monsoon collection, which already contains work by fellow Biennalian, the Brazilian Beatriz Milhazes.

MODERN PAINTERS, Periodicals Pending, ISSN number 0953-6698, is published quarterly (4 times per year: September, December, March, June) by Fine Art Journals Ltd, USA agent USACAN at 1320 Route 9, Champlain, NY 12919. Subscription price in US$41.00 per annum. Periodicals postage paid at Champlain NY and at additional mailing offices. POSTMASTER: send address changes to MODERN PAINTERS, c/o Express Mag, PO BOX 2769, Plattsburgh, NY, USA 12901- 0239.